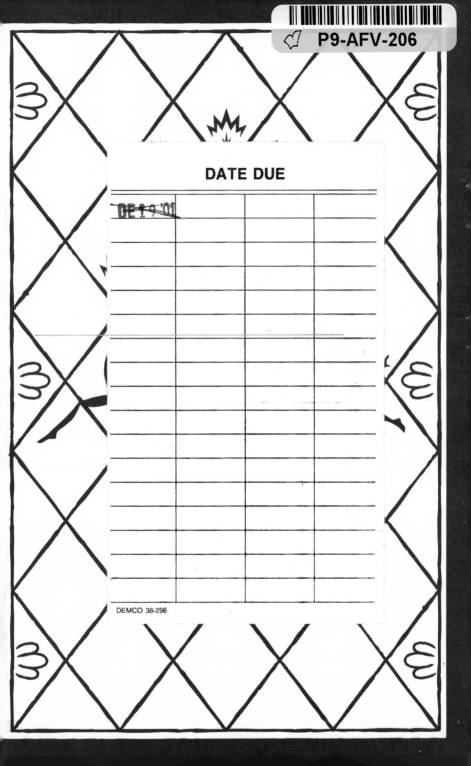

THE
COMPLEAT
ANGLER

IZAAK WALTON

THE COMPLEAT ANGLER

OR

THE CONTEMPLATIVE MAN'S RECREATION

IZAAK WALTON AND CHARLES COTTON

INTRODUCTION BY
HOWELL RAINES

THE MODERN LIBRARY

NEW YORK

1996 Modern Library Edition

Biographical note copyright © 1996 by Random House, Inc.
Introduction copyright © 1996 by Howell Raines

Jacket painting: (detail) *A View of the Lake District* by John Rathbone,
courtesty of Bridgeman /Art Resource, N.Y. Spine of jacket portrait
courtesy of Culver Pictures.

Library of Congress Cataloging-in-Publication Data is available.

ISBN 0-679-60203-8

Modern Library website address:
http://www.randomhouse.com/modernlibrary

Printed in the United States of America on acid-free paper
2 4 6 8 9 7 5 3 1

IZAAK WALTON

Izaak Walton, one of the earliest English biographers who is best remembered as the author of *The Compleat Angler*, was born in the parish of St. Mary's, at Stafford, on August 9, 1593. His father, Gervase Walton, was an innkeeper who died when the boy was five. By the time Walton was twenty he was living in London, apprenticed to his brother-in-law, a prosperous clothier. His marriage to Rachel Floud, a relative of Archbishop Thomas Cranmer, in 1626 allied him with a prominent clerical family, and as a parishioner at St. Dunstan's Church Walton became a close friend of its vicar, John Donne.

Among Walton's earliest surviving literary efforts is an elegy written in 1633 for the initial collection of Donne's poems. The poet-clergyman was the subject of the first of Walton's great biographical essays: *Life of Donne* served as the preface to the 1640 edition of the minister's sermons and was filled with anecdotes and personal impressions. Over the years Walton's loyalty to the Church of England, coupled with his genius for friendship, inspired him to write biographies of four other eminent theologians: Sir Henry Wotton (1651), Richard Hooker (1665), George Herbert (1670), and Dr. Robert Sanderson (1678). Each is distinguished by the intimacy and vivacity characteristic of the *Life of Donne*. It is little wonder that Samuel Johnson rated Walton's five *Lives* among "his most favourite books."

Walton's reputation as a biographer is overshadowed by the enduring popularity of *The Compleat Angler*. First published in 1653, during the Civil War that forced Walton and other royalists to flee London, the work is more than an engaging discourse on the art of fishing. It reflects a thoughtful, sensitive Englishman's abiding concern with leading a contemplative life. Indeed, many have read Walton's unique celebration of angling throughout the English countryside as a veiled satire against Cromwell and the Puritans. Four revised editions appeared in the author's lifetime, and *The Compleat Angler* has enjoyed a wide following ever since. Samuel Johnson praised the book in the eighteenth century as did the Scottish philosopher Lord Home. Later, Charles Lamb recommended *The Compleat Angler* to Samuel Taylor Coleridge. "It breathes the very spirit of innocence, purity, and simplicity of heart," he noted. "It would sweeten a man's temper at any time to read it; it would Christianise every angry, discordant passion; pray make yourself acquainted with it."

Walton remained active well into old age. The Restoration of Charles II in 1660 returned many of his friends in the Anglican clergy to positions of influence, and they were quick to reciprocate the acts of goodwill he had displayed during Cromwell's reign. Following the death of his second wife in 1662, Walton was employed as steward to the bishop of Worcester. At the bishop's residence of Farnham Castle in Wincester Walton continued to write and revise his published works.

In 1676 Walton asked a young follower, the poet Charles Cotton, to furnish a supplement on fly-fishing for the fifth edition of *The Compleat Angler,* and the two pursued the project at a cottage on the banks of the Dove River in Derbyshire. On August 9, 1683, the inveterate angler marked his ninetieth birthday by drafting a will and securing it with a seal given him by John Donne. Izaak Walton died three months later on December 15, 1683 and was buried at Winchester Cathedral.

INTRODUCTION
BY HOWELL RAINES

It is a dangerous act to ask a failed English professor to expound on a genuine monument of literature. But the Modern Library has taken the risk by inviting me to introduce *The Compleat Angler*. Years ago, before I was seduced by the adrenalating charms of the newsroom, I planned to spend my life in the world of carrels and classrooms, studying and expounding upon the masterworks of English literature. This particular masterwork, of course, is the foundation document of all fishing literature, and that means I am doubly whetted for the task. For I have been from childhood what our learned author, Izaak Walton, called "a brother of the angle." So, our lesson commences—briefly, I promise.

We must ask ourselves two questions. Who was Izaak Walton? Why has this book become the most reprinted book in the language except for the Holy Bible and *Pilgrim's Progress*? Let's dispense with the first question as quickly as possible. Izaak Walton was born in 1593, ten years before the end of Queen Elizabeth's reign. Like many authors of the time, he was self-educated. Walton was a Fleet Street shopkeeper whose learning came from reading and from fortuitous friendships with a gang of writers that included Ben

Jonson and the great poet-preacher John Donne. Walton worshiped in Donne's parish, St. Dunstan's, and helped keep the great man's church clean. He progressed from "scavenger," or volunteer janitor, to vestryman. When a more important, titled parishioner—the poet and royal ambassador Sir Henry Wotton—died, Walton inherited the job of writing Donne's biography. His *Life of John Donne*, published in 1640, would have earned Walton a paragraph in A. C. Baugh's history of English literature if *The Compleat Angler* had never appeared.

But it did appear in 1653, when Walton was sixty, and we have the English Civil War to thank for the timing. Walton left London in 1643 or 1644 for very good reason. King Charles had fled town in 1642. Oliver Cromwell and the Puritans were gaining control of the capital, and as the historian G. M. Trevelyan wrote, "men began to choose their side." Izaak Walton chose the side of the streams that flowed through the safely Royalist strongholds of the English countryside. *The Compleat Angler* is the record of a happy decade of enforced retirement. Its author's appreciation of the pastoral beauties of the streamside and the milkmaid's sweet songs was no doubt sharpened by the fact that unlike other supporters of the famously foolish Charles I, Izaak Walton was sticking hooks into worms rather than having his own head displayed on the end of a New Model Army pike.

Let us now abandon the sullen precincts of history, let us shed the inconvenient baggage of biographical fact and mount the uplands of literary speculation. Here we may address the second and more interesting question. Why, indeed, has this sometimes fey and gassy volume been through almost five hundred editions? I speculate that there is one reason you will not find in the scholarly literature. The book has what is known in the book trade as a selling title. We inhabit a world in which Richard Brautigan's hippie tome *Trout Fishing in America* was lofted onto the bestseller lists by innocent anglers who thought they were buying a how-to book. Generations of their forebears bought *The Compleat Angler* in the faith that it would tell them how to catch more fish. In fact, the book can serve that purpose for anyone who thinks that knowing how to fatten a maggot or weave a leader out of a mare's tail is the road to contentment.

But the real reason for the book's popularity lies elsewhere. My friend Tom McGuane says that Walton's book endures because it "is not about how to fish, but about how to be." I will amend that slightly to say that *The Compleat Angler* is about how to dream, and that is why we love it. You see, the search for fish is really a search for a grail: the place of perfect companionship and flawless contentment. Walton promises that if we follow "the gallant fisher's life," we will be free of the torments invented by "money-getting men." We will savor the peace once tasted by "such men as lived in those times when there were fewer lawyers."

With his powerful incantatory language about the fraternal bond among anglers, Walton may have invented the most enduring conceit of fishing literature. That is the conceit of exceptionalism—the idea that people who fish are especially blessed, more gifted and more sensitive than other citizens. This idea is expressed in what another angling writer, Nick Lyons, who was once a *real* English professor, identifies as the signature passage of the book. "No life, my honest scholar, no life so happy and so pleasant as the life of a well-governed angler, for when the lawyer is swallowed up with business, and the statesman is preventing or contriving plots, then we sit on cowslip banks, hear the birds sing, and possess ourselves in as much quietness as these silent silver streams, which we now see glide so quietly by us. Indeed, my good scholar, we may say of angling as Dr. Boteler said of strawberries, 'Doubtless God could have made a better berry, but doubtless God never did'; and so (if I might judge) 'God never did make a more calm, quiet, innocent recreation than angling.'"

Sweet stuff, that, but the alert scholar may be asking why I said above that Walton *may* have invented the conceit of exceptionalism that has informed virtually all angling writers for the past five centuries. The question brings us willy-nilly to a subset of the subject Izaak Walton, writer. That is Izaak Walton, liar. It is no news that fishermen, like politicians, preachers and pyramid salesman, like to dress up their facts by telling what Mark Twain called "stretchers." In all these cases, ornamental mendacity seems an unavoidable condition of the enterprise, although it might be argued that the former three lie for a purpose while only the angler lies for the sport of it. In any event, Walton's whoppers have always been a delicate subject for the angling hagiographers. After all, the man is a venerated author and a

Christian so notoriously devout as to be buried in a cathedral.

But even Charles Cotton, the aristocratic young admirer who wrote the fly-fishing appendage added to the book in 1676, could not resist a subtle dig about his teacher's truthfulness. You have to understand angling code words to spot the accusation. Cotton was offended by Walton's theory that the way to whip a big trout was simply to toss one's pole in the water, forcing the fish to exhaust itself by dragging the object around like a buoy. Cotton condemned the practice described by "your Master and mine" as unsporting and probably impossible. Then catching himself he added, "I am satisfied he has sometimes done it, because he says so." Translation: Don't try this trick unless you want to lose your big fish. The old man is lying again.

Lying about fishing exploits is one thing, plagiarism another. Since 1954, Walton's admirers have been wrestling with the inconvenient discovery in an English attic of a book entitled *The Arte of Angling*. Like *The Compleat Angler,* this book takes the form of a dialogue between a master, Piscator (Angler), and a student, Viator (Wanderer). In later editions of Walton, Viator became Venator (Hunter). So the question arises of whether Walton cribbed his format and chief characters, as well as his subject matter, from a book published seventy-six years earlier. Desperate to vindicate Walton, one scholar observed that Walton set his dialogue on a "fine, fresh May morning" rather than the "whisteling cold morning" described in *The Arte of Angling*. Also, the older book featured a churlish wife instead of

Walton's affably flirtatious milkmaid. But despite such dodges, the two books contain many "exactly parallel passages," to use the delicate language of A. J. McClane's fishing encyclopedia.

The evidence is clear. Izaak Walton cribbed from his anonymous predecessor. But he brought his own gifts to the project, and those gifts went beyond having a randier imagination when it came to milkmaids. Walton had a sweeter, more conversational writing style. In the end, it is that style and Walton's hallmark skill at evoking every fisher's dream of endless vernal contentment that has made this book endure. Copying from earlier works was commonplace in his time; and in our own century, no less an authority than William Faulkner has asserted that a writer will take anything useful that is not nailed down. The raw stuff of *The Compleat Angler* was provided by the sporting literature of the Elizabethan age, the transforming touch was purely Walton.

So my scholarly conclusion is that Izaak Walton was a fibber, an acceptably inventive plagiarist and a genuine, if raw and redundant genius when it came to describing the green and pleasant land and clear waters that gave birth to the Anglo-American style of fly fishing. What James Russell Lowell called Walton's "living and naturally cadenced voice" speaks to us across five centuries and across the ocean that separates his waters from the American rivers where the goal defined by Charles Cotton—"to fish fine, and far off"—has reached its highest refinement. For notwithstanding the usual British pretensions, Americans have long since become the most expert and most ardently purist fly fishers in the world. Walton was not a pioneer of refined technique, but he defined a way of connecting with nature that still shapes the aestethics of angling.

This edition of *The Compleat Angler* becomes part of a chain that has kept this book in print continuously since 1750. The book has lasted so long because fishing has a mystery at its heart. The quest for fish mirrors a more ambitious quest, that search for dreaming contentment that kept Walton on the stream well into the last decade of his ninety years. "Oh, sir, this is a war where you sometimes win, and must sometimes expect to lose," Charles Cotton wrote in the fifth edition. Like his master, Cotton spoke of fishing and something greater and more elusive, our yearning to grasp the home truths that glide into view and fade away like the largest trout in the most beautiful river in the endless meadows of a country we never quite find.

Here ends the lesson of the failed English professor. Now you are on your own with the grand Piscator, the old man who awaits each of us always on the bank of the unfindable river, Sir Izaak Walton.

A NOTE ON THE TEXT.

The first edition of *The Compleat Angler* was published in 1653. In Walton's lifetime, four further editions were made. The last of these, the fifth edition of 1676, included a new, second section written by Walton's adopted son Charles Cotton. This Modern Library volume includes the text of the fifth edition as presented in the work compiled by James Russell Lowell in 1889. Many of the notes (with the Linnæan Arrangement of the Fish) and the illustrations were taken from the earlier edition of John Major, completed in 1844. Eight etchings have been taken from the Major edition—these are marked by an asterisk in the list of illustrations. The rest of the illustrations are the woodcuts from the Major edition that are repeated in the Lowell edition.

CONTENTS.

PART II.

INSTRUCTIONS HOW TO ANGLE FOR A TROUT OR
GRAYLING IN A CLEAR STREAM.

LIST OF ILLUSTRATIONS.

THE RIGHT WORSHIPFUL

JOHN OFFLEY, ESQ.

OF

MADELY MANOR, IN THE COUNTY OF STAFFORD,

My most Honored Friend.

SIR,—

I HAVE made so ill use of your former favors, as by them to be encouraged to intreat that they may be enlarged to the Patronage and Protection of this Book: and I have put on a modest confidence, that I shall not be denied, because it is a Discourse of Fish and Fishing, which you know so well, and both love and practise so much.

You are assured, though there be ignorant men of another belief, that Angling is an Art; and you know that Art better than others: and that this truth is demonstrated by the fruits of that pleasant labor which you enjoy when you purpose to give rest to your mind, and divest yourself of your more serious business, and, which is often, dedicate a day or two to this recreation.

At which time, if common Anglers should attend you, and be eyewitnesses of the success, not of your fortune, but your skill, it would doubtless beget in them an emulation to be like you, and that emulation might beget an industrious diligence to be so; but I know it is not attainable by common capacities. And there be now many men of great wisdom, learning, and experience, which love and practise this Art, that know I speak the truth.

Sir,—This pleasant curiosity of Fish and Fishing, of which you are so great a master, has been thought worthy the pens and practices of divers in other nations that have been reputed men of great learning and wisdom; and amongst those of this nation, I remember Sir Henry Wotton, a dear lover of this Art, has told me that his intentions were to write a Discourse of the Art, and in praise of Angling. And doubtless he had done so, if death had not prevented him; the remembrance of which hath often made me sorry: for, if he had lived to do it, then the unlearned Angler had seen some better Treatise of this Art, a Treatise that might have proved worthy his perusal; which, though some have undertaken, I could never yet see in English.

But mine may be thought as weak, and as unworthy of common view: and I do here freely confess that I should rather excuse myself, than censure others, my own discourse being liable to so many exceptions; against which, you, Sir, might make this one,—that it can contribute nothing to your knowledge. And, lest a longer Epistle may diminish your pleasure, I shall make this no longer than to add this following truth,

That I am really, Sir,

Your affectionate Friend,

And most humble Servant,

Iz. Wa.

READERS OF THIS DISCOURSE,

THE HONEST ANGLER.

I THINK fit to tell thee these following truths,—that I did neither undertake, nor write, nor publish, and much less own, this Discourse to please myself: and having been too easily drawn to do all to please others, as I proposed not the gaining of credit by this undertaking, so I would not willingly lose any part of that to which I had a just title before I begun it; and do therefore desire and hope, if I deserve not commendations, yet I may obtain pardon.

And though this Discourse may be liable to some exceptions, yet I cannot doubt but that most Readers may receive so much pleasure or profit by it, as may make it worthy the time of their perusal, if they be not too grave or too busy men. And this is all the confidence that I can put on, concerning the merit of what is here offered to their consideration and censure; and if the last prove too severe, as I have a liberty, so I am resolved to use it and neglect all sour censures.

And I wish the Reader also to take notice, that in writing of it I have made myself a recreation of a recreation. And that it might prove so to him, and not read dull and tediously, I have in several places mixed, not any scurrility, but some innocent, harmless mirth: of which, if thou be a severe, sour-complexioned man, then I here disallow thee to be a competent judge; for divines say, There are offences given, and offences not given but taken.

And I am the willinger to justify the pleasant part of it, because, though it is known I can be serious at seasonable times, yet the whole Discourse is, or rather was, a picture of my own disposition; especially in such days and times as I have laid aside business, and gone a-fishing with honest Nat. and R. Roe: but they are gone, and with them most of my pleasant hours, even as a shadow that passeth away and returns not.

And next let me add this, that he that likes not the book should like the excellent picture of the Trout, and some of the other fish; which I may take a liberty to commend, be-cause they concern not myself.

Next let me tell the Reader, that in that which is the more useful part of this Discourse, that is to say, the observations of the nature, and breeding, and seasons, and catching of fish, I am not so simple as not to know that a captious Reader may find exceptions against something said of some of these: and therefore I must entreat him to consider, that experience teaches us to know that several countries alter the time, and I think almost the manner, of fishes' breeding, but doubtless of their being in season: as may appear by three rivers in Monmouthshire, namely, Severn, Wye, and Usk; where Camden (*Brit.*, fol. 633) observes, that in the river Wye, Salmon are in season from September to April; and we are certain that in Thames, and Trent, and in most other rivers, they be in season the six hotter months.

Now for the Art of Catching Fish, that is to say, how to make a man that was none to be an Angler by a book; he that undertakes it shall undertake a harder task than Mr. Hales, a most valiant and excellent fencer, who in a printed book, called "A Private School of Defence," undertook to teach that art or science, and was laughed at for his labor. Not but that many useful things might be learned by that book, but he was laughed at, because that art was not to be taught by words, but practice: and so must Angling. And note also, that in this Discourse I do not undertake to say all that is known, or may be said of it, but I undertake to acquaint the Reader with many things that are not usually known to every Angler; and I shall leave gleanings and observations enough to be made out of the experience of all that love and practise this recreation, to which I shall encourage them. For Angling may be said to be so like the Mathematics that it can never be fully learned; at least not so fully but that there will still be more new experiments left for the trial of other men that succeed us.

But I think all that love this game may here learn something that may be worth their money, if they be not poor and needy men; and in case they be, I then wish them to forbear to buy it: for I write not to get money, but for pleasure, and this Discourse boasts of no more; for I hate to promise much and deceive the Reader.

And however it proves to him, yet I am sure I have found a high content in the search and conference of what is here offered to the Reader's view and censure; I wish him as much in the perusal of it. And so I might here take my leave;

but will stay a little and tell him, that whereas it is said by many, that, in fly-fishing for a Trout, the Angler must observe his twelve several flies for the twelve months of the year; I say, he that follows that rule shall be as sure to catch fish, and be as wise, as he that makes hay by the fair days in an almanac, and no surer; for those very flies that use to appear about and on the water in one month of the year, may the following year come almost a month sooner or later, as the same year proves colder or hotter: and yet in the following Discourse I have set down the twelve flies that are in reputation with many Anglers, and they may serve to give him some observations concerning them. And he may note, that there are in Wales and other countries peculiar flies proper to the particular place or country; and doubtless, unless a man makes a fly to counterfeit that very fly in that place, he is like to lose his labor, or much of it: but for the generality, three or four flies neat and rightly made, and not too big, serve for a Trout in most rivers all the summer. And for winter fly-fishing, it is as useful as an almanac out of date. And of these, because as no man is born an artist, so no man is born an Angler, I thought fit to give thee this notice.

When I have told the Reader, that in this fifth impression there are many enlargements, gathered both by my own observations and the communication with friends, I shall stay him no longer than to wish him a rainy evening to read this following Discourse; and that, if he be an honest Angler, the east wind may never blow when he goes a-fishing.

I. W.

THE
COMPLEAT ANGLER

PART I

THE FIRST DAY.

CHAP. I.—*A Conference betwixt an* ANGLER, *a* HUNTER, *and a* FALCONER, *each commending his Recreation.*[1]

PISCATOR, VENATOR, AUCEPS.

PISCATOR.

OU are well overtaken, Gentlemen: a good morning to you both: I have stretched my legs up Tottenham Hill to overtake you, hoping your business may occasion you towards Ware, whither I am going this fine, fresh May morning.

VENATOR. Sir, I, for my part, shall almost answer your hopes; for my purpose is to drink my morning's draught at the Thatched House in Hoddesden[2]; and I think not to rest till I come thither, where I have appointed a friend or two to meet me: but for this gentleman that you see with me, I know not how far he intends his journey; he came so lately into my company, that I have scarce had time to ask him the question.

Auceps. Sir, I shall, by your favor, bear you company as far as Theobald's[3]; and there leave you, for then I turn up to a friend's house who mews a hawk for me, which I now long to see.

Ven. Sir, we are all so happy as to have a fine, fresh, cool morning, and I hope we shall each be the happier in the others' company. And, Gentlemen, that I may not lose yours, I shall either abate or amend my pace to enjoy it; knowing that, as the Italians say, "Good company in a journey makes the way to seem the shorter."

Auc. It may do so, Sir, with the help of good discourse, which, methinks, we may promise from you that both look and speak so cheerfully; and, for my part, I promise you as an invitation to it, that I will be as free and open-hearted as discretion will allow me to be with strangers.

Ven. And, Sir, I promise the like.

Pisc. I am right glad to hear your answers: and in confidence you speak the truth, I shall put on a boldness to ask you, Sir, whether business or pleasure caused you to be so early up, and walk so fast; for this other gentleman hath declared he is going to see a hawk, that a friend mews for him.[4]

Ven. Sir, mine is a mixture of both, a little business and more pleasure: for I intend this day to do all my business, and then bestow another day or two in hunting the otter, which a friend, that I go to meet, tells me is much pleasan-

ter than any other chase whatsoever; howsoever, I mean to
try it; for to-morrow morning we shall meet a pack of otter-
dogs of noble Mr. Sadler's,[5] upon Amwell Hill, who will be
there so early, that they intend to prevent the sun rising.

Pisc. Sir, my fortune has answered my desires; and my
purpose is to bestow a day or two in helping to destroy some
of those villanous vermin; for I hate them perfectly, because
they love fish so well, or rather, because they destroy so
much; indeed, so much, that, in my judgment, all men that
keep otter-dogs ought to have pensions from the King to
encourage them to destroy the very breed of those base otters, they do so much mischief.

Ven. But what say you to the foxes of the nation? Would
not you as willingly have them destroyed? for doubtless
they do as much mischief as otters do.

Pisc. O Sir, if they do, it is not so much to me and my fraternity as those base vermin the otters do.

Auc. Why, Sir, I pray, of what fraternity are you, that you
are so angry with the poor otters?

Pisc. I am, Sir, a Brother of the Angle, and therefore an
enemy to the otter: for you are to note that we Anglers all
love one another, and therefore do I hate the otter, both for
my own and their sakes who are of my brotherhood.

Ven. And I am a lover of hounds; I have followed many
a pack of dogs many a mile, and heard many merry huntsmen make sport and scoff at Anglers.

Auc. And I profess myself a Falconer, and have heard
many grave, serious men pity them, 't is such a heavy, contemptible, dull recreation.

Pisc. You know, Gentlemen, 't is an easy thing to scoff at any art or recreation: a little wit, mixed with ill-nature, confidence, and malice, will do it; but though they often venture boldly, yet they are often caught, even in their own trap, according to that of Lucian,[6] the father of the family of scoffers.

> "Lucian, well skilled in scoffing, this hath writ:
> Friend, that's your folly which you think your wit:
> This you vent oft, void both of wit and fear,
> Meaning another, when yourself you jeer."

If to this you add what Solomon says of scoffers, that "they are an abomination to mankind" (Prov. xxiv. 9), let him that thinks fit scoff on, and be a scoffer still; but I account them enemies to me, and to all that love virtue and Angling.

And for you that have heard many grave, serious men pity Anglers, let me tell you, Sir, there be many men that are by others taken to be serious and grave men, which we contemn and pity. Men that are taken to be grave, because nature hath made them of a sour complexion, money-getting men,—men that spend all their time, first in getting, and next in anxious care to keep it; men that are condemned to be rich, and then always busy or discontented: for these poor-rich-men, we Anglers pity them perfectly, and stand in no need to borrow their thoughts to think ourselves so happy. No, no, Sir, we enjoy a contentedness above the reach of such dispositions, and as the learned and ingenious Montaigne[7] says like himself freely, "When my cat and I

entertain each other with mutual apish tricks, as playing
with a garter, who knows but that I make my cat more sport
than she makes me? Shall I conclude her to be simple, that
has her time to begin or refuse to play as freely as I myself
have? Nay, who knows but that it is a defect of my not un-

derstanding her language (for doubtless cats talk and reason
with one another) that we agree no better? And who knows
but that she pities me for being no wiser than to play with
her, and laughs and censures my folly for making sport for
her, when we two play together?"

Thus freely speaks Montaigne concerning cats, and I
hope I may take as great a liberty to blame any man, and
laugh at him too, let him be never so grave, that hath not
heard what Anglers can say in the justification of their art
and recreation; which I may again tell you is so full of pleasure, that we need not borrow their thoughts to think ourselves happy.

VEN. Sir, you have almost amazed me: for though I am no scoffer, yet I have, I pray let me speak it without offence, always looked upon Anglers as more patient and more simple men than I fear I shall find you to be.

PISC. Sir, I hope you will not judge my earnestness to be impatience: and for my simplicity, if by that you mean a harmlessness, or that simplicity which was usually found in the primitive Christians, who were, as most Anglers are, quiet men and followers of peace,—men that were so simply-wise as not to sell their consciences to buy riches, and with them vexation and a fear to die; if you mean such simple men as lived in those times when there were fewer lawyers, when men might have had a lordship safely conveyed to them in a piece of parchment no bigger than your hand, though several sheets will not do it safely in this wiser age,—I say, Sir, if you take us Anglers to be such simple men as I have spoken of, then myself and those of my profession will be glad to be so understood: but if by simplicity you meant to express a general defect in those that profess and practice the excellent art of Angling, I hope in time to disabuse you, and make the contrary appear so evidently, that, if you will but have patience to hear me, I shall remove all the anticipations that discourse, or time, or prejudice, have possessed you with against that laudable and ancient art; for I know it is worthy the knowledge and practice of a wise man.

But, Gentlemen, though I be able to do this, I am not so unmannerly as to engross all the discourse to myself: and, therefore, you two having declared yourselves, the one to be a lover of Hawks, the other of Hounds, I shall be most glad to hear what you can say in the commendation of that recreation which each of you love and practise; and having heard what you can say, I shall be glad to exercise your attention with what I can say concerning my own recreation and art of Angling, and by this means we shall make the way to seem the shorter: and if you like my motion, I would have Mr. Falconer to begin.

Auc. Your motion is consented to with all my heart; and, to testify it, I will begin as you have desired me.

And first for the element that I use to trade in, which is the Air, an element of more worth than weight, an element that doubtless exceeds both the earth and water; for though I sometimes deal in both, yet the air is most properly mine,—I and my Hawks use that most, and it yields us most recreation. It stops not the high soaring of my noble, generous Falcon: in it she ascends to such an height, as the dull eyes of beasts and fish are not able to reach to; their bodies are too gross for such high elevations: in the air my troops of Hawks soar up on high, and when they are lost in the sight of men, then they attend upon and converse with the Gods; therefore I think my Eagle is so justly styled *Jove's servant in ordinary:* and that very Falcon, that I am now going to see, deserves no meaner a title, for she usually in her flight endangers herself, like the son of Dædalus, to have her wings scorched by the sun's heat, she flies so near it, but her mettle makes her careless of danger; for she then heeds nothing, but makes her nimble pinions cut the fluid air, and so makes her high way over the steepest mountains and deepest rivers, and in her glorious career looks with contempt upon those high steeples and magnificent palaces which we adore and wonder at; from which height I can make her to descend by a word from my mouth, which she both knows and obeys, to accept of meat from my hand, to own me for her master, to go home with me, and be willing the next day to afford me the like recreation.

And more: this element of air which I profess to trade in, the worth of it is such, and it is of such necessity, that no creature whatsoever, not only those numerous creatures that feed on the face of the earth, but those various creatures that have their dwelling within the waters,—every creature that hath life in its nostrils stands in need of my element. The waters cannot preserve the fish without air, witness the not breaking of ice in an extreme frost: the reason is, for that if the inspiring and expiring organ of any animal be stopped, it suddenly yields to nature, and dies. Thus necessary is air to the existence both of fish and beasts, nay, even to man himself; that air, or breath of life with which God at first inspired mankind (Gen. ii. 7), he, if he wants it, dies presently, becomes a sad object to all that loved and beheld him, and in an instant turns to putrefaction.

Nay, more, the very birds of the air, those that be not Hawks, are both so many and so useful and pleasant to mankind, that I must not let them pass without some observations: they both feed and refresh him; feed him with their choice bodies, and refresh him with their heavenly voices. I will not undertake to mention the several kinds of fowl by which this is done; and his curious palate pleased by day, and which with their very excrements afford him a soft

HAWKING

lodging at night. These I will pass by, but not those little nimble musicians of the air, that warble forth their curious ditties, with which Nature hath furnished them to the shame of Art.

As first the Lark, when she means to rejoice, to cheer herself and those that hear her, she then quits the earth and sings as she ascends higher into the air; and, having ended her heavenly employment, grows then mute and sad to think she must descend to the dull earth, which she would not touch but for necessity.

How do the Blackbird and Thrassel with their melodious voices bid welcome to the cheerful spring, and in their fixed mouths warble forth such ditties as no art or instrument can reach to!

Nay, the smaller birds also do the like in their particular seasons, as namely the Laverock, the Titlark, the little Linnet, and the honest Robin, that loves mankind both alive and dead.

But the Nightingale, another of my airy creatures, breathes such sweet loud music out of her little instrumental throat, that it might make mankind to think miracles are not ceased. He that at midnight, when the very laborer sleeps securely, should hear, as I have very often, the clear airs, the sweet descants, the natural rising and falling, the doubling and redoubling of her voice, might well be lifted above earth, and say, "Lord, what music hast thou provided for the saints in heaven, when thou affordest bad men such music on earth!"

And this makes me the less to wonder at the many

aviaries in Italy, or at the great charge of Varro[8] his aviary, the ruins of which are yet to be seen in Rome, and is still so famous there, that it is reckoned for one of those notables which men of foreign nations either record, or lay up in their memories when they return from travel.

This for the birds of pleasure, of which very much more might be said. My next shall be of birds of political use; I think 't is not to be doubted that Swallows have been taught to carry letters between two armies. But 't is certain that, when the Turks besieged Malta or Rhodes, I now remember not which 't was, Pigeons are then related to carry and recarry letters. And Mr. G. Sandys,[9] in his Travels, relates it to be done betwixt Aleppo and Babylon. But if that be disbelieved, 't is not to be doubted that the Dove was sent out of the ark by Noah, to give him notice of land, when to him all appeared to be sea; and the Dove proved a faithful and comfortable messenger. And for the sacrifices of the Law, a pair of Turtle-doves or young Pigeons were as well accepted as costly bulls and rams. And when God would feed the Prophet Elijah (I Kings xvii. 4–6) after a kind of miraculous manner, he did it by Ravens, who brought him meat morning and evening. Lastly, the Holy Ghost, when he descended visibly upon our Saviour, did it by assuming the shape of a Dove. And, to conclude this part of my discourse, pray remember these wonders were done by birds of the air, the element in which they and I take so much pleasure.

There is also a little contemptible winged creature, an inhabitant of my aerial element, namely the laborious Bee, of whose prudence, policy, and regular government of their own commonwealth I might say much, as also of their several kinds, and how useful their honey and wax are both for meat and medicines to mankind; but I will leave them to their sweet labor, without the least disturbance, believing them to be all very busy at this very time amongst the herbs and flowers that we see Nature puts forth this May morning.

And now to return to my Hawks, from whom I have made too long a digression; you are to note, that they are usually distinguished into two kinds; namely, the Long-winged and the Short-winged Hawk; of the first kind, there be chiefly in use amongst us in this nation,

> The Gerfalcon and Jerkin,
> The Falcon and Tassel-gentle,
> The Laner and Laneret,
> The Bockerel and Bockeret,
> The Saker and Sacaret,
> The Merlin and Jack. Merlin,
> The Hobby and Jack;
> There is the Stelletto of Spain,
> The Blood-red Rook from Turkey,
> The Waskite from Virginia.

And there is of Short-winged Hawks,

> The Eagle and Iron,
> The Goshawk and Tarcel,
> The Sparhawk and Musket,
> The French Pye of two sorts.

These are reckoned Hawks of note and worth, but we have also of an inferior rank,

The Stanyel, the Ringtail,
The Raven, the Buzzard,
The Forked Kite, the Bald Buzzard,
The Hen-driver, and others that I forbear to name.

Gentlemen, if I should enlarge my discourse to the observation of the Eires, the Brancher, the Ramish Hawk, the
Haggard, and the two sorts of Lentners, and then treat of
their several ayries, their mewings, rare order of casting, and
the renovation of their feathers; their reclaiming, dieting,
and then come to their rare stories of practice;—I say, if I
should enter into these, and many other observations that I
could make, it would be much, very much pleasure to me:
but lest I should break the rules of civility with you, by taking up more than the proportion of time allotted to me, I
will here break off, and entreat you, Mr. Venator, to say what
you are able in the commendation of Hunting, to which you
are so much affected; and if time will serve, I will beg your
favor for a further enlargement of some of those several
heads of which I have spoken. But no more at present.

VEN. Well, Sir, and I will now take my turn, and will first
begin with a commendation of the Earth, as you have done
most excellently of the Air; the earth being that element
upon which I drive my pleasant, wholesome, hungry trade.
The earth is a solid, settled element; an element most uni-
versally beneficial both to man and beast: to men who have
their several recreations upon it, as horse-races, hunting,
sweet smells, pleasant walks: the earth feeds man, and all
those several beasts that both feed him and afford him

recreation. What pleasure doth man take in hunting the
stately Stag, the generous Buck, the Wild-Boar, the cunning Otter, the crafty Fox, and the fearful Hare! And if I
may descend to a lower game, what pleasure is it sometimes
with gins to betray the very vermin of the earth! as namely,
the Fitchet, the Fulimart, the Ferret, the Polecat, the
Mouldwarp, and the like creatures that live upon the face
and within the bowels of the earth! How doth the earth
bring forth herbs, flowers, and fruits, both for physic and
the pleasure of mankind! and above all, to me at least, the
fruitful vine, of which when I drink moderately it clears my
brain, cheers my heart, and sharpens my wit. How could
Cleopatra have feasted Mark Antony with eight wild-boars
roasted whole at one supper, and other meat suitable, if the
earth had not been a bountiful mother? But to pass by the
mighty Elephant, which the earth breeds and nourisheth,
and descend to the least of creatures, how doth the earth afford us a doctrinal example in the little Pismire, who in the
summer provides and lays up her winter provision, and
teaches man to do the like! The earth feeds and carries
those horses that carry us. If I would be prodigal of my time
and your patience, what might not I say in commendations
of the earth? that puts limits to the proud and raging sea,
and by that means preserves both man and beast that it destroys them not, as we see it daily doth those that venture
upon the sea, and are there shipwrecked, drowned, and left
to feed haddocks; when we that are so wise as to keep ourselves on earth, walk, and talk, and live, and eat, and drink,
and go a hunting: of which recreation I will say a little, and

then leave Mr. Piscator to the commendation of Angling.

Hunting is a game for Princes and noble persons; it hath been highly prized in all ages; it was one of the qualifications that Xenophon bestowed on his Cyrus, that he was a hunter of wild beasts. Hunting trains up the younger nobility to the use of manly exercises in their riper age. What more manly exercise than hunting the Wild-Boar, the Stag, the Buck, the Fox, or the Hare! How doth it preserve health, and increase strength and activity!

And for the dogs that we use, who can commend their excellency to that height which they deserve? How perfect is the Hound at smelling, who never leaves or forsakes his first scent, but follows it through so many changes and varieties of other scents, even over and in the water, and into the earth! What music doth a pack of dogs then make to any man, whose heart and ears are so happy as to be set to the tune of such instruments! How will a right Greyhound fix his eye on the best Buck in a herd, single him out, and follow him, and him only, through a whole herd of rascal game, and still know and then kill him! For my Hounds, I know the language of them, and they know the language and meaning of one another, as perfectly as we know the voices of those with whom we discourse daily.

I might enlarge myself in the commendation of Hunting, and of the noble Hound especially, as also of the docibleness of dogs in general; and I might make many observations of land-creatures, that for composition, order, figure, and constitution approach nearest to the completeness and understanding of man; especially of those crea-

tures which Moses in the Law permitted to the Jews (Lev.
ix. 2–8), which have cloven hoofs and chew the cud, which
I shall forbear to name, because I will not be so uncivil to
Mr. Piscator as not to allow him a time for the commendation of Angling, which he calls an Art; but doubtless 't is an
easy one: and, Mr. Auceps, I doubt we shall hear a watery
discourse of it, but I hope 't will not be a long one.

AUC. And I hope so too, though I fear it will.

PISC. Gentlemen, let not prejudice prepossess you. I confess my discourse is like to prove suitable to my recreation,
calm and quiet; we seldom take the name of God into our
mouths, but it is either to praise him or pray to him: if others use it vainly in the midst of their recreations, so vainly
as if they meant to conjure, I must tell you it is neither our
fault nor our custom; we protest against it. But pray remember, I accuse nobody; for as I would not make "a watery discourse," so I would not put too much vinegar into it;
nor would I raise the reputation of my own art by the
diminution or ruin of another's. And so much for the pro-
logue to what I mean to say.

And now for the Water, the element that I trade in. The
Water is the eldest daughter of the creation, the element
upon which the Spirit of God did first move (Gen. i. 2), the
element which God commanded to bring forth living creatures abundantly; and without which, those that inhabit the
land, even all creatures that have breath in their nostrils,
must suddenly return to putrefaction. Moses, the great law-
giver and chief philosopher, skilled in all the learning of the
Egyptians, who was called the friend of God, and knew the

mind of the Almighty, names this element the first in the creation; this is the element upon which the Spirit of God did first move, and is the chief ingredient in the creation: many philosophers have made it to comprehend all the other elements, and most allow it the chiefest in the mixtion of all living creatures.

There be that profess to believe that all bodies are made of water, and may be reduced back again to water only; they endeavor to demonstrate it thus:—

Take a willow, or any like speedy-growing plant, newly rooted in a box or barrel full of earth, weigh them all together exactly when the trees begin to grow, and then weigh all together after the tree is increased from its first rooting to weigh an hundred pound weight more than when it was first rooted and weighed; and you shall find this augment of the tree to be without the diminution of one drachm weight of the earth. Hence they infer this increase of wood to be from water of rain, or from dew, and not to be from any other element. And they affirm, they can reduce this wood back again to water; and they affirm, also, the same may be done in any animal or vegetable. And this I take to be a fair testimony of the excellency of my element of Water.

The Water is more productive than the earth. Nay, the earth hath no fruitfulness without showers or dews; for all the herbs and flowers and fruits are produced and thrive by the water; and the very minerals are fed by streams that run underground, whose natural course carries them to the tops of many high mountains, as we see by several springs breaking forth on the tops of the highest hills; and this is also witnessed by the daily trial and testimony of several miners.

Nay, the increase of those creatures that are bred and fed in the water are not only more and more miraculous, but more advantageous to man, not only for the lengthening of his life, but for the preventing of sickness; for 't is observed by the most learned physicians, that the casting off of Lent and other fish days,—which hath not only given the lie to so many learned, pious, wise founders of colleges, for which we should be ashamed,—hath doubtless been the chief cause of those many putrid, shaking, intermitting agues, unto which this nation of ours is now more subject than those wiser countries that feed on herbs, salads, and plenty of fish; of which it is observed in story, that the greatest part of the world now do. And it may be fit to remember that Moses (Lev. xi. 9, Deut. xiv. 9) appointed fish to be the chief diet for the best commonwealth that ever yet was.

And it is observable, not only that there are fish,—as namely, the Whale, three times as big as the mighty Elephant, that is so fierce in battle,—but that the mightiest feasts have been of fish. The Romans in the height of their glory have made fish the mistress of all their entertainments; they have had music to usher in their Sturgeons, Lampreys, and Mullets, which they would purchase at rates rather to be wondered at than believed. He that shall view the writings of Macrobius,[10] or Varro,[11] may be confirmed and informed of this, and of the incredible value of their fish and fish-ponds.

But, Gentlemen, I have almost lost myself, which I confess I may easily do in this philosophical discourse; I met with most of it very lately, and, I hope, happily, in a conference with a most learned physician, Dr. Wharton, a dear friend, that loves both me and my art of Angling. But however, I will wade no deeper in these mysterious arguments, but pass to such observations as I can manage with more pleasure, and less fear of running into error. But I must not yet forsake the waters, by whose help we have so many known advantages.

And first, to pass by the miraculous cures of our known baths, how advantageous is the sea for our daily traffic, without which we could not now subsist! How does it not only furnish us with food and physic for the bodies, but with such observations for the mind as ingenious persons would not want!

How ignorant had we been of the beauty of Florence, of the monuments, urns, and rarities that yet remain in and near unto old and new Rome, so many as it is said will take up a year's time to view, and afford to each of them but a convenient consideration; and therefore it is not to be wondered at, that so learned and devout a father as St. Jerome, after his wish to have seen Christ in the flesh, and to have heard St. Paul preach, makes his third wish to have seen Rome in her glory; and that glory is not yet all lost, for what pleasure is it to see the monuments of Livy, the choicest of the historians; of Tully, the best of orators; and to see the bay-trees that now grow out of the very tomb of Virgil! These, to any that love learning, must be pleasing. But what pleasure is it to a devout Christian to see there the humble house in which St. Paul was content to dwell, and to view

the many rich statues that are there made in honor of his
memory! Nay, to see the very place in which St. Peter and
he lie buried together! These are in and near to Rome. And
how much more doth it please the pious curiosity of a
Christian, to see that place on which the blessed Saviour of
the world was pleased to humble himself, and to take our
nature upon him, and to converse with men,—to see
Mount Sion, Jerusalem, and the very Sepulchre of our Lord
Jesus! How may it beget and heighten the zeal of a Christian, to see the devotions that are daily paid to him at that
place! Gentlemen, lest I forget myself I will stop here, and
remember you, that, but for my element of Water, the inhabitants of this poor island must remain ignorant that
such things ever were, or that any of them have yet a being.

Gentlemen, I might both enlarge and lose myself in such
like arguments; I might tell you that Almighty God is said
to have spoken to a fish, but never to a beast; that he hath
made a Whale a ship to carry and set his prophet Jonah safe
on the appointed shore. Of these I might speak, but I must
in manners break off, for I see Theobald's house. I cry you
mercy for being so long, and thank you for your patience.

Auc. Sir, my pardon is easily granted you; I except against
nothing that you have said; nevertheless, I must part with
you at this park-wall, for which I am very sorry; but I assure
you, Mr. Piscator, I now part with you full of good
thoughts, not only of yourself, but your recreation. And so,
Gentlemen, God keep you both!

Pisc. Well, now, Mr. Venator, you shall neither want time

nor my attention to hear you enlarge your discourse concerning Hunting.

Ven. Not I, Sir; I remember you said that Angling itself was of great antiquity, and a perfect art, and an art not easily attained to; and you have so won upon me in your former discourse, that I am very desirous to hear what you can say further concerning those particulars.

Pisc. Sir, I did say so, and I doubt not but if you and I did converse together but a few hours, to leave you possessed with the same high and happy thoughts that now possess me of it; not only of the antiquity of Angling, but that it deserves commendations, and that it is an art, and an art worthy the knowledge and practice of a wise man.

Ven. Pray, Sir, speak of them what you think fit, for we have yet five miles to the Thatched House, during which walk I dare promise you my patience and diligent attention shall not be wanting. And if you shall make that to appear which you have undertaken; first, that it is an art, and an art worth the learning, I shall beg that I may attend you a day or two a-fishing, and that I may become your scholar, and be instructed in the art itself which you so much magnify.

Pisc. O Sir, doubt not but that Angling is an art; is it not an art to deceive a Trout with an artificial fly?—a Trout! that is more sharp-sighted than any Hawk you have named, and more watchful and timorous than your high-mettled Merlin is bold? and yet I doubt not to catch a brace or two to-morrow, for a friend's breakfast: doubt not therefore, Sir, but that Angling is an art, and an art worth your learning: the question is rather, whether you be capable of learning it?

for Angling is somewhat like Poetry, men are to be born so: I mean with inclinations to it, though both may be heightened by discourse and practice; but he that hopes to be a good Angler must not only bring an inquiring, searching, observing wit, but he must bring a large measure of hope and patience, and a love and propensity to the art itself; but having once got and practised it, then doubt not but Angling will prove to be so pleasant, that it will prove to be like virtue, a reward to itself.

VEN. Sir, I am now become so full of expectation, that I long much to have you proceed; and in the order that you propose.

PISC. Then first, for the antiquity of Angling,[12] of which I shall not say much, but only this: some say it is as ancient as Deucalion's flood; others, that Belus, who was the first inventor of godly and virtuous recreations, was the first inventor of Angling; and some others say, for former times have had their disquisitions about the antiquity of it, that Seth, one of the sons of Adam, taught it to his sons, and that by them it was derived to posterity; others say, that he left it engraven on those pillars which he erected, and trusted to preserve the knowledge of the mathematics, music, and the rest of that precious knowledge, and those useful arts which by God's appointment or allowance and his noble industry were thereby preserved from perishing in Noah's flood.

These, Sir, have been the opinions of several men, that have possibly endeavored to make Angling more ancient than is needful, or may well be warranted; but for my part, I shall content myself in telling you, that Angling is much more ancient than the incarnation of our Saviour; for in the Prophet Amos mention is made of fish-hooks; and in the Book of Job, which was long before the days of Amos, for that book is said to be writ by Moses, mention is made also of fish-hooks, which must imply Anglers in those times.

But, my worthy friend, as I would rather prove myself a gentleman by being learned and humble, valiant and inoffensive, virtuous and communicable, than by any fond ostentation of riches, or, wanting those virtues myself, boast that these were in my ancestors,—and yet I grant that where a noble and ancient descent and such merits meet in any man, it is a double dignification of that person:—so if this antiquity of Angling, which for my part I have not forced, shall, like an ancient family, be either an honor or an ornament to this virtuous art which I profess to love and practise, I shall be the gladder that I made an accidental mention of the antiquity of it; of which I shall say no more, but proceed to that just commendation which I think it deserves.

And for that I shall tell you, that in ancient times a debate hath risen, and it remains yet unresolved, whether the happiness of man in this world doth consist more in contemplation or action.

Concerning which, some have endeavored to maintain their opinion of the first, by saying, that the nearer we mortals come to God by way of imitation, the more happy we are. And they say, that God enjoys himself only by a contemplation of his own Infiniteness, Eternity, Power, and Goodness, and the like. And upon this ground, many cloisteral men of great learning and devotion prefer contemplation before action. And many of the fathers seem to approve this opinion, as may appear in their commentaries upon the words of our Saviour to Martha (Luke x. 41, 42).

And, on the contrary, there want not men of equal authority and credit, that prefer action to be the more excellent: as namely, experiments in physic, and the application of it, both for the ease and prolongation of man's life; by which each man is enabled to act and do good to others, either to serve his country, or do good to particular persons: and they say also, that action is doctrinal, and teaches both art and virtue, and is a maintainer of humane society; and for these, and other like reasons, to be preferred before contemplation.

Concerning which two opinions I shall forbear to add a third by declaring my own, and rest myself contented in telling you, my very worthy friend, that both these meet together, and do most properly belong to the most honest, ingenuous, quiet, and harmless art of Angling.

And first, I shall tell you what some have observed, and I have found it to be a real truth, that the very sitting by the river's side is not only the quietest and fittest place for contemplation, but will invite an Angler to it; and this seems to be maintained by the learned Peter du Moulin,[13] who, in his discourse of the Fulfilling of Prophecies, observes, that when God intended to reveal any future events or high notions to his prophets, he then carried them either to the deserts or the sea-shore, that having so separated them from amidst the press of people and business, and the cares of the world, he might settle their mind in a quiet repose, and there make them fit for revelation.

And this seems also to be intimated by the children of Israel (Psal. 137), who, having in a sad condition banished all mirth and music from their pensive hearts, and having hung up their then mute harps upon the willow-trees growing by the rivers of Babylon, sat down upon those banks bemoaning the ruins of Sion, and contemplating their own sad condition.

And an ingenious Spaniard says,[14] that "rivers and the inhabitants of the watery element were made for wise men to contemplate, and fools to pass by without consideration." And though I will not rank myself in the number of the first, yet give me leave to free myself from the last, by offering to you a short contemplation, first of rivers and then of fish; concerning which I doubt not but to give you many observations that will appear very considerable: I am sure they have appeared so to me, and made many an hour pass away more pleasantly, as I have sat quietly on a flowery bank by a calm river, and contemplated what I shall now relate to you.

And first concerning Rivers; there be so many wonders reported and written of them, and of the several creatures that be bred and live in them, and those by authors of so good credit, that we need not to deny them an historical faith.

As namely of a river in Epirus, that puts out any lighted torch, and kindles any torch that was not lighted. Some waters being drank cause madness, some drunkenness, and some laughter to death. The river Selarus in a few hours turns a rod or wand to stone; and our Camden mentions the like in England, and the like in Lochmere in Ireland. There is also a river in Arabia, of which all the sheep that drink thereof have their wool turned into a vermilion color. And one of no less credit than Aristotle[15] tells us of a merry river, the river Elusina, that dances at the noise of music, for with music it bubbles, dances, and grows sandy, and so continues till the music ceases, but then it presently returns to its wonted calmness and clearness. And Camden tells us of a well near to Kirby in Westmoreland, that ebbs and flows several times every day; and he tells us of a river in Surrey, it is called Mole, that after it has run several miles, being opposed by hills, finds or makes itself a way under ground, and breaks out again so far off, that the inhabitants thereabouts boast, as the Spaniards do of their river Anus, that they feed divers flocks of sheep upon a bridge. And lastly, for I would not tire your patience, one of no less authority than Josephus, that learned Jew, tells us of a river in Judæa that runs swiftly all the six days of the week, and stands still and rests all their Sabbath.

But I will lay aside my discourse of rivers,[16] and tell you some things of the monsters, or fish, call them what you will, that they breed and feed in them. Pliny the philosopher says, in the third chapter of his ninth book, that in the Indian Sea the fish called the Balæna, or Whirlpool, is so long and broad as to take up more in length and breadth than two acres of ground, and of other fish of two hundred cubits long; and that in the river Ganges, there be Eels of thirty foot long. He says there, that these monsters appear in that sea only when the tempestuous winds oppose the torrents of waters falling from the rocks into it, and so turning what lay at the bottom to be seen on the water's top.

And he says, that the people of Cadara, an island near this place, make the timber for their houses of those fish-bones. He there tells us, that there are sometimes a thousand of these great Eels found wrapped or interwoven together. He tells us there, that it appears that Dolphins love music, and will come, when called for, by some men or boys, that know and use to feed them, and that they can swim as swift as an arrow can be shot out of a bow; and much of this is spoken concerning the Dolphin, and other fish, as may be found also in learned Dr. Casaubon's[17] discourse "Of Credulity and Incredulity," printed by him about the year 1670.

I know we islanders are averse to the belief of these wonders; but there be so many strange creatures to be now seen, many collected by John Tradescant,[18] and others added by my friend Elias Ashmole, Esq.,[19] who now keeps them

carefully and methodically at his house near to Lambeth near London, as may get some belief of some of the other wonders I mentioned. I will tell you some of the wonders that you may now see, and not till then believe, unless you think fit.

You may there see the Hog-fish, the Dog-fish, the Dolphin, the Coney-fish, the Parrot-fish, the Shark, the Poison-fish, Sword-fish, and not only other incredible fish, but you may there see the Salamander, several sorts of Barnacles, of Solan geese, the Bird of Paradise, such sorts of Snakes, and such bird's-nests, and of so various forms, and so wonderfully made, as may beget wonder and amusement in any beholder: and so many hundred of other rarities in that collection, as will make the other wonders I spake of the less incredible; for you may note, that the waters are Nature's storehouse, in which she locks up her wonders.

But, Sir, lest this discourse may seem tedious, I shall give it a sweet conclusion out of that holy poet, Mr. George Herbert, his divine "Contemplation on God's Providence."

> "Lord! who hath praise enough? Nay, who hath any?
> None can express thy works but he that knows them;
> And none can know thy works they are so many
> And so complete, but only he that owes them!
>
> "We all acknowledge both thy power and love
> To be exact, transcendent, and divine;
> Who dost so strongly and so sweetly move,
> Whilst all things have their end, yet none but thine.
>
> "Wherefore, most sacred Spirit, I here present
> For me, and all my fellows, praise to thee;
> And just it is that I should pay the rent,
> Because the benefit accrues to me."

And as concerning fish in that Psalm (Psal. civ.), wherein for height of poetry and wonders the prophet David seems even to exceed himself, how doth he there express himself in choice metaphors, even to the amazement of a contemplative reader, concerning the sea, the rivers, and the fish therein contained! And the great naturalist, Pliny, says, "That Nature's great and wonderful power is more demonstrated in the sea than on the land." And this may appear by the numerous and various creatures inhabiting both in and about that element; as to the readers of Gesner, Rondeletius, Pliny, Ausonius,[20] Aristotle, and others, may be demonstrated. But I will sweeten this discourse also out of a contemplation in divine Du Bartas,[21] who says:—

"God quickened in the sea and in the rivers
So many fishes of so many features,
That in the waters we may see all creatures,
Ev'n all that on the earth are to be found,
As if the world were in deep waters drowned.
For Seas, as well as Skies, have Sun, Moon, Stars;
As well as Air—Swallows, Rooks, and Stares;
As well as Earth—Vines, Roses, Nettles, Melons,
Mushrooms, Pinks, Gilliflowers, and many millions
Of other plants, more rare, more strange than these,
As very fishes living in the seas:
As also Rams, Calves, Horses, Hares, and Hogs,
Wolves, Urchins, Lions, Elephants, and Dogs;
Yea, Men and Maids, and, which I most admire,
The mitred Bishop, and the cowled Friar:
Of which examples but a few years since
Were shown the Norway and Polonian Prince."

These seem to be wonders, but have had so many confir-
mations from men of learning and credit, that you need not
doubt them: nor are the number nor the various shapes of
fishes more strange or more fit for contemplation, than
their different natures, inclinations, and actions; concerning
which I shall beg your patient ear a little longer.

The Cuttle-fish will cast a long gut out of her throat,
which, like as an Angler doth his line, she sendeth forth and
pulleth in again at her pleasure, according as she sees some
little fish come near to her; and the Cuttle-fish, being then
hid in the gravel, lets the smaller fish nibble and bite the
end of it, at which time she by little and little draws the
smaller fish so near to her, that she may leap upon her, and
then catches and devours her: and for this reason some have
called this fish the Sea-Angler.*

And there is a fish called a Hermit,[22] that at a certain age
gets into a dead fish's shell, and like a hermit dwells there
alone, studying the wind and weather, and so turns her shell
that she makes it defend her from the injuries that they
would bring upon her.

There is also a fish called, by Ælian,[23] in his ninth Book
of Living Creatures, Ch. 16, the Adonis, or Darling of the
Sea; so called because it is a loving and innocent fish, a fish
that hurts nothing that hath life, and is at peace with all the
numerous inhabitants of that vast watery element: and
truly I think most Anglers are so disposed to most of
mankind.

*Montaigne, Essays, and others affirm this.

And there are also lustful and chaste fishes, of which I shall give you examples.

And first, what Du Bartas says of a fish called the Sargus: which because none can express it better than he does, I shall give you in his own words; supposing it shall not have the less credit for being verse, for he hath gathered this and other observations out of authors that have been great and industrious searchers into the secrets of Nature.

> "The adult'rous Sargus doth not only change
> Wives every day in the deep streams, but, strange!
> As if the honey of sea-love delight
> Could not suffice his raging appetite,
> Goes courting she-goats on the grassy shore,
> Horning their husbands that had horns before."

And the same author writes concerning the Cantharus, that which you shall also hear in his own words:—

> "But contrary, the constant Cantharus
> Is ever constant to his faithful spouse;
> In nuptial duties spending his chaste life,
> Never loves any but his own dear wife."

Sir, but a little longer, and I have done.

VEN. Sir, take what liberty you think fit, for your discourse seems to be music, and charms me to an attention.

PISC. Why then, Sir, I will take a little liberty to tell, or rather to remember you, what is said of Turtle-Doves; first, that they silently plight their troth and marry; and that then the survivor scorns, as the Thracian women are said to do, to outlive his or her mate, and this is taken for a truth, and if the survivor shall ever couple with another, then not only the living but the dead, be it either the he or the she, is denied the name and honor of a true Turtle-Dove.

And to parallel this land-rarity, and teach mankind moral faithfulness, and to condemn those that talk of religion, and yet come short of the moral faith of fish and fowl; men that violate the law affirmed by St. Paul (Rom. ii. 14, 15, 16), to be writ in their hearts, and which, he says, shall at the last day condemn and leave them without excuse;—I pray hearken to what Du Bartas sings, for the hearing of such conjugal faithfulness will be music to all chaste ears, and therefore I pray hearken to what Du Bartas sings of the Mullet.

> "But for chaste love the Mullet hath no peer;
> For, if the fisher hath surprised her pheer,
> As mad with woe, to shore she followeth,
> Prest to consort him both in life and death."

On the contrary, what shall I say of the House-Cock, which treads any hen; and then, contrary to the Swan, the Partridge, and Pigeon, takes no care to hatch, to feed, or to cherish his own brood, but is senseless, though they perish.

And 't is considerable, that the Hen, which, because she also takes any Cock, expects it not, who is sure the chickens be her own, hath by a moral impression her care and affection to her own brood more than doubled, even to such a height, that our Saviour, in expressing his love to Jerusalem (Matt. xxiii. 37), quotes her for an example of tender affection; as his father had done Job for a pattern of patience.

And to parallel this Cock, there be divers fishes that cast their spawn on flags or stones, and then leave it uncovered, and exposed to become a prey, and be devoured by vermin, or other fishes; but other fishes, as namely the Barbel, take such care for the preservation of their seed, that, unlike to the Cock or the Cuckoo, they mutually labor, both the spawner and the melter, to cover their spawn with sand, or watch it, or hide it in some secret place, unfrequented by vermin or by any fish but themselves.

Sir, these examples may, to you and others, seem strange; but they are testified, some by Aristotle, some by Pliny, some by Gesner, and by many others of credit, and are believed and known by divers, both of wisdom and experience, to be a truth; and indeed are, as I said at the beginning, fit for the contemplation of a most serious and a most pious man. And, doubtless, this made the Prophet David say (Psal. cvii. 23, 24), "They that occupy themselves in deep waters see the wonderful works of God:" indeed, such wonders and pleasures too as the land affords not.

And that they be fit for the contemplation of the most prudent, and pious, and peaceable men, seems to be testified by the practice of so many devout and contemplative men, as the Patriarchs and Prophets of old, and of the Apostles of our Saviour in our latter times; of which twelve, we are sure he chose four that were simple Fishermen, whom he inspired and sent to publish his blessed will to the

Gentiles, and inspired them also with a power to speak all languages, and by their powerful eloquence to beget faith in the unbelieving Jews, and themselves to suffer for that Saviour whom their forefathers and they had crucified; and, in their sufferings, to preach freedom from the incumbrances of the law, and a new way to everlasting life. This was the employment of these happy Fishermen, concerning which choice some have made these observations.

First, that he never reproved these for their employment or calling, as he did scribes and the money-changers. And secondly, he found that the hearts of such men by nature were fitted for contemplation and quietness; men of mild, and sweet, and peaceable spirits, as indeed most Anglers are: these men, our blessed Saviour, who is observed to love to plant grace in good natures, though indeed nothing be too hard for him, yet these men he chose to call from their irreprovable employment of fishing, and gave them grace to be his disciples, and to follow him and do wonders; I say four of twelve.

And it is observable, that it was our Saviour's will, that these our four Fishermen should have a priority of nomination in the catalogue of his Twelve Apostles (Matt. x. 2–4, Acts i. 13), as namely, first St. Peter, St. Andrew, St. James, and St. John, and then the rest in their order.

And it is yet more observable, that when our blessed Saviour went up into the mount, when he left the rest of his disciples and chose only three to bear him company at his Transfiguration, that those three were all Fishermen. And it is to be believed, that all the other Apostles, after they be-

took themselves to follow Christ, betook themselves to be
Fishermen too; for it is certain that the greater number of
them were found together fishing by Jesus after his Resurrection, as it is recorded in the twenty-first chapter of St.
John's Gospel, v. 3, 4.

And since I have your promise to hear me with patience,
I will take a liberty to look back upon an observation that
hath been made by an ingenious and learned man; who observes, that God hath been pleased to allow those whom he
himself hath appointed to write his holy will in Holy Writ,
yet, to express his will in such metaphors as their former affections or practice had inclined them to: and he brings
Solomon for an example, who before his conversion was re-
markably carnally amorous; and after by God's appointment wrote that spiritual dialogue or holy amorous
love-song, the Canticles, betwixt God and his Church; in
which he says his beloved had eyes like the fish-pools of
Heshbon.

And if this hold in reason, as I see none to the contrary,
then it may be probably concluded, that Moses, who, I told
you before, writ the Book of Job, and the Prophet Amos,
who was a shepherd, were both Anglers; for you shall in all
the Old Testament find fish-hooks, I think, but twice mentioned; namely, by meek Moses, the friend of God, and by
the humble Prophet Amos.

Concerning which last, namely, the Prophet Amos, I
shall make but this observation,—that he that shall read the
humble, lowly, plain style of that prophet, and compare it
with the high, glorious, eloquent style of the Prophet Isa-

iah, though they be both equally true, may easily believe
Amos to be, not only a shepherd, but a good-natured, plain
fisherman. Which I do the rather believe by comparing the
affectionate, loving, lowly, humble Epistles of St. Peter, St.
James, and St. John, whom we know were all Fishers, with
the glorious language and high metaphors of St. Paul, who
we may believe was not.

And for the lawfulness of fishing, it may very well be
maintained by our Saviour's bidding St. Peter cast his hook
into the water and catch a fish, for money to pay tribute to
Cæsar. And let me tell you, that Angling is of high esteem,
and of much use in other nations. He that reads the Voyages of Ferdinand Mendez Pinto[24] shall find that there he
declares to have found a king and several priests a-fishing.

And he that reads Plutarch[25] shall find that Angling was
not contemptible in the days of Mark Antony and Cleopatra, and that they in the midst of their wonderful glory used
Angling as a principal recreation. And let me tell you, that
in the Scripture Angling is always taken in the best sense;
and that, though Hunting may be sometimes so taken, yet
it is but seldom to be so understood. And let me add this
more,—he that views the ancient Ecclesiastical Canons
shall find Hunting to be forbidden to churchmen, as being
a turbulent, toilsome, perplexing recreation; and shall find
Angling allowed to clergymen, as being a harmless recreation, a recreation that invites them to contemplation and
quietness.

I might here enlarge myself by telling you what commendations our learned Perkins bestows on Angling; and

how dear a lover and great a practiser of it our learned Doctor Whitaker was, as indeed many others of great learning have been. But I will content myself with two memorable men, that lived near to our own time, whom I also take to have been ornaments to the art of Angling.

The first is Doctor Nowel,[26] sometime Dean of the

Cathedral Church of St. Paul in London, where his monument stands yet undefaced: a man that in the Reformation of Queen Elizabeth, not that of Henry VIII., was so noted for his meek spirit, deep learning, prudence, and piety, that the then Parliament and Convocation both chose, enjoined, and trusted him to be the man to make a Catechism for public use, such a one as should stand as a rule for faith and manners to their posterity. And the good old man, though he was very learned, yet knowing that God leads us not to heaven by many nor by hard questions, like an honest Angler, made that good, plain, unperplexed Catechism which is printed with our good old Service-Book. I say, this good man was a dear lover and constant practiser of Angling as any age can produce; and his custom was to spend, besides his fixed hours of prayer, those hours which by command of the Church were enjoined the clergy, and voluntarily dedicated to devotion by many primitive Christians,—I say, beside those hours, this good man was observed to spend a tenth part of his time in Angling; and also, for I have conversed with those which have conversed with him, to bestow a tenth part of his revenue, and usually all his fish, amongst the poor that inhabited near to those rivers in which it was caught; saying often, "that Charity gave life to Religion:" and at his return to his house would praise God he had spent that day free from worldly trouble; both harmlessly, and in a recreation that became a churchman. And this good man was well content, if not desirous, that posterity should know he was an Angler, as may appear by his picture now to be seen, and carefully kept in Brazennose College, to which he was a liberal benefactor; in which picture he is drawn leaning on a desk with his Bible before him, and on one hand of him his lines, hooks, and other tackling, lying in a round; and on his other hand are his Angle-rods of several sorts: and by them this is written, "that he died 13 Feb. 1601, being aged ninety-five years, forty-four of which he had been Dean of St. Paul's Church; and that his age had neither impaired his hearing, nor dimmed his eyes, nor weakened his memory, nor made any of the faculties of his mind weak or useless." 'T is said that Angling and temperance were great causes of these blessings, and I wish the like to all that imitate him and love the memory of so good a man.

My next and last example shall be that undervaluer of money, the late Provost of Eton College, Sir Henry Wotton; a man with whom I have often fished and conversed, a man whose foreign employments in the service of this nation, and whose experience, learning, wit, and cheerfulness made his company to be esteemed one of the delights of mankind. This man, whose very approbation of Angling were sufficient to convince any modest censurer of it, this man was also a most dear lover, and a frequent practiser, of the art of Angling; of which he would say, " 'T was an employment for his idle time, which was then not idly spent:" for Angling was, after tedious study, "a rest to his mind, a cheerer of his spirits, a diverter of sadness, a calmer of unquiet thoughts, a moderator of passions, a procurer of contentedness;" and "that it begat habits of peace and patience in those that professed and practised it." Indeed, my friend, you will find Angling to be like the virtue of humility, which has a calmness of spirit, and a world of other blessings attending upon it.

Sir, this was the saying of that learned man, and I do easily believe that peace, and patience, and a calm content, did cohabit in the cheerful heart of Sir Henry Wotton, because I know that, when he was beyond seventy years of age, he made this description of a part of the present pleasure that possessed him, as he sat quietly in a summer's evening on a bank a-fishing. It is a description of the Spring, which because it glided as soft and sweetly from his pen as that river does at this time, by which it was then made, I shall repeat it unto you.

"This day Dame Nature seemed in love:
The lusty sap began to move;
Fresh juice did stir th' embracing vines,
And birds had drawn their valentines.
The jealous Trout, that low did lie,
Rose at a well-dissembled fly:
There stood my friend, with patient skill,
Attending of his trembling quill.
Already were the eaves possest
With the swift Pilgrim's daubed nest:
The groves already did rejoice
In Philomel's triumphing voice:
The showers were short, the weather mild,
The morning fresh, the evening smiled.
      Joan takes her neat rubbed pail, and now
She trips to milk the sand-red cow;
Where, for some sturdy foot-ball swain,
Joan strokes a syllabub or twain.
The fields and gardens were beset
With tulips, crocus, violet;
And now, though late, the modest rose
Did more than half a blush disclose.
Thus all looks gay, and full of cheer,
To welcome the new-liveried year."

These were the thoughts that then possessed the undisturbed mind of Sir Henry Wotton. Will you hear the wish
of another Angler, and the commendation of his happy life,
which he also sings in verse? viz. Jo. Davors, Esq.:—

"Let me live harmlessly, and near the brink
    Of Trent or Avon have a dwelling-place;
Where I may see my quill or cork down sink

With eager bite of Perch, or Bleak, or Dace;
And on the world and my Creator think:
　　Whilst some men strive ill-gotten goods t' embrace,
And others spend their time in base excess
Of wine, or, worse, in war and wantonness.

"Let them that list these pastimes still pursue,
　　And on such pleasing fancies feed their fill,
So I the fields and meadows green may view,
　　And daily by fresh rivers walk at will,
Among the daisies and the violets blue,
　　Red hyacinth, and yellow daffodil,
Purple Narcissus like the morning rays,
Pale gander-grass, and azure culver-keys.

"I count it higher pleasure to behold
　　The stately compass of the lofty sky,
And in the midst thereof, like burning gold,
　　The flaming chariot of the world's great eye;
The watery clouds that in the air up-rolled
　　With sundry kinds of painted colors fly;
And fair Aurora lifting up her head,
Still blushing, rise from old Tithonus' bed;

"The hills and mountains raised from the plains,
　　The plains extended level with the ground,
The grounds divided into sundry veins,
　　The veins enclosed with rivers running round;
These rivers making way through Nature's chains
　　With headlong course into the sea profound;
The raging sea, beneath the valleys low,
Where lakes and rills and rivulets do flow;

"The lofty woods, the forests wide and long,
　　Adorned with leaves, and branches fresh and green,

In whose cool bowers the birds with many a song
    Do welcome with their quire the Summer's Queen;
The meadows fair where Flora's gifts among
    Are intermixed, with verdant grass between;
The silver-scaled fish that softly swim
Within the sweet brook's crystal watery stream.

"All these, and many more of His creation
    That made the heavens, the Angler oft doth see;
Taking therein no little delectation,
    To think how strange, how wonderful, they be!
Framing thereof an inward contemplation,
    To set his heart from other fancies free;
And whilst he looks on these with joyful eye,
His mind is rapt above the starry sky."

Sir, I am glad my memory has not lost these last verses, because they are somewhat more pleasant and more suitable to May-day than my harsh discourse; and I am glad your patience hath held out so long as to hear them and me, for both together have brought us within the sight of the Thatched House; and I must be your debtor, if you think it worth your attention, for the rest of my promised discourse, till some other opportunity and a like time of leisure.

VEN. Sir, you have Angled me on with much pleasure to the Thatched House; and I now find your words true, that "good company makes the way seem short:" for trust me, Sir, I thought we had wanted three miles of this house till you showed it to me; but now we are at it, we 'll turn into it, and refresh ourselves with a cup of drink and a little rest.

Pisc. Most gladly, Sir, and we'll drink a civil cup to all the Otter-hunters that are to meet you to-morrow.

Ven. That we will, Sir, and to all the lovers of Angling too, of which number I am now willing to be one myself; for, by the help of your good discourse and company, I have put on new thoughts both of the art of Angling, and of all that profess it: and if you will but meet me to-morrow at the time and place appointed, and bestow one day with me and my friends in hunting the Otter, I will dedicate the next two days to wait upon you, and we two will for that time do nothing but angle, and talk of fish and fishing.

Pisc. 'T is a match, Sir; I'll not fail you, God willing, to be at Amwell Hill to-morrow morning before sun-rising.

THE SECOND DAY.

CHAP. II.—*Observations of the* OTTER *and* CHUB.

VENATOR.

MY friend Piscator, you have kept time with my thoughts; for the sun is just rising, and I myself just now come to this place, and the dogs have just now put down an Otter. Look down at the bottom of the hill there in that meadow, checkered with water-lilies and lady-smocks; there you may see what work they make. Look! look! you may see all busy, men and dogs, dogs and men, all busy.

PISC. Sir, I am right glad to meet you, and glad to have so fair an entrance into this day's sport, and glad to see so many dogs, and more men all in pursuit of the Otter. Let's compliment no longer, but join unto them. Come, honest Venator, let's be gone, let us make haste; I long to be doing: no reasonable hedge or ditch shall hold me.

VEN. Gentleman Huntsman, where found you this Otter?

HUNT. Marry, Sir, we found her a mile from this place, a-fishing: she has this morning eaten the greatest part of this Trout; she has only left thus much of it, as you see, and was fishing for more. When we came, we found her just at it: but we were here very early, we were here an hour before sunrise, and have given her no rest since we came; sure she will hardly escape all these dogs and men. I am to have the skin if we kill her.

VEN. Why, Sir, what's the skin worth?

Hunt. 'T is worth ten shillings to make gloves; the gloves of an Otter are the best fortification for your hands that can be thought on against wet weather.

Pisc. I pray, honest Huntsman, let me ask you a pleasant question: Do you hunt a beast or a fish?

Hunt. Sir, it is not in my power to resolve you. I leave it to be resolved by the College of Carthusians, who have made vows never to eat flesh. But I have heard the question hath been debated among many great clerks, and they seem to differ about it; yet most agree that her tail is fish: and if her body be fish too, then I may say that a fish will walk upon land, for an Otter does so sometimes five, or six, or ten miles in a night, to catch for her young ones, or to glut herself with fish, and I can tell you that pigeons will fly forty miles for a breakfast; but, Sir, I am sure the Otter devours much fish, and kills and spoils much more than he eats: and I can tell you that this Dog-fisher, for so the Latins call him, can smell a fish in the water an hundred yards from him: Gesner says much farther, and that his stones are good against the falling-sickness; and that there is an herb, Benione, which being hung in a linen-cloth near a fish-pond, or any haunt that he uses, makes him to avoid the place; which proves he smells both by water and land. And I can tell you there is brave hunting this water-dog in Cornwall; where there have been so many, that our learned Camden says there is a river called Ottersey, which was so named by reason of the abundance of Otters that bred and fed in it.

And thus much for my knowledge of the Otter, which you may now see above water at vent, and the dogs close with him; I now see he will not last long: follow, therefore, my masters, follow, for Sweetlips was like to have him at this last vent.

VEN. Oh me! all the horse are got over the river. What shall we do now? shall we follow them over the water?

HUNT. No, Sir, no, be not so eager: stay a little and follow me, for both they and the dogs will be suddenly on this side again, I warrant you; and the Otter too, it may be. Now have at him with Kilbuck, for he vents again.

VEN. Marry, so he does, for look, he vents in that corner. Now, now Ringwood has him: now he 's gone again, and has bit the poor dog. Now Sweetlips has her; hold her, Sweetlips! Now all the dogs have her, some above and some under water; but now, now she 's tired, and past losing: come, bring her to me, Sweetlips. Look, 't is a Bitch-Otter, and she has lately whelped: let 's go to the place where she was put down, and not far from it you will find all her young ones, I dare warrant you, and kill them all too.

Hunt. Come, Gentlemen! come all! let 's go to the place where we put down the Otter. Look you, hereabout it was that she kennelled; look you, here it was indeed, for here 's her young ones, no less than five: come, let's kill them all.

Pisc. No, I pray, Sir, save me one, and I'll try if I can make her tame, as I know an ingenious gentleman in Leicester-shire, Mr. Nich. Seagrave, has done; who hath not only made her tame, but to catch fish, and do many other things of much pleasure.

Hunt. Take one with all my heart, but let us kill the rest. And now let's go to an honest alehouse, where we may have a cup of good barley-wine, and sing "Old Rose," and all of us rejoice together.

Ven. Come, my friend Piscator, let me invite you along with us. I 'll bear your charges this night, and you shall bear mine to-morrow; for my intention is to accompany you a day or two in fishing.

Pisc. Sir, your request is granted, and I shall be right glad, both to exchange such a courtesy, and also to enjoy your company.

Ven. Well, now let 's go to your sport of Angling.

Pisc. Let 's be going with all my heart. God keep you all, Gentlemen, and send you meet this day with another Bitch-Otter, and kill her merrily, and all her young ones too.

Ven. Now, Piscator, where will we begin to fish?

Pisc. We are not yet come to a likely place: I must walk a mile further yet, before I begin.

Ven. Well then, I pray, as we walk, tell me freely how do

you like your lodging, and mine host, and the company? Is
not mine host a witty man?

PISC. Sir, I will tell you presently what I think of your host;
but first I will tell you, I am glad these Otters were killed,
and I am sorry that there are no more otter-killers: for I
know that the want of otter-killers, and the not keeping the
Fence-months for the preservation of fish, will in time prove
the destruction of all rivers; and those very few that are left,
that make conscience of the laws of the nation,[28] and of
keeping days of abstinence, will be forced to eat flesh, or suffer more inconveniences than are yet foreseen.

VEN. Why, Sir, what be those that you call the Fence-
months?

PISC. Sir, they be principally three, namely, March, April,
and May; for these be the usual months that Salmon come
out of the sea to spawn in most fresh rivers, and their fry
would about a certain time return back to the salt water, if
they were not hindered by weirs and unlawful gins, which
the greedy fishermen set, and so destroy them by thousands;
as they would, being so taught by Nature, change the fresh
for salt water. He that shall view the wise statutes made in
the 13th of Edward I., and the like in Richard II., may see
several provisions made against the destruction of fish; and
though I profess no knowledge of the law, yet I am sure the
regulation of these defects might be easily mended. But I
remember that a wise friend of mine did usually say, "That
which is everybody's business is nobody's business;" if it
were otherwise, there could not be so many nets and fish
that are under the statute size sold daily amongst us, and of

which the conservators of the waters should be ashamed.

But above all, the taking fish in spawning-time may be said to be against nature; it is like the taking the dam on the nest when she hatches her young; a sin so against nature, that Almighty God hath in the Levitical law (Deuteronomy xxii. 6, 7) made a law against it.

But the poor fish have enemies enough beside such unnatural Fishermen, as namely, the Otters that I spake of, the Cormorant, the Bittern, the Osprey, the Sea-gull, the Heron, the Kingfisher, the Gorara, the Puet, the Swan, Goose, Ducks, and the Craber, which some call the Water-rat: against all which any honest man may make a just quarrel, but I will not, I will leave them to be quarrelled with and killed by others; for I am not of a cruel nature,—I love to kill nothing but fish.

And now to your question concerning your host. To speak truly, he is not to me a good companion: for most of his conceits were either Scripture jests, or lascivious jests; for which I count no man witty, for the Devil will help a man that way inclined, to the first, and his own corrupt nature, which he always carries with him, to the latter: but a companion that feasts the company with wit and mirth, and leaves out the sin which is usually mixed with them, he is the man; and indeed such a companion should have his charges borne, and to such company I hope to bring you this night; for at Trout Hall, not far from this place, where I purpose to lodge to-night,[29] there is usually an Angler that proves good company. And let me tell you, good company and good discourse are the very sinews of virtue: but for such discourse as we heard last night, it infects others; the very boys will learn to talk and swear as they heard mine host, and another of the company that shall be nameless; I am sorry the other is a gentleman, for less religion will not save their souls than a beggar's: I think more will be required at the last great day. Well, you know what example is able to do; and I know what the poet says in the like case, which is worthy to be noted by all parents and people of civility:—

> "Many a one
> Owes to his country his religion:
> And in another would as strongly grow,
> Had but his nurse or mother taught him so."

This is reason put into verse, and worthy the consideration of a wise man. But of this no more, for though I love civility, yet I hate severe censures: I'll to my own art, and I doubt not but at yonder tree I shall catch a Chub, and then we'll turn to an honest cleanly hostess, that I know right well, rest ourselves there, and dress it for our dinner.

VEN. O Sir! a Chub is the worst fish that swims; I hoped for a Trout to my dinner.

PISC. Trust me, Sir, there is not a likely place for a Trout hereabout, and we stayed so long to take our leave of your huntsmen this morning, that the sun is got so high, and shines so clear, that I will not undertake the catching of a Trout till evening. And though a Chub be by you and many others reckoned the worst of fish, yet you shall see I'll make it a good fish by dressing it.

VEN. Why, how will you dress him?

Pisc. I'll tell you by and by, when I have caught him. Look you here, Sir, do you see?—but you must stand very close,—there lie upon the top of the water in this very hole twenty Chubs. I'll catch only one, and that shall be the biggest of them all; and that I will do so I 'll hold you twenty to one, and you shall see it done.

Ven. Ay, marry, Sir! now you talk like an artist; and I 'll say you are one, when I shall see you perform what you say you can do: but I yet doubt it.

Pisc. You shall not doubt it long, for you shall see me do it presently. Look, the biggest of these Chubs has had some bruise upon his tail, by a pike or some other accident, and that looks like a white spot; that very Chub I mean to put into your hands presently; sit you but down in the shade, and stay but a little while, and I 'll warrant you I 'll bring him to you.

Ven. I 'll sit down and hope well, because you seem to be so confident.

Pisc. Look you, Sir, there is a trial of my skill; there he is:

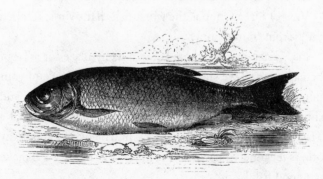

that very Chub that I showed you with the white spot on
his tail; and I 'll be as certain to make him a good dish of
meat, as I was to catch him. I 'll now lead you to an honest
ale-house, where we shall find a cleanly room, lavender in
the windows, and twenty ballads stuck about the wall:
there my hostess, which I may tell you is both cleanly, and
handsome, and civil, hath dressed many a one for me, and
shall now dress it after my fashion, and I warrant it good
meat.

VEN. Come, Sir, with all my heart, for I begin to be hungry, and long to be at it, and indeed to rest myself too; for
though I have walked but four miles this morning, yet I
begin to be weary; yesterday's hunting hangs still upon me.

PISC. Well, Sir, and you shall quickly be at rest, for yonder is the house I mean to bring you to.

Come, Hostess, how do you? Will you first give us a cup
of your best drink, and then dress this Chub, as you dressed
my last, when I and my friend were here about eight or ten
days ago? But you must do me one courtesy, it must be done
instantly.

HOSTESS. I will do it, Mr. Piscator, and with all the speed
I can.

PISC. Now, Sir, has not my hostess made haste? and does
not the fish look lovely?

VEN. Both, upon my word, Sir; and therefore let 's say
grace, and fall to eating of it.

PISC. Well, Sir, how do you like it?

VEN. Trust me, 't is as good meat as I ever tasted: but now

let me thank you for it, drink to you, and beg a courtesy of you; but it must not be denied me.

Pisc. What is it, I pray, Sir? You are so modest, that methinks I may promise to grant it before it is asked.

Ven. Why, Sir, it is that from henceforth you would allow me to call you Master, and that really I may be your scholar; for you are such a companion, and have so quickly caught and so excellently cooked this fish, as makes me ambitious to be your scholar.

Pisc. Give me your hand; from this time forward I will be your master, and teach you as much of this art as I am able; and will, as you desire me, tell you somewhat of the nature of most of the fish that we are to angle for; and I am sure I both can and will tell you more than any common Angler yet knows.

THE THIRD DAY.

CHAP. III.—*How to fish for, and to dress, the* CHAVENDER, *or* CHUB.

PISCATOR.

THE Chub, though he eat well thus dressed, yet as he is usually dressed he does not: he is objected against, not only for being full of small forked bones, dispersed through all his body, but that he eats waterish, and that the flesh of him is not firm, but short and tasteless. The French esteem him so mean, as to call him *un Vilain;* nevertheless he may be so dressed as to make him very good meat: as, namely, if he be a large Chub, then dress him thus:—

First scale him, and then wash him clean, and then take out his guts; and to that end make the hole as little and near to his gills as you may conveniently, and especially make clean his throat from the grass and weeds that are usually in it, for if that be not very clean, it will make him to taste very sour. Having so done, put some sweet herbs into his belly; and then tie him with two or three splinters to a spit, and roast him, basted often with vinegar, or rather verjuice and butter, with good store of salt mixed with it.

Being thus dressed, you will find him a much better dish of meat than you, or most folk, even than Anglers themselves, do imagine; for this dries up the fluid watery humor with which all Chubs do abound.

But take this rule with you, that a Chub newly taken and newly dressed is so much better than a Chub of a day's keeping after he is dead, that I can compare him to nothing so fitly as to cherries newly gathered from a tree, and others that have been bruised and lain a day or two in water. But the Chub being thus used and dressed presently, and not washed after he is gutted,—for note, that, lying long in water, and washing the blood out of any fish after they be gutted, abates much of their sweetness,—you will find the Chub, being dressed in the blood and quickly, to be such meat as will recompense your labor, and disabuse your opinion.

Or you may dress the Chavender or Chub thus:—

When you have scaled him, and cut off his tail and fins, and washed him very clean, then chine or slit him through the middle, as a salt fish is usually cut; then give him three or four cuts or scotches on the back with your knife, and broil him on charcoal, or wood-coal that is free from smoke; and all the time he is a-broiling, baste him with the best sweet butter, and good store of salt mixed with it; and to this add a little thyme cut exceeding small, or bruised into the butter. The Cheven thus dressed hath the watery taste taken away, for which so many except against him. Thus was the Cheven dressed that you now liked so well, and commended so much. But note again, that if this Chub that you ate of had been kept till to-morrow, he had not been worth a rush. And remember that his throat be washed very clean,—I say very clean,—and his body not washed after he is gutted, as indeed no fish should be.

Well, Scholar, you see what pains I have taken to recover the lost credit of the poor, despised Chub. And now I will give you some rules how to catch him: and I am glad to enter you into the art of Fishing by catching a Chub, for there is no fish better to enter a young Angler, he is so easily caught; but then it must be this particular way.

Go to the same hole in which I caught my Chub, where in most hot days you will find a dozen or twenty Chevens floating near the top of the water. Get two or three grasshoppers as you go over the meadow; and get secretly behind the tree, and stand as free from motion as is possible. Then put a grasshopper on your hook, and let your hook hang a quarter of a yard short of the water, to which end you must rest your rod on some bough of the tree. But it is likely the Chubs will sink down towards the bottom of the water at the first shadow of your rod, for a Chub is the fearfullest of fishes, and will do so if but a bird flies over him, and makes the least shadow on the water; but they will presently rise up to the top again, and there lie soaring till some shadow affrights them again. I say, when they lie upon the top of the water, look out the best Chub, which you, setting yourself in a fit place, may very easily see, and move your rod as softly as a snail moves to that Chub you intend to catch: let your bait fall gently upon the water three or four inches before him, and he will infallibly take the bait. And you will be as sure to catch him; for he is one of the leather-mouthed fishes, of which a hook does scarcely ever lose its hold; and, therefore, give him play enough before you offer to take him out of the water. Go your way presently; take my rod, and do as I bid you, and I will sit down and mend my tackling till you return back.

VEN. Truly, my loving Master, you have offered me as fair as I could wish. I 'll go and observe your directions.

Look you, Master, what I have done! that which joys my heart, caught just such another Chub as yours was.

PISC. Marry, and I am glad of it; I am like to have a towardly scholar of you. I now see that, with advice and practice, you will make an Angler in a short time. Have but a love to it, and I 'll warrant you.

VEN. But, Master, what if I could not have found a grasshopper?

PISC. Then I may tell you, that a black snail, with his belly slit to show his white, or a piece of soft cheese, will usually do as well. Nay, sometimes a worm, or any kind of fly, as the Ant-fly, the Flesh-fly, or Wall-fly, or the Dor or Beetle, which you may find under cow-dung, or a Bob, which you will find in the same place, and in time will be a Beetle,—it is a short white worm, like to and bigger than a gentle,—or a Cod-worm, or a Case-worm,—any of these will do very well to fish in such a manner.

And after this manner you may catch a Trout in a hot evening; when, as you walk by a brook, and shall see or hear him leap at flies, then if you get a grasshopper, put it on your hook, with your line about two yards long, standing behind a bush or tree where his hole is, and make your bait stir up and down on the top of the water. You may, if you stand close, be sure of a bite, but not sure to catch him, for he is not a leather-mouthed fish: and after this manner you may fish for him with almost any kind of live fly, but especially with a grasshopper.

VEN. But before you go further, I pray, good Master, what mean you by a leather-mouthed fish?

PISC. By a leather-mouthed fish, I mean such as have their teeth in their throat, as the Chub or Cheven; and so the Barbel, the Gudgeon, and Carp, and divers others have; and the hook, being stuck into the leather, or skin, of the mouth of such fish, does very seldom or never lose its hold: but on the contrary, a Pike, a Perch, or Trout, and so some other fish,—which have not their teeth in their throats, but in their mouths, which you shall observe to be very full of bones, and the skin very thin, and little of it;—I say, of these fish the hook never takes so sure hold but you often lose your fish, unless he have gorged it.

VEN. I thank you, good Master, for this observation; but now what shall be done with my Chub or Cheven that I have caught?

PISC. Marry, Sir, it shall be given away to some poor body, for I 'll warrant you I 'll give you a Trout for your supper: and it is a good beginning of your art to offer your first-fruits to the poor, who will both thank God and you for it, which I see by your silence you seem to consent to. And for your willingness to part with it so charitably, I will also teach you more concerning Chub-fishing. You are to note that in March and April he is usually taken with worms; in May, June, and July he will bite at any fly, or at cherries, or at beetles with their legs and wings cut off, or at any kind of snail, or at the black bee that breeds in clay-walls; and he never refuses a grasshopper on the top of a swift stream, nor, at the bottom, the young humble-bee that breeds in long grass, and is ordinarily found by the mower of it. In August, and in the cooler months, a yellow paste, made of the strongest cheese, and pounded in a mortar with a little butter and saffron, so much of it as being beaten small will turn it to a lemon color. And some make a paste for the winter months,—at which time the Chub is accounted best, for then it is observed that the forked bones are lost or turned into a kind of gristle, especially if he be baked,—of cheese and turpentine. He will bite also at a Minnow or Penk, as a Trout will; of which I shall tell you more hereafter, and of divers other baits. But take this for a rule, that in hot weather he is to be fished for towards the mid-water, or near the top; and in colder weather nearer the bottom. And if you fish for him on the top with a beetle or any fly, then be sure to let your line be very long, and to keep out of sight. And having told you that his spawn is excellent meat, and that the head of a large Cheven, the throat being well washed, is the best part of him, I will say no more of this fish at the present, but wish you may catch the next you fish for.

But lest you may judge me too nice in urging to have the Chub dressed so presently after he is taken, I will commend to your consideration how curious former times have been in the like kind.

You shall read in Seneca his "Natural Questions," Lib. iii. cap. 17, that the ancients were so curious in the newness of their fish, that that seemed not new enough that was not put alive into the guest's hand; and he says that to that end

they did usually keep them living in glass bottles in their
dining-rooms; and they did glory much, in their entertain-
ing of friends, to have that fish taken from under their table
alive, that was instantly to be fed upon. And he says they
took great pleasure to see their Mullets change to several
colors, when they were dying. But enough of this, for I
doubt I have stayed too long from giving you some observations of the Trout, and how to fish for him, which shall
take up the next of my spare time.

THE THIRD DAY.

CHAP. IV.—*Observations of the* NATURE *and* BREEDING *of the* TROUT, *and how to fish for him. And the Milk-maid's Song.*

PISCATOR.

THE Trout is a fish highly valued both in this and foreign nations. He may be justly said, as the old poet said of wine, and we English say of venison, to be a generous fish: a fish that is so like the buck that he also has his seasons; for it is observed, that he comes in and goes out of season with the stag and buck. Gesner says his name is of a German offspring, and says he is a fish that feeds clean and purely, in the swiftest streams, and on the hardest gravel; and that he may justly contend with all fresh-water fish, as the Mullet may with all sea-fish, for precedency and daintiness of taste, and that, being in right season, the most dainty palates have allowed precedency to him.

And before I go further in my discourse, let me tell you that you are to observe, that, as there be some barren does, that are good in summer, so there be some barren Trouts that are good in winter, but there are not many that are so, for usually they be in their perfection in the month of May, and decline with the buck. Now you are to take notice, that in several countries, as in Germany and in other parts, compared to ours, fish do differ much in their bigness, and

shape, and other ways, and so do Trouts. It is well known
that in the Lake Leman, the Lake of Geneva, there are
Trouts taken of three cubits long,[30] as is affirmed by Gesner, a writer of good credit; and Mercator[31] says, the Trouts

that are taken in the Lake of Geneva are a great part of the
merchandise of that famous city. And you are further to
know, that there be certain waters that breed Trouts remarkable both for their number and smallness. I know a little brook in Kent that breeds them to a number incredible,
and you may take them twenty or forty in an hour, but none
greater than about the size of a gudgeon. There are also in
divers rivers, especially that relate to, or be near to the sea,
as Winchester, or the Thames about Windsor, a little Trout
called a Samlet or Skegger-Trout,—in both which places I
have caught twenty or forty at a standing,—that will bite as
fast and as freely as minnows; these be by some taken to be
young Salmons, but in those waters they never grow to be
bigger than a herring.

There is also in Kent near to Canterbury a Trout called
there a Fordidge Trout, a Trout that bears the name of the
town where it is usually caught, that is accounted the rarest

of fish; many of them near the bigness of a Salmon, but known by their different color, and in their best season they cut very white: and none of these have been known to be caught with an angle, unless it were one that was caught by Sir George Hastings, an excellent Angler, and now with God; and he hath told me, he thought that Trout bit not for hunger but wantonness; and is the rather to be believed, because both he then, and many others before him, have been curious to search into their bellies, what the food was by which they lived: and have found out nothing by which they might satisfy their curiosity.

Concerning which you are to take notice, that it is reported by good authors, that grasshoppers, and some fish, have no mouths, but are nourished and take breath by the porousness of their gills, man knows not how; and this may be believed, if we consider that, when the Raven hath hatched her eggs, she takes no further care, but leaves her young ones to the care of the God of nature, who is said in the Psalms (Psal. cxlvii. 9) "to feed the young ravens that call upon him." And they be kept alive, and fed by a dew, or worms that breed in their nests, or some other ways that we mortals know not; and this may be believed of the Fordidge Trout, which, as it is said of the Stork (Jere. viii. 7), that "he knows his season," so he knows his times, I think almost his day of coming into that river out of the sea; where he lives, and, it is like, feeds, nine months of the year, and fasts three in the river of Fordidge. And you are to note that those townsmen are very punctual in observing the time of beginning to fish for them; and boast much that their river affords a Trout that exceeds all others. And just so does Sussex boast of several fish; as namely, a Shelsey Cockle, a Chichester Lobster, an Arundel Mullet, and an Amerly Trout.

And now for some confirmation of the Fordidge Trout: you are to know that this Trout is thought to eat nothing in the fresh water; and it may be the better believed, because it is well known that swallows and bats and wagtails, which are called half-year birds, and not seen to fly in England for six months in the year, but about Michaelmas leave us for a hotter climate; yet some of them that have been left behind their fellows have been found, many thousands at a time, in hollow trees, or clay caves, where they have been observed to live and sleep out the whole winter without meat. And so Albertus[32] observes, that there is one kind of frog that hath her mouth naturally shut up about the end of August, and that she lives so all the winter: and though it be strange to some, yet it is known to too many among us to be doubted.

And so much for these Fordidge Trouts, which never afford an Angler sport, but either live their time of being in the fresh water by their meat formerly gotten in the sea, not unlike the swallow or frog, or by the virtue of the fresh water only; or as the Bird of Paradise and the Chameleon are said to live, by the sun and the air.

There is also in Northumberland a Trout called a Bull-Trout, of a much greater length and bigness than any in these southern parts: and there are in many rivers that relate to the sea Salmon-Trouts, as much different from others, both in shape and in their spots, as we see sheep in some

countries differ one from another in their shape and bigness, and in the fineness of their wool; and certainly, as
some pastures breed larger sheep, so do some rivers, by reason of the ground over which they run, breed larger Trouts.

Now the next thing that I will commend to your consideration is, that the Trout is of a more sudden growth than
other fish: concerning which you are also to take notice,
that he lives not so long as the Perch and divers other fishes
do, as Sir Francis Bacon hath observed in his "History of
Life and Death."

And next you are to take notice, that he is not like the
Crocodile, which, if he lives never so long, yet always
thrives till his death: but 't is not so with the Trout; for after
he has come to his full growth, he declines in his body, and
keeps his bigness or thrives only in his head, till his death.
And you are to know, that he will about, especially before,
the time of his spawning, get almost miraculously through
weirs and flood-gates against the streams: even through
such high and swift places as is almost incredible. Next, that
the Trout usually spawns about October or November, but
in some rivers a little sooner or later: which is the more observable, because most other fish spawn in the spring or
summer, when the sun hath warmed both the earth and
water, and made it fit for generation. And you are to note,
that he continues many months out of season: for it may be
observed of the Trout, that he is like the Buck or the Ox,
that will not be fat in many months, though he go in the
very same pasture that horses do, which will be fat in one
month; and so you may observe, that most other fishes re-

cover strength, and grow sooner fat and in season, than the Trout doth.

And next you are to note, that till the sun gets to such a height as to warm the earth and the water, the Trout is sick, and lean, and lousy, and unwholesome: for you shall in winter find him to have a big head, and then to be lank, and thin, and lean: at which time many of them have sticking on them Sugs, or Trout-lice, which is a kind of a worm, in shape like a clove or pin, with a big head, and sticks close to him and sucks his moisture; those, I think, the Trout breeds himself, and never thrives till he free himself from them, which is when warm weather comes; and then, as he grows stronger, he gets from the dead still water into the sharp streams and the gravel, and there rubs off these worms or lice; and then, as he grows stronger, so he gets him into swifter and swifter streams, and there lies at the watch for any fly or minnow that comes near to him: and he especially loves the May-fly, which is bread of the Cod-worm, or Cadis; and these make the Trout bold and lusty, and he is usually fatter and better meat at the end of that month than at any time of the year.

Now you are to know, that it is observed that usually the best Trouts are either red or yellow; though some, as the Fordidge Trout, be white and yet good; but that is not usual: and it is a note observable, that the female Trout hath usually a less head and a deeper body than the male Trout, and is usually the better meat. And note, that a hog-back and a little head, to either Trout, Salmon, or any other fish, is a sign that that fish is in season.

But yet you are to note, that as you see some willows, or palm-trees, bud and blossom sooner than others do, so some Trouts be in rivers sooner in season: and as some hollies or oaks are longer before they cast their leaves, so are some Trouts in rivers longer before they go out of season.

And you are to note, that there are several kinds of Trouts; but these several kinds are not considered but by very few men, for they go under the general name of Trouts: just as Pigeons do in most places; though it is certain there are tame and wild Pigeons: and of the tame, there be Helmits and Runts, and Carriers and Cropers, and indeed too many to name. Nay, the Royal Society have found and published lately, that there be thirty and three kinds of Spiders: and yet all, for aught I know, go under that one general name of Spider.[33] And 't is so with many kinds of fish, and of Trouts especially, which differ in their bigness, and shape, and spots, and color. The great Kentish Hens may be an instance compared to other hens; and doubtless there is a kind of small Trout, which will never thrive to be big, that breeds very many more than others do that be of a larger size: which you may rather believe, if you consider that the little Wren or Titmouse will have twenty young ones at a time, when usually the noble Hawk, or the musical Thrassel or Blackbird, exceed not four or five.

And now you shall see me try my skill to catch a Trout, and at my next walking, either this evening or to-morrow morning, I will give you direction how you yourself shall fish for him.

VEN. Trust me, Master, I see now it is a harder matter to

catch a Trout than a Chub: for I have put on patience, and followed you these two hours, and not seen a fish stir, neither at your minnow nor your worm.

PISC. Well, Scholar, you must endure worse luck some time, or you will never make a good Angler. But what say you now? there is a Trout now, and a good one too, if I can but hold him, and two or three turns more will tire him. Now you see he lies still, and the sleight is to land him: reach me that landing-net. So, Sir, now he is mine own, what say you now? is not this worth all my labor and your patience?

VEN. On my word, Master, this is a gallant Trout; what shall we do with him?

PISC. Marry, e'en eat him to supper: we'll go to my Hostess, from whence we came: she told me, as I was going out of door, that my brother Peter, a good Angler and a cheerful companion, had sent word he would lodge there tonight, and bring a friend with him. My Hostess has two beds, and I know you and I may have the best: we'll rejoice with my brother Peter and his friend, tell tales, or sing ballads, or make a catch, or find some harmless sport to content us, and pass away a little time without offence to God or man.

VEN. A match, good Master: Let's go to that house, for the linen looks white, and smells of lavender, and I long to lie in a pair of sheets that smell so. Let's be going, good Master, for I am hungry again with fishing.

PISC. Nay, stay a little, good Scholar: I caught my last

Trout with a worm; now I will put on a minnow and try a
quarter of an hour about yonder trees for another, and so
walk towards our lodging. Look you, Scholar, thereabout
we shall have a bite presently, or not at all. Have with you,
Sir, o' my word, I have hold of him. Oh! it is a great logger-
headed Chub; come, hang him upon that willow-twig, and
let's be going. But turn out of the way a little, good Scholar,
towards yonder high honeysuckle hedge; there we'll sit and
sing whilst this shower falls so gently upon the teeming
earth, and gives yet a sweeter smell to the lovely flowers that
adorn these verdant meadows.

Look, under that broad beech-tree I sat down, when I
was last this way a-fishing, and the birds in the adjoining
grove seemed to have a friendly contention with an echo,
whose dead voice seemed to live in a hollow tree, near to the
brow of that primrose hill; there I sat viewing the silver
streams glide silently towards their centre, the tempestuous
sea; yet sometimes opposed by rugged roots, and pebble-
stones, which broke their waves, and turned them into
foam: and sometimes I beguiled time by viewing the harmless lambs, some leaping securely in the cool shade, whilst
others sported themselves in the cheerful sun; and saw others craving comfort from the swollen udders of their bleating dams. As I thus sat, these and other sights had so fully
possessed my soul with content, that I thought, as the poet
has happily expressed it,

> "I was for that time lifted above earth,
> And possessed joys not promised in my birth."

As I left this place, and entered into the next field, a second pleasure entertained me; 't was a handsome Milkmaid that had not yet attained so much age and wisdom as to load her mind with any fears of many things that will never be, as too many men too often do; but she cast away all care, and sung like a nightingale. Her voice was good, and the ditty fitted for it; 't was that smooth song, which was made by Kit Marlowe, now at least fifty years ago: and the Milkmaid's mother sung an answer to it, which was made by Sir Walter Raleigh in his younger days.

They were old-fashioned poetry, but choicely good, I think much better than the strong lines that are now in fashion in this critical age. Look yonder! on my word, yonder they both be a-milking again. I will give her the Chub, and persuade them to sing those two songs to us.

God speed you, good woman! I have been a-fishing, and am going to Bleak Hall[34] to my bed; and having caught more fish than will sup myself and my friend, I will bestow this upon you and your daughter, for I use to sell none.

Milk-w. Marry, God requite you! Sir, and we'll eat it cheerfully; and if you come this way a-fishing two months hence, a-grace of God I'll give you a syllabub of new verjuice in a new-made hay-cock for it, and my Maudlin shall sing you one of her best ballads; for she and I both love all Anglers, they be such honest, civil, quiet men. In the mean time will you drink a draught of red cow's milk? you shall have it freely.

Pisc. No, I thank you; but I pray do us a courtesy that shall stand you and your daughter in nothing, and yet we will think ourselves still something in your debt: it is but to sing us a song that was sung by your daughter when I last passed over this meadow, about eight or nine days since.

MILK-W. What song was it, I pray? Was it "Come, Shepherds, deck your herds"? or "As at noon Dulcina rested"? or "Philida flouts me"? or Chevy Chace? or Johnny Armstrong? or Troy Town?

PISC. No, it is none of those: it is a song that your daughter sung the first part, and you sung the answer to it.

MILK-W. O, I know it now; I learned the first part in my golden age, when I was about the age of my poor daughter; and the latter part, which indeed fits me best now, but two or three years ago, when the cares of the world began to take hold of me: but you shall, God willing, hear them both, and sung as well as we can, for we both love Anglers. Come, Maudlin, sing the first part to the gentlemen with a merry heart, and I'll sing the second, when you have done.

"THE MILK-MAID'S SONG.

"Come, live with me, and be my love,
And we will all the pleasure prove
That valleys, groves, or hills, or field,
Or woods and steepy mountains yield.

"Where we will sit upon the rocks,
And see the shepherds feed our flocks,
By shallow rivers, to whose falls
Melodious birds sing madrigals.

"And I will make thee beds of roses,
And then a thousand fragrant posies;

A cap of flowers, and a kirtle
Embroidered all with leaves of myrtle;

"A gown made of the finest wool,
Which from our pretty lambs we pull;
Slippers lined choicely for the cold,
With buckles of the purest gold;

"A belt of straw, and ivy-buds,
With coral clasps and amber studs;—
And if these pleasures may thee move,
Come, live with me, and be my love.

"Thy silver dishes for thy meat,
As precious as the Gods do eat,
Shall on an ivory table be
Prepared each day for thee and me.

"The shepherd swains shall dance and sing
For thy delight each May morning:
If these delights thy mind may move,
Then live with me, and be my love."

VEN. Trust me, Master, it is a choice song, and sweetly sung by honest Maudlin. I now see it was not without cause that our good Queen Elizabeth did so often wish herself a Milkmaid all the month of May, because they are not troubled with fears and cares, but sing sweetly all the day, and sleep securely all the night: and, without doubt, honest, innocent, pretty Maudlin does so. I'll bestow Sir Thomas Overbury's Milkmaid's wish upon her,—"that she may die in the Spring; and, being dead, may have good store of flowers stuck round about her winding-sheet."

"THE MILK-MAID'S MOTHER'S ANSWER.

"If all the world and love were young,
And truth in every shepherd's tongue,
These pretty pleasures might me move
To live with thee, and be thy love.

"But time drives flocks from field to fold:
When rivers rage, and rocks grow cold,
Then Philomel becometh dumb,
And age complains of cares to come.

"The flowers do fade, and wanton fields
To wayward Winter reckoning yields:
A honey tongue, a heart of gall,
Is fancy's spring, but sorrow's fall.

"Thy gowns, thy shoes, thy beds of roses,
Thy cap, thy kirtle, and thy posies,
Soon break, soon wither, soon forgotten;
In folly ripe, in reason rotten.

"Thy belt of straw, and ivy-buds,
Thy coral clasps and amber studs,
All these in me no means can move
To come to thee, and be thy Love.

"What should we talk of dainties then,
Of better meat than 's fit for men?
These are but vain: that's only good
Which God hath blest, and sent for food.

"But could youth last, and love still breed,
Had joys no date, nor age no need,—

THE MILKMAID'S SONG

Then those delights my mind might move,
To live with thee, and be thy love."

MOTHER. Well, I have done my song. But stay, honest
Anglers, for I will make Maudlin to sing you one short song
more. Maudlin, sing that song that you sung last night,
when young Coridon the Shepherd played so purely on his
oaten pipe to you and your Cousin Retty.

MAUD. I will, Mother.

"I married a wife of late,
The more 's my unhappy fate:
    I married her for love,
    As my fancy did me move,
And not for a worldly estate:

"But oh! the green-sickness
    Soon changed her likeness,
And all her beauty did fail.
    But 't is not so
    With those that go,
    Through frost and snow,
    As all men know,
And carry the milking-pail."

PISC. Well sung! Good woman, I thank you. I'll give you
another dish of fish one of these days; and then beg another song of you. Come, Scholar, let Maudlin alone: do
not you offer to spoil her voice. Look! yonder comes mine
Hostess, to call us to supper. How now! is my brother Peter
come?

HOST. Yes, and a friend with him; they are both glad to hear that you are in these parts, and long to see you, and long to be at supper, for they be very hungry.

THE THIRD AND FOURTH DAYS.

CHAP. V.—*More Directions how to fish for, and how to make for the* TROUT *an* ARTIFICIAL MINNOW *and* FLIES, *with some Merriment.*

PISCATOR.

WELL met, Brother Peter! I heard you and a friend would lodge here to-night, and that hath made me to bring my friend to lodge here too. My friend is one that would fain be a Brother of the Angle: he hath been an Angler but this day, and I have taught him how to catch a Chub by daping with a grasshopper; and the Chub he caught was a lusty one of nineteen inches long. But pray, Brother Peter, who is your companion?

PETER. Brother Piscator, my friend is an honest Countryman, and his name is Coridon, and he is a downright witty companion, that met me here purposely to be pleasant and eat a Trout; and I have not yet wetted my line since we met together: but I hope to fit him with a Trout for his breakfast, for I 'll be early up.

PISC. Nay, brother, you shall not stay so long: for, look you! here is a Trout will fill six reasonable bellies.

Come, Hostess, dress it presently, and get us what other meat the house will afford, and give us some of your best barley-wine, the good liquor that our honest forefathers did use to drink of; the drink which preserved their health,

and made them live so long, and do so many good deeds.

PETER. O' my word, this Trout is perfect in season. Come, I thank you, and here is a hearty draught to you, and to all the Brothers of the Angle wheresoever they be, and to my young brother's good fortune to-morrow. I will furnish him with a rod, if you will furnish him with the rest of the tackling; we will set him up and make him a fisher. And I will tell him one thing for his encouragement, that his fortune hath made him happy to be scholar to such a master; a master that knows as much both of the nature and breeding of fish as any man: and can also tell him as well how to catch and cook them, from the Minnow to the Salmon, as any that I ever met withal.

PISC. Trust me, Brother Peter, I find my Scholar to be so suitable to my own humor, which is to be free, and pleasant, and civilly merry, that my resolution is to hide nothing that I know from him. Believe me, Scholar, this is my resolution; and so here 's to you a hearty draught, and to all that love us, and the honest art of Angling.

VEN. Trust me, good Master, you shall not sow your seed in barren ground; for I hope to return you an increase answerable to your hopes: but, however, you shall find me obedient, and thankful, and serviceable to my best ability.

PISC. 'T is enough, honest Scholar: come, let 's to supper. Come, my friend Coridon, this Trout looks lovely; it was twenty-two inches when it was taken; and the belly of it looked, some part of it as yellow as a marigold, and part of it as white as a lily; and yet methinks it looks better in this good sauce.

CORIDON. Indeed, honest friend, it looks well, and tastes well: I thank you for it, and so doth my friend Peter, or else he is to blame.

PET. Yes, and so I do; we all thank you, and when we have supped, I will get my friend Coridon to sing you a song for requital.

COR. I will sing a song, if anybody will sing another; else, to be plain with you, I will sing none: I am none of those that sing for meat, but for company: I say, " 'T is merry in hall, when men sing all."

PISC. I 'll promise you I 'll sing a song that was lately made, at my request, by Mr. William Basse, one that hath made the choice songs of the "Hunter in his career," and of "Tom of Bedlam," and many others of note; and this that I will sing is in praise of Angling.[35]

COR. And then mine shall be the praise of a countryman's life. What will the rest sing of?

PET. I will promise you, I will sing another song in praise

of Angling to-morrow night; for we will not part till then; but fish to-morrow, and sup together, and the next day every man leave fishing, and fall to his business.

VEN. 'T is a match; and I will provide you a song or a catch against then, too, which shall give some addition of mirth to the company; for we will be civil, and as merry as beggars.

PISC. 'T is a match, my masters. Let's even say grace, and turn to the fire, drink the other cup to wet our whistles, and so sing away all sad thoughts.

Come on, my masters, who begins? I think it is best to draw cuts, and avoid contention.

PET. It is a match. Look, the shortest cut falls to Coridon.

COR. Well, then, I will begin, for I hate contention.

CORIDON'S SONG.

"O the sweet contentment
The countryman doth find!
   Heigh trolollie lollie loe,
   Heigh trolollie lee,
That quiet contemplation
Possesseth all my mind:
   Then care away,
   And wend along with me.

"For courts are full of flattery,
As hath too oft been tried;
   Heigh trolollie lollie loe, etc.
The city full of wantonness,
And both are full of pride:
   Then care away, etc.

"But oh! the honest countryman
Speaks truly from his heart,
    Heigh trolollie lollie loe, etc.
His pride is in his tillage,
His horses, and his cart:
    Then care away, etc.

"Our clothing is good sheep-skins,
Gray russet for our wives,
    Heigh trolollie lollie loe, etc.
'T is warmth, and not gay clothing,
That doth prolong our lives:
    Then care away, etc.

"The ploughman, though he labor hard,
Yet on the holiday,
    Heigh trolollie lollie loe, etc.
No emperor so merrily
Does pass his time away:
    Then care away, etc.

"To recompense our tillage,
The heavens afford us showers;
    Heigh trolollie lollie loe, etc.
And for our sweet refreshments
The earth affords us bowers:
    Then care away, etc.

"The cuckoo and the nightingale
Full merrily do sing,
    Heigh trolollie lollie loe, etc.
And with their pleasant roundelays
Bid welcome to the spring:
    Then care away, etc.

"This is not half the happiness
The countryman enjoys;
   Heigh trolollie lollie loe, etc.
Though others think they have as much,
Yet he that says so lies:
   Then come away, turn
   Countryman with me."

                      Jo. Chalkhill.

Pisc. Well sung! Coridon, this song was sung with mettle; and it was choicely fitted to the occasion: I shall love you for it as long as I know you. I would you were a Brother of the Angle, for a companion that is cheerful, and free from swearing and scurrilous discourse, is worth gold. I love such mirth as does not make friends ashamed to look upon one another next morning; nor men, that cannot well bear it, to repent the money they spend when they be warmed with drink. And take this for a rule, you may pick out such times and such companies, that you may make yourselves merrier for a little than a great deal of money; for " 'T is the company and not the charge that makes the feast:" and such a companion you prove; I thank you for it.

But I will not compliment you out of the debt that I owe you, and therefore I will begin my song, and wish it may be so well liked.

THE ANGLER'S SONG.

"As inward love breeds outward talk,
The hound some praise, and some the hawk:
Some, better pleased with private sport,

Use tennis, some a mistress court:
> But these delights I neither wish,
> Nor envy, while I freely fish.

"Who hunts, doth oft in danger ride;
Who hawks, lures oft both far and wide;
Who uses games shall often prove
A loser; but who falls in love
> Is fettered in fond Cupid's snare:
> My angle breeds me no such care.

"Of recreation there is none
So free as Fishing is alone;
All other pastimes do no less
Than mind and body both possess:
> My hand alone my work can do,
> So I can fish and study too.

"I care not, I, to fish in seas;
Fresh rivers best my mind do please,
Whose sweet calm course I contemplate,
And seek in life to imitate:
> In civil bounds I fain would keep,
> And for my past offences weep.

"And when the timorous Trout I wait
To take, and he devours my bait,
How poor a thing sometimes I find
Will captivate a greedy mind!
> And when none bite, I praise the wise,
> Whom vain allurements ne'er surprise.

"But yet, though while I fish I fast,
I make good fortune my repast;

And thereunto my friend invite,
In whom I more than that delight:
    Who is more welcome to my dish,
    Than to my angle was my fish.

"As well content no prize to take,
As use of taken prize to make:
For so our Lord was pleased when
He fishers made fishers of men:
    Where, which is in no other game,
    A man may fish and praise his name.

"The first men that our Saviour dear
Did choose to wait upon him here
Blest fishers were, and fish the last
Food was that he on earth did taste:
    I therefore strive to follow those
    Whom he to follow him hath chose."

Cor. Well sung, Brother! you have paid your debt in good coin. We Anglers are all beholden to the good man that made this song. Come, Hostess, give us more ale, and let's drink to him.

And now let's every one go to bed that we may rise early: but first let's pay our reckoning, for I will have nothing to hinder me in the morning; for my purpose is to prevent the sun rising.

Pet. A match. Come, Coridon, you are to be my bedfellow: I know, Brother, you and your Scholar will lie together. But where shall we meet to-morrow night? for my friend Coridon and I will go up the water towards Ware.

PISC. And my Scholar and I will go down towards Waltham.

COR. Then let 's meet here, for here are fresh sheets that smell of lavender; and I am sure we cannot expect better meat or better usage in any place.

PET. 'T is a match. Good night to everybody!

PISC. And so say I.

VEN. And so say I.

THE FOURTH DAY.

PISC. Good morrow, good Hostess! I see my Brother Peter is still in bed: come, give my Scholar and me a morning drink, and a bit of meat to breakfast, and be sure to get a good dish of meat or two against supper, for we shall come home as hungry as hawks. Come, Scholar, let 's be going.

VEN. Well now, good Master, as we walk towards the river give me direction, according to your promise, how I shall fish for a Trout.

PISC. My honest Scholar, I will take this very convenient opportunity to do it.

The Trout is usually caught with a worm or a minnow, which some call a Penk, or with a fly, viz. either a natural or an artificial fly: concerning which three I will give you some observations and directions.

And, first, for worms: of these there be very many sorts; some breed only in the earth, as the Earth-worm; others of or amongst plants, as the Dug-worm; and others breed either out of excrements, or in the bodies of living creatures, as in the horns of sheep or deer; or some of dead flesh, as the maggot or gentle, and others.

Now these be most of them particularly good for particular fishes: but for the Trout, the Dew-worm, which some also call the Lob-worm, and the Brandling, are the chief; and especially the first for a great Trout, and the latter for a less. There be also of Lob-worms some called Squirrel-tails, a worm that has a red head, a streak down the back, and a broad tail, which are noted to be the best, because they are the toughest and most lively, and live longest in the water: for you are to know, that a dead worm is but a dead bait, and like to catch nothing, compared to a lively, quick, stirring worm. And for a Brandling, he is usually found in an old dunghill, or some very rotten place near to it: but most usually in cow-dung, or hog's dung, rather than horse-dung, which is somewhat too hot and dry for that worm. But the best of them are to be found in the bark of the tanners, which they cast up in heaps after they have used it about their leather.

There are also divers other kinds of worms, which for color and shape alter even as the ground out of which they are got; as the Marsh-worm, the Tag-tail, the Flag-worm, the Dock-worm, the Oak-worm, the Gilt-tail, the Twachel or Lob-worm, which of all others is the most excellent bait for a Salmon, and too many to name, even as many sorts as some think there be of several herbs or shrubs, or of several kinds of birds in the air: of which I shall say no more, but tell you, that what worms soever you fish with are the bet-

ter for being well scoured, that is, long kept before they be
used: and in case you have not been so provident, then the
way to cleanse and scour them quickly is to put them all
night in water, if they be Lob-worms, and then put them
into your bag with fennel; but you must not put your
Brandlings above an hour in water, and then put them into
fennel for sudden use; but if you have time, and purpose to
keep them long, then they be best preserved in an earthen
pot with good store of moss, which is to be fresh every three
or four days in summer, and every week or eight days in
winter; or at least the moss taken from them, and clean
washed, and wrung betwixt your hands till it be dry, and
then put it to them again. And when your worm, especially
the Brandling, begins to be sick and lose of his bigness, then
you may recover him by putting a little milk or cream, about
a spoonful in a day, into them by drops on the moss; and if
there be added to the cream an egg beaten and boiled in it,
then it will both fatten and preserve them long. And note,
that when the knot, which is near to the middle of the
Brandling, begins to swell, then he is sick, and, if he be not
well looked to, is near dying. And for moss you are to note,
that there be divers kinds of it, which I could name to you,
but will only tell you that that which is likest a buck's horn
is the best, except it be soft white moss, which grows on
some heaths, and is hard to be found. And note, that in a
very dry time, when you are put to an extremity for worms,
walnut-tree leaves squeezed into water, or salt in water, to
make it bitter or salt, and then that water poured on the
ground where you shall see worms are used to rise in the

night, will make them to appear above ground presently. And you may take notice, some say that camphor put into your bag with your moss and worms gives them a strong and so tempting a smell, that the fish fare the worse and you the better for it.

And now I shall show you how to bait your hook with a worm, so as shall prevent you from much trouble, and the loss of many a hook too, when you fish for a Trout with a running-line; that is to say, when you fish for him by hand at the ground. I will direct you in this as plainly as I can, that you may not mistake.

Suppose it be a big Lob-worm; put your hook into him somewhat above the middle, and out again a little below the middle: having so done, draw your worm above the arming of your hook; but note, that at the entering of your hook it must not be at the head-end of the worm, but at the tail-end of him, that the point of your hook may come out toward the head-end, and having drawn him above the arming of your hook, then put the point of your hook again into the very head of the worm, till it come near to the place where the point of the hook first came out: and then draw back that part of the worm that was above the shank or arming of your hook, and so fish with it. And if you mean to fish with two worms, then put the second on before you turn back the hook's head of the first worm. You cannot lose above two or three worms before you attain to what I direct you; and having attained it, you will find it very useful, and thank me for it, for you will run on the ground without tangling.

Now for the Minnow or Penk; he is not easily found and caught till March, or in April, for then he appears first in the river; Nature having taught him to shelter and hide himself in the winter in ditches that be near to the river, and there both to hide and keep himself warm in the mud or in the weeds, which rot not so soon as in a running river, in which place if he were in winter, the distempered floods that are usually in that season would suffer him to take no rest, but carry him headlong to mills and weirs, to his confusion. And of these Minnows, first you are to know, that the biggest size is not the best; and next, that the middle size and the whitest are the best: and then you are to know, that your Minnow must be so put on your hook, that it must turn round when 't is drawn against the stream, and that it may turn nimbly, you must put it on a big-sized hook as I shall now direct you, which is thus. Put your hook in at his mouth and out at his gill; then, having drawn your hook two or three inches beyond or through his gill, put it again into his mouth, and the point and beard out at his tail; and then tie the hook and his tail about very neatly with a white thread, which will make it the apter to turn quick in the water: that done, pull back that part of your line which was slack when you did put your hook into the Minnow the second time; I say, pull that part of your line back so that it shall fasten the head so that the body of the Minnow shall be almost straight on your hook; this done, try how it will turn by drawing it across the water or against a stream; and if it do not turn nimbly, then turn the tail a little to the right or left hand, and try again, till it turn quick; for if not, you are in danger to catch nothing; for know, that it is impossible that it should turn too quick. And you are yet to know, that in case you want a Minnow, then a small Loach or a Sticklebag, or any other small fish that will turn quick, will serve as well. And you are yet to know, that you may salt them, and by that means keep them ready and fit for use three or four days, or longer; and that of salt, bay-salt is the best.

And here let me tell you, what many old Anglers know right well, that at some times, and in some waters, a Minnow is not to be got, and therefore let me tell you, I have— which I will show to you—an artificial Minnow, that will catch a Trout as well as an artificial fly; and it was made by a handsome woman, that had a fine hand, and a live Minnow lying by her: the mould or body of the Minnow was cloth, and wrought upon or over it thus with a needle; the back of it with very sad French green silk, and paler green silk towards the belly, shadowed as perfectly as you can imagine, just as you see a Minnow; the belly was wrought also with a needle, and it was a part of it white silk, and another part of it with silver thread: the tail and fins were of a quill, which was shaven thin; the eyes were of two little black beads, and the head was so shadowed, and all of it so curiously wrought, and so exactly dissembled, that it would beguile any sharp-sighted Trout in a swift stream. And this Minnow I will now show you; look, here it is: and if you like it, lend it you, to have two or three made by it, for they be easily carried about an Angler and be of excellent use; for note, that a large Trout will come as fiercely at a Minnow, as the highest mettled hawk doth seize on a partridge, or a greyhound on a hare. I have been told, that one hundred and sixty Minnows have been found in a Trout's belly; either the Trout had devoured so many, or the miller that gave it a friend of mine had forced them down his throat after he had taken him.

Now for Flies, which is the third bait wherewith Trouts are usually taken. You are to know, that there are so many sorts of flies as there be of fruits: I will name you but some of them; as the Dun-fly, the Stone-fly, the Red-fly, the Moor-fly, the Tawny-fly, the Shell-fly, the Cloudy or Blackish-fly, the Flag-fly, the Vine-fly: there be of flies, Caterpillars, and Canker-flies, and Bear-flies; and indeed too many either for me to name or for you to remember: and their breeding is so various and wonderful, that I might easily amaze myself and tire you in a relation of them.

And yet I will exercise your promised patience by saying a little of the Caterpillar, or the Palmer-fly or worm, that by them you may guess what a work it were in a discourse but to run over those very many flies, worms, and little living creatures with which the sun and summer adorn and beautify the river-banks and meadows, both for the recreation and contemplation of us Anglers: pleasures which, I think, myself enjoy more than any other man that is not of my profession.

Pliny holds an opinion, that many have their birth or being from a dew, that in the spring falls upon the leaves of trees; and that some kinds of them are from a dew left upon herbs or flowers; and others from a dew left upon coleworts or cabbages; all which kinds of dews being thickened and

condensed, are by the sun's generative heat most of them
hatched, and in three days made living creatures: and these
of several shapes and colors; some being hard and tough,
some smooth and soft; some are horned in their head, some
in their tail, some have none: some have hair, some none:
some have sixteen feet, some less, and some have none: but,
as our Topsel[36] hath, with great diligence, observed, those
which have none move upon the earth, or upon broad
leaves, their motion being not unlike to the waves of the
sea. Some of them he also observes to be bred of the eggs of
other caterpillars, and that those in their time turn to be
butterflies; and again, that their eggs turn the following year
to be caterpillars. And some affirm, that every plant has his
particular fly or caterpillar, which it breeds and feeds. I have
seen, and may therefore affirm it, a green caterpillar, or
worm, as big as a small peascod, which had fourteen legs;
eight on the belly, four under the neck, and two near the
tail. It was found on a hedge of privet; and was taken
thence, and put into a large box, and a little branch or two
of privet put to it, on which I saw it feed as sharply as a dog
gnaws a bone: it lived thus five or six days, and thrived, and
changed the color two or three times; but, by some neglect
in the keeper of it, it then died and did not turn to a fly: but
if it had lived, it had doubtless turned to one of those flies
that some call Flies-of-prey, which those that walk by the
rivers may, in summer, see fasten on smaller flies, and, I
think, make them their food. And 't is observable, that, as
there be these Flies-of-prey which be very large, so there be
others, very little, created, I think, only to feed them, and

breed out of I know not what; whose life, they say, Nature intended not to exceed an hour; and yet that life is thus made shorter by other flies, or accident.

'T is endless to tell you what the curious searchers into Nature's productions have observed of these worms and flies: but yet I shall tell you what Aldrovandus,[37] our Topsel, and others, say of the Palmer-worm or Caterpillar: that whereas others content themselves to feed on particular herbs or leaves,—for most think those very leaves that gave them life and shape give them a particular feeding and nourishment, and that upon them they usually abide;—yet he observes that this is called a Pilgrim or Palmer-worm, for his very wandering life and various food; not contenting himself, as others do, with any one certain place for his abode, nor any certain kind of herb or flower for his feeding; but will boldly and disorderly wander up and down, and not endure to be kept to a diet, or fixed to a particular place.

Nay, the very colors of Caterpillars are, as one has observed, very elegant and beautiful. I shall, for a taste of the rest, describe one of them, which I will some time the next month show you feeding on a willow-tree, and you shall find him punctually to answer this very description: his lips and mouth somewhat yellow, his eyes black as jet, his forehead purple, his feet and hinder parts green, his tail two-forked and black; the whole body stained with a kind of red spots which run along the neck and shoulder-blade, not unlike the form of Saint Andrew's cross, or the letter X, made thus crosswise, and a white line drawn down his back to his tail; all which add much beauty to his whole body. And it is to me observable, that at a fixed age this Caterpillar gives over to eat, and towards winter comes to be covered over with a strange shell or crust, called an Aurelia; and so lives a kind of dead life, without eating, all the winter. And, as others of several kinds turn to be several kinds of flies and vermin the spring following, so this caterpillar then turns to be a painted butterfly.

Come, come, my Scholar, you see the river stops our morning walk, and I will also here stop my discourse: only, as we sit down under this honey-suckle hedge, whilst I look a line to fit the rod that our Brother Peter hath lent you, I shall, for a little confirmation of what I have said, repeat the observation of Du Bartas:—

"God, not contented to each kind to give,
And to infuse the virtue generative,
By his wise power made many creatures breed
Of lifeless bodies, without Venus' deed.

"So the cold humor breeds the Salamander;
Who, in effect, like to her birth's commander,
With child with hundred winters, with her touch
Quencheth the fire, though glowing ne'er so much.

"So in the fire, in burning furnace, springs
The fly Perausta with the flaming wings:
Without the fire it dies; in it it joys;
Living in that which all things else destroys.

"So, slow Boötes underneath him sees
In th' icy islands goslings hatched of trees;

Whose fruitful leaves, falling into the water,
Are turned, 't is known, to living fowls soon after.

"So rotten planks of broken ships do change
To barnacles. O transformation strange!
'T was first a green tree, then a broken hull,
Lately a mushroom, now a flying gull."

VEN. O my good Master! this morning walk has been spent to my great pleasure and wonder: but I pray, when shall I have your direction how to make Artificial Flies, like to those that the Trout loves best? and also how to use them?

PISC. My honest Scholar, it is now past five of the clock; we will fish till nine, and then go to breakfast. Go you to yonder sycamore-tree, and hide your bottle of drink under the hollow root of it; for about that time, and in that place, we will make a brave breakfast with a piece of powdered beef, and a radish or two that I have in my fish-bag: we shall, I warrant you, make a good, honest, wholesome, hungry breakfast; and I will then give you direction for the making and using of your flies: and in the mean time there is your rod and line; and my advice is, that you fish as you see me do, and let 's try which can catch the first fish.

VEN. I thank you, Master, I will observe and practise your direction, as far as I am able.

PISC. Look you, Scholar; you see I have hold of a good fish: I now see it is a Trout. I pray put that net under him, and touch not my line, for if you do, then we break all. Well done, Scholar, I thank you.

Now for another. Trust me I have another bite. Come, Scholar, come, lay down your rod, and help me to land this, as you did the other. So now we shall be sure to have a good dish of fish to supper.

VEN. I am glad of that; but I have no fortune: sure, Master, your's is a better rod and better tackling.

PISC. Nay, then, take mine, and I will fish with yours. Look you, Scholar, I have another. Come, do as you did before. And now I have a bite at another. Oh me! he has broke all; there's half a line and a good hook lost.

VEN. Ay, and a good Trout too.

PISC. Nay, the Trout is not lost; for pray take notice, no man can lose what he never had.

VEN. Master, I can neither catch with the first nor second angle: I have no fortune.

PISC. Look you, Scholar, I have yet another. And now, having caught three brace of Trouts, I will tell you a short tale as we walk towards our breakfast. A scholar, a preacher I should say, that was to preach to procure the approbation of a parish, that he might be their lecturer, had got from his fellow-pupil the copy of a sermon that was first preached with great commendation by him that composed it: and though the borrower of it preached it word for word, as it was at first, yet it was utterly disliked as it was preached by the second to his congregation; which the sermon-borrower complained of to the lender of it, and was thus answered: "I lent you indeed my fiddle, but not my fiddlestick; for you are to know, that every one cannot make music with my words, which are fitted for my own mouth." And so, my

Scholar, you are to know, that as the ill pronunciation or ill accenting of words in a sermon spoils it, so the ill carriage of your line, or not fishing even to a foot in a right place, makes you lose your labor; and you are to know, that though you have my fiddle, that is, my very rod and tacklings with which you see I catch fish, yet you have not my fiddlestick: that is, you yet have not skill to know how to carry your hand and line, nor how to guide it to a right place: and this must be taught you,—for you are to remember I told you Angling is an art,—either by practice, or a long observation, or both. But take this for a rule, when you fish for a Trout with a worm, let your line have so much, and not more lead than will fit the stream in which you fish; that is to say, more in a great troublesome stream than in a smaller that is quieter: as near as may be, so much as will sink the bait to the bottom, and keep it still in motion, and not more.

But now let 's say grace and fall to breakfast. What say you, Scholar, to the providence of an old Angler? Does not this meat taste well? and was not this place well chosen to eat it? for this sycamore-tree will shade us from the sun's heat.

Ven. All excellent good; and my stomach excellent good too. And now I remember, and find that true which devout Lessius[38] says, "that poor men, and those that fast often, have much more pleasure in eating than rich men and gluttons, that always feed before their stomachs are empty of their last meat, and call for more; for by that means they rob themselves of that pleasure that hunger brings to poor men." And I do seriously approve of that saying of yours, "that you had rather be a civil, well-governed, well-grounded, temperate, poor Angler, than a drunken lord:" but I hope there is none such. However, I am certain of this, that I have been at many very costly dinners that have not afforded me half the content that this has done, for which I thank God and you.

And now, good Master, proceed to your promised direction for making and ordering my Artificial Fly.

Pisc. My honest Scholar, I will do it, for it is a debt due unto you by my promise. And because you shall not think yourself more engaged to me than indeed you really are, I will freely give you such directions as were lately given to me by an ingenious Brother of the Angle, an honest man, and a most excellent fly-fisher.[39]

You are to note, that there are twelve kinds of artificial-made Flies to angle with upon the top of the water. Note by the way, that the fittest season of using these is a blustering, windy day, when the waters are so troubled that the natural fly cannot be seen, or rest upon them. The first is the Dun-fly, in March: the body is made of dun wool, the wings of the partridge's feathers. The second is another Dun-fly: the body of black wool, and the wings made of the black drake's feathers, and of the feathers under his tail. The third is the Stone-fly, in April: the body is made of black wool, made yellow under the wings, and under the tail, and so made with wings of the drake. The fourth is the Ruddy-fly, in the beginning of May: the body made of red wool wrapt about with black silk, and the feathers are the wings of the drake; with the feathers of a red capon also, which hang dangling on his sides next to the tail. The fifth is the yellow or greenish fly, in May likewise: the body made of yellow wool, and the wings made of the red cock's hackle or tail. The sixth is the Black-fly, in May also: the body made of black wool, and lapped about with the herle of a peacock's tail; the wings are made of the wings of a brown capon with his blue feathers in his head. The seventh is the Sad-yellow-fly in June: the body is made of black wool, with a yellow list on either side, and the wings taken off the wings of a buzzard, bound with black braked hemp. The eighth is the Moorish-fly: made with the body of duskish wool, and the wings made of the blackish mail of the drake. The ninth is the Tawny-fly, good until the middle of June: the body made of tawny wool, the wings made contrary one against the other, made of the whitish mail of the wild-drake. The tenth is the Wasp-fly, in July: the body made of black wool, lapped about with yellow silk; the wings made of the feathers of the drake, or of the buzzard. The eleventh is the Shell-fly, good in mid-July: the body made of greenish wool, lapped about with the herle of a peacock's tail, and the wings made of the wings of the buzzard. The twelfth is the dark Drake-fly, good in August: the body made with black wool, lapped about with black silk; his wings are made with the mail of the black-drake, with a black head. Thus have you a jury of flies likely to betray and condemn all the Trouts in the river.

I shall next give you some other directions for fly-fishing, such as are given by Mr. Thomas Barker,[40] a gentleman that

hath spent much time in fishing; but I shall do it with a little variation.

First, let your rod be light, and very gentle: I take the
best to be of two pieces. And let not your line exceed,—
especially for three or four links next to the hook,—I say,
not exceed three or four hairs at the most, though you may
fish a little stronger above in the upper part of your line;
but if you can attain to angle with one hair, you shall have
more rises and catch more fish. Now you must be sure not
to cumber yourself with too long a line, as most do. And
before you begin to angle, cast to have the wind on your
back, and the sun, if it shines, to be before you, and to fish
down the stream; and carry the point or top of your rod
downward, by which means the shadow of yourself, and
rod too, will be the least offensive to the fish; for the sight
of any shade amazes the fish, and spoils your sport, of
which you must take a great care.

In the middle of March, till which time a man should not
in honesty catch a Trout; or in April, if the weather be dark,
or a little windy or cloudy, the best fishing is with the
Palmer-worm, of which I last spoke to you; but of these
there be divers kinds, or at least of divers colors: these and
the May-fly are the ground of all fly-angling, which are to
be thus made.

First, you must arm your hook with the line in the inside
of it; then take your scissors, and cut so much of a brown
mallard's feather as in your own reason will make the wings
of it, you having withal regard to the bigness or littleness of
your hook: then lay the outmost part of your feather next to

your hook, then the point of your feather next the shank of your hook; and, having so done, whip it three or four times about the hook with the same silk with which your hook was armed; and, having made the silk fast, take the hackle of a cock or capon's neck, or a plover's top, which is usually better: take off the one side of the feather, and then take the hackle, silk, or crewel, gold or silver thread, make these fast at the bent of the hook, that is to say, below your arming; then you must take the hackle, the silver or gold thread, and work it up to the wings, shifting or still removing your finger as you turn the silk about the hook; and still looking at every stop or turn, that your gold, or what materials soever you make your fly of, do lie right and neatly, and if you find they do so, then, when you have made the head, make all fast: and then work your hackle up to the head, and make that fast: and then, with a needle or pin, divide the wing into two; and then with the arming silk whip it about cross-ways betwixt the wings; and then with your thumb you must turn the point of the feather towards the bent of the hook; and then work three or four times about the shank of the hook; and then view the proportion, and if all be neat and to your liking, fasten.

I confess, no direction can be given to make a man of a dull capacity able to make a fly well: and yet I know this, with a little practice, will help an ingenious Angler in a good degree: but to see a fly made by an artist in that kind, is the best teaching to make it. And, then, an ingenious Angler may walk by the river and mark what flies fall on the water that day, and catch one of them, if he see the Trouts

leap at a fly of that kind: and then having always hooks
ready-hung with him, and having a bag also always with
him, with bear's hair, or the hair of a brown or sad-colored
heifer, hackles of a cock or a capon, several colored silk and
crewel to make the body of the fly, the feathers of a drake's
head, black or brown sheep's wool, or hog's wool, or hair,
thread of gold and of silver, silk of several colors, especially
sad-colored, to make the fly's head; and there be also other
colored feathers both of little birds and of speckled fowl:—
I say, having those with him in a bag, and trying to make a
fly, though he miss at first, yet shall he at last hit it better,
even to such a perfection as none can well teach him. And
if he hit to make his fly right, and have the luck to hit also
where there is store of Trouts, a dark day, and a right wind,
he will catch such store of them as will encourage him to
grow more and more in love with the art of fly-making.

Ven. But, my loving Master, if any wind will not serve,
then I wish I were in Lapland, to buy a good wind of one of
the honest witches, that sell so many winds there, and so
cheap.

Pisc. Marry, Scholar, but I would not be there, nor indeed
from under this tree: for look how it begins to rain, and by
the clouds, if I mistake not, we shall presently have a smok-
ing shower: and therefore sit close; this sycamore-tree will
shelter us: and I will tell you, as they shall come into my
mind, more observations of Fly-fishing for a Trout.

But first for the wind: you are to take notice, that of the
winds the south wind is said to be best. One observes, that

> "when the wind is south,
> It blows your bait into a fish's mouth."

Next to that, the west wind is believed to be the best: and having told you that the east wind is the worst, I need not tell you which wind is the best in the third degree: and yet, as Solomon observes (Eccles. xi. 4), that "he that considers the wind shall never sow;" so he that busies his head too much about them, if the weather be not made extreme cold by an east wind, shall be a little superstitious: for as it is observed by some, that there is no good horse of a bad color, so I have observed that if it be a cloudy day, and not extreme cold, let the wind sit in what corner it will, and do its worst, I heed it not. And yet take this for a rule, that I would willingly fish standing on the lee-shore: and you are to take notice, that the fish lies or swims nearer the bottom, and in deeper water, in winter than in summer; and also nearer the bottom in a cold day, and then gets nearest the lee-side of the water.

But I promised to tell you more of the Fly-fishing for a Trout, which I may have time enough to do, for you see it rains May butter. First for a May-fly: you may make his body with greenish-colored crewel, or willowish color; darkening it in most places with waxed silk, or ribbed with black hair, or some of them ribbed with silver thread; and such wings, for the color, as you see the fly to have at that season,—nay, at that very day on the water. Or you may make the Oak-fly with an orange tawny and black ground, and the brown of a mallard's feather for the wings; and you are to know, that these two are most excellent flies, that is, the May-fly and the Oak-fly. And let me again tell you, that you keep as far from the water as you can possibly, whether you fish with a fly or worm, and fish down the stream: and when you fish with a fly, if it be possible, let no part of your line touch the water, but your fly only; and be still moving your fly upon the water, or casting it into the water, you yourself being also always moving down the stream.

Mr. Barker commends several sorts of the Palmer-flies; not only those ribbed with silver and gold, but others that have their bodies all made of black, or some with red, and a red hackle. You may also make the Hawthorn-fly, which is all black, and not big, but very small, the smaller the better: or the Oak-fly, the body of which is orange-color and black crewel, with a brown wing: or a fly made with a peacock's feather is excellent in a bright day. You must be sure you want not in your magazine-bag the peacock's feather, and grounds of such wool and crewel as will make the Grasshopper; and note, that usually the smallest flies are the best. And note also, that the light fly does usually make most sport in a dark day, and the darkest and least fly in a bright or clear day: and lastly note, that you are to repair upon any occasion to your magazine-bag; and upon any occasion vary, and make them lighter or sadder according to your fancy or the day.

And now I shall tell you, that the fishing with a natural fly is excellent, and affords much pleasure. They may be found thus: the May-fly usually in and about that month near to the river-side, especially against rain: the Oak-fly on the but or body of an oak or ash, from the beginning of May to the end of August; it is a brownish fly, and easy to be so found, and stands usually with his head downward, that is to say, towards the root of the tree: the small black fly, or Hawthorn-fly, is to be had on any hawthorn-bush after the leaves be come forth: with these and a short line, as I showed to angle for a Chub, you may dape or dop; and also with a grasshopper behind a tree, or in any deep hole; still making it to move on the top of the water, as if it were alive, and still keeping yourself out of sight, you shall certainly have sport if there be Trouts; yea, in a hot day, but especially in the evening of a hot day, you will have sport.

And now, Scholar, my direction for fly-fishing is ended with this shower, for it has done raining. And now look about you, and see how pleasantly that meadow looks; nay, and the earth smells as sweetly too. Come, let me tell you what holy Mr. Herbert says of such days and flowers as these; and then we will thank God that we enjoy them, and walk to the river, and sit down quietly, and try to catch the other brace of Trouts.

> "Sweet day, so cool, so calm, so bright,
> The bridal of the earth and sky,
> Sweet dews shall weep thy fall to-night,—
>   For thou must die!

> "Sweet rose, whose hue, angry and brave,
> Bids the rash gazer wipe his eye,
> Thy root is ever in its grave,—
>   And thou must die!

"Sweet spring, full of sweet days and roses,
A box where sweets compacted lie;
My music shows you have your closes,—
                    And all must die!

"Only a sweet and virtuous soul,
Like seasoned timber, never gives,
But when the whole world turns to coal,—
                    Then chiefly lives!"

VEN. I thank you, good Master, for your good direction for fly-fishing, and for the sweet enjoyment of the pleasant day, which is so far spent without offence to God or man: and I thank you for the sweet close of your discourse with Mr. Herbert's verses; who, I have heard, loved Angling: and I do the rather believe it, because he had a spirit suitable to Anglers, and to those primitive Christians that you love, and have so much commended.

PISC. Well, my loving Scholar, and I am pleased to know that you are so well pleased with my direction and discourse.

And since you like these verses of Mr. Herbert's so well, let me tell you what a reverend and learned divine that professes to imitate him, and has indeed done so most excellently, hath writ of our Book of Common Prayer: which I know you will like the better because he is a friend of mine, and I am sure no enemy to Angling.

"What? Prayer by the Book? and Common? Yes; why not?
        The spirit of grace
        And supplication

Is not left free alone
For time and place,
But manner too: to read or speak by rote,
Is all alike to him, that prays
In 's heart what with his mouth he says.

"They that in private by themselves alone
Do pray, may take
What liberty they please,
In choosing of the ways
Wherein to make
Their soul's most intimate affections known
To Him that sees in secret, when
Th' are most concealed from other men.

"But he that unto others leads the way
In public prayer,
Should do it so,
As all that hear may know
They need not fear
To tune their hearts unto his tongue, and say,
Amen! not doubt they were betrayed
To blaspheme, when they meant to have prayed.

"Devotion will add life unto the letter,
And why should not
That which authority
Prescribes esteemed be
Advantage got?
If th' prayer be good, the commoner the better,
Prayer in the Church's words, as well
As sense, of all prayers bears the bell."

CH. HARVIE.[41]

And now, Scholar, I think it will be time to repair to our angle-rods, which we left in the water to fish for themselves; and you shall choose which shall be yours; and it is an even lay one of them catches.

And let me tell you, this kind of fishing with a dead-rod, and laying night-hooks, are like putting money to use; for they both work for the owners when they do nothing but sleep, or eat, or rejoice; as you know we have done this last hour, and sat as quietly and as free from cares under this sycamore, as Virgil's Tityrus and his Melibœus did under their broad beech-tree. No life, my honest Scholar, no life so happy and so pleasant as the life of a well-governed Angler; for when the lawyer is swallowed up with business, and the statesman is preventing or contriving plots, then we sit on cowslip banks, hear the birds sing, and possess ourselves in as much quietness as these silent silver streams, which we now see glide so quietly by us. Indeed, my good Scholar, we may say of Angling, as Dr. Boteler[42] said of strawberries: "Doubtless God could have made a better berry, but doubtless God never did:" and so, if I might be judge, "God never did make a more calm, quiet, innocent recreation than Angling."

I'll tell you, Scholar, when I sat last on this primrose-bank, and looked down these meadows, I thought of them as Charles the Emperor did of the city of Florence,—"that they were too pleasant to be looked on, but only on holy-days:" as I then sat on this very grass, I turned my present thoughts into verse: 't was a Wish, which I 'll repeat to you.

THE ANGLER'S WISH.

I in these flowery meads would be;
These crystal streams should solace me;
To whose harmonious, bubbling noise
I with my angle would rejoice:
    Sit here, and see the turtle-dove
    Court his chaste mate to acts of love:

Or, on that bank, feel the west wind
Breathe health and plenty; please my mind
To see sweet dew-drops kiss these flowers,
And then washed off by April showers:
    Here, hear my Kenna sing*[43] a song;
    There, see a blackbird feed her young,

Or a leverock build her nest;
Here, give my weary spirits rest,
And raise my low-pitched thoughts above
Earth, or what poor mortals love:
    Thus free from lawsuits, and the noise
    Of princes' courts, I would rejoice:

Or, with my Bryan, and a book,
Loiter long days near Shawford Brook;
There sit by him, and eat my meat,
There see the sun both rise and set:
There bid good morning to next day,
There meditate my time away:
    And angle on, and beg to have
    A quiet passage to a welcome grave.

*Like Hermit poor.[44]

When I had ended this composure, I left this place, and saw a Brother of the Angle sit under that honeysuckle hedge, one that will prove worth your acquaintance. I sat down by him, and presently we met with an accidental piece of merriment which I will relate to you; for it rains still.

On the other side of this very hedge sat a gang of Gypsies, and near to them sat a gang of beggars. The Gypsies were then to divide all the money that had been got that week, either by stealing linen or poultry, or by fortune-telling, or legerdemain, or, indeed, by any other sleights and secrets belonging to their mysterious government. And the sum that was got that week proved to be but twenty and some odd shillings. The odd money was agreed to be distributed amongst the poor of their own corporation: and for the remaining twenty shillings, that was to be divided unto four Gentlemen-gypsies, according to their several degrees in their commonwealth.

And the first or chiefest Gypsy was by consent to have a third part of the twenty shillings, which all men know is 6s. 8d.

The second was to have a fourth part of the 20s., which all men know to be 5s.

The third was to have a fifth part of the 20s., which all men know to be 4s.

The fourth and last Gypsy was to have a sixth part of the 20s., which all men know to be 3s. 4d.

As, for example
   3 times 6s. 8d. is . . . . 20s.
And so is 4 times 5s. . . . . 20s.
And so is 5 times 4s. . . . . 20s.
And so is 6 times 3s. 4d. . . . . 20s.

And yet he that divided the money was so very a Gypsy, that, though he gave to every one these said sums, yet he kept one shilling of it for himself.

	s.	d.
As, for example,	6	8
	5	0
	4	0
	3	4
make but	19	0

But now you shall know, that when the four Gypsies saw that he had got one shilling by dividing the money, though not one of them knew any reason to demand more, yet, like lords and courtiers, every Gypsy envied him that was the gainer, and wrangled with him; and every one said the remaining shilling belonged to him: and so they fell to so high a contest about it, as none that knows the faithfulness of one Gypsy to another will easily believe; only we that have lived these last twenty years are certain that money has been able to do much mischief. However, the Gypsies were too wise to go to law, and did therefore choose their choice friends Rook and Shark, and our late English Gusman,[45] to be their arbitrators and umpires. And so they left this honeysuckle hedge; and went to tell fortunes, and cheat, and get more money and lodging in the next village.

When these were gone, we heard as high a contention amongst the beggars, whether it was easiest to rip a cloak, or to unrip a cloak? One beggar affirmed it was all one: but that was denied, by asking her if doing and undoing were all one. Then another said, 't was easiest to unrip a cloak, for that was to let it alone: but she was answered by asking her how she unripped it, if she let it alone? and she confessed herself mistaken. These and twenty such like questions were proposed, and answered with as much beggarly logic and earnestness as was ever heard to proceed from the mouth of the most pertinacious schismatic; and sometimes all the beggars, whose number was neither more nor less than the poets' nine Muses, talked all together about this ripping and unripping, and so loud that not one heard what the other said: but at last one Beggar craved audience, and told them, that old Father Clause, whom Ben Jonson in his Beggar's Bush[46] created king of their corporation, was that night to lodge at an ale-house, called Catch-her-by-the-way, not far from Waltham Cross, and in the high-road towards London; and he therefore desired them to spend no more time about that and such like questions, but to refer all to Father Clause at night, for he was an upright judge, and in the mean time draw cuts what song should be next sung, and who should sing it. They all agreed to the motion, and the lot fell to her that was the youngest, and veriest virgin of the company, and she sung Frank Davison's[47] song, which he made forty years ago; and all the others of the company joined to sing the burden with her. The ditty was this,—but first the burden:—

> "Bright shines the sun: play, beggars, play,
> Here's scraps enough to serve to-day.

> "What noise of viols is so sweet
>   As when our merry clappers ring?
> What mirth doth want when beggars meet?
>   A beggar's life is for a king.
> Eat, drink, and play; sleep when we list,
> Go where we will,—so stocks be mist.
>   Bright shines the sun: play, beggars, play,
>   Here's scraps enough to serve to-day.

> "The world is ours, and ours alone,
>   For we alone have world at will;
> We purchase not, all is our own,
>   Both fields and streets we beggars fill:
> Nor care to get, nor fear to keep,
> Did ever break a beggar's sleep.
>   Bright shines the sun: play, beggars, play,
>   Here's scraps enough to serve to-day

> "A hundred herds of black and white
>   Upon our gowns securely feed;
> And yet if any dare us bite,
>   He dies therefore as sure as creed.
> Thus beggars lord it as they please,
> And only beggars live at ease.
>   Bright shines the sun: play, beggars, play,
>   Here's scraps enough to serve to-day."

VEN. I thank you, good Master, for this piece of merriment, and this song, which was well humored by the maker, and well remembered by you.

PISC. But I pray forget not the catch which you promised to make against night; for our countryman, honest Coridon, will expect your catch and my song, which I must be forced to patch up, for it is so long since I learned it that I have forgot a part of it. But come, now it hath done raining, let's stretch our legs a little in a gentle walk to the river, and try what interest our angles will pay us for lending them so long to be used by the Trouts: lent them indeed, like usurers, for our profit and their destruction.

VEN. O me! look you Master, a fish, a fish! O alas, Master, I have lost her!

PISC. Ay, marry, Sir, that was a good fish indeed: if I had had the luck to have taken up that rod, then 't is twenty to one he should not have broke my line by running to the rod's end, as you suffered him. I would have held him within the bent of my rod, unless he had been fellow to the great Trout that is near an ell long, which was of such a length and depth that he had his picture drawn, and is now to be seen at mine Host Rickabie's, at the George in Ware; and it may be, by giving that very great Trout the rod, that is, by casting it to him into the water, I might have caught him at the long run; for so I use always to do when I meet with an overgrown fish, and you will learn to do so too hereafter: for I tell you, Scholar, fishing is an art, or, at least, it is an art to catch fish.

VEN. But, Master, I have heard that the great Trout you speak of is a Salmon.

PISC. Trust me, Scholar, I know not what to say to it. There are many country people that believe Hares change sexes every year; and there be very many learned men think so too, for in their dissecting them they find many reasons to incline them to that belief. And to make the wonder seem yet less, that Hares change sexes, note that Doctor Mer. Casaubon affirms, in his book "Of Credible and Incredible Things," that Gaspar Peucerus,[48] a learned physician, tells us of a people that once a year turn wolves, partly in shape, and partly in conditions. And so, whether this were a Salmon when he came into the fresh water, and his not returning into the sea hath altered him to another color or kind, I am not able to say; but I am certain he hath all the signs of being a Trout, both for his shape, color, and spots; and yet many think he is not.

VEN. But, Master, will this Trout which I had hold of die? for it is like he hath the hook in his belly.

PISC. I will tell you, Scholar, that unless the hook be fast in his very gorge, 't is more than probable he will live; and a little time, with the help of the water, will rust the hook, and it will in time wear away, as the gravel doth in the horse-hoof, which only leaves a false quarter.

And now, Scholar, let 's go to my rod. Look you, Scholar, I have a fish too, but it proves a logger-head Chub; and this is not much amiss, for this will pleasure some poor body, as we go to our lodgings to meet our brother Peter and honest Coridon. Come, now bait your hook again, and lay it into the water, for it rains again; and we will even retire to the sycamore-tree, and there I will give you more directions concerning fishing, for I would fain make you an artist.

VEN. Yes, good Master, I pray let it be so.

PISC. Well, Scholar, now we are sat down and are at ease, I shall tell you a little more of Trout-fishing, before I speak of the Salmon, which I purpose shall be next, and then of the Pike or Luce.

You are to know, there is night as well as day fishing for a Trout, and that in the night the best Trouts come out of their holes; and the manner of taking them is, on the top of the water with a great lob or garden-worm, or rather two, which you are to fish with in a place where the waters run somewhat quietly, for in a stream the bait will not be so well discerned. I say in a quiet or dead place near to some swift, there draw your bait over the top of the water, to and fro, and if there be a good Trout in the hole, he will take it, especially if the night be dark: for then he is bold and lies near the top of the water, watching the motion of any frog or water-rat or mouse that swims betwixt him and the sky; these he hunts after, if he sees the water but wrinkle or move in one of these dead holes, where these great old Trouts usually lie near to their holds: for you are to note, that the great old Trout is both subtle and fearful, and lies close all day, and does not usually stir out of his hold, but lies in it as close in the day as the timorous Hare does in her form; for the chief feeding of either is seldom in the day, but usually in the night, and then the great Trout feeds very boldly.

And you must fish for him with a strong line, and not a little hook; and let him have time to gorge your hook, for he does not usually forsake it, as he oft will in the day fishing. And if the night be not dark, then fish so with an artificial fly of a light color, and at the snap: nay, he will sometimes rise at a dead mouse, or a piece of cloth, or anything that seems to swim cross the water, or to be in motion. This is a choice way, but I have not oft used it, because it is void of the pleasures that such days as these, that we two now enjoy, afford an Angler.

And you are to know, that in Hampshire, which I think exceeds all England for swift, shallow, clear, pleasant brooks, and store of Trouts, they use to catch Trouts in the night by the light of a torch or straw, which when they have discovered, they strike with a trout-spear or other ways. This kind of way they catch very many; but I would not believe it till I was an eyewitness of it, nor do I like it now I have seen it.

VEN. But, Master, do not Trouts see us in the night?

PISC. Yes, and hear and smell too, both then and in the day-time; for Gesner observes, the Otter smells a fish forty furlongs off him in the water: and that it may be true seems to be affirmed by Sir Francis Bacon, in the Eighth Century of his Natural History, who there proves that waters may be the medium of sounds, by demonstrating it thus: "That if you knock two stones together very deep under the water, those that stand on a bank near to that place may hear the noise without any diminution of it by the water." He also offers the like experiment concerning the letting an anchor fall, by a very long cable or rope, on a rock or the sand within the sea. And this being so well observed and demonstrated, as it is by that learned man, has made me to believe that Eels unbed themselves, and stir at the noise of thunder, and not only, as some thing, by the motion or stirring of the earth which is occasioned by that thunder.

And this reason of Sir Francis Bacon, Exper. 792, has made me crave pardon of one that I laughed at for affirming, that he knew Carps come to a certain place in a pond, to be fed, at the ringing of a bell or the beating of a drum: and however, it shall be a rule for me to make as little noise as I can when I am fishing, until Sir Francis Bacon be confuted; which I shall give any man leave to do.

And, lest you may think him singular in this opinion, I will tell you, this seems to be believed by our learned Doctor Hakewill,[49] who in his Apology of God's Power and Providence, fol. 360, quotes Pliny to report, that one of the Emperors had particular fish-ponds, and in them several fish, that appeared and came when they were called by their particular names. And St. James tells us, Chap. iii. 7, that all things in the sea have been tamed by mankind. And Pliny tells us, Lib. ix. 35, that Antonia, the wife of Drusus, had a Lamprey, at whose gills she hung jewels, or earrings: and that others have been so tender-hearted as to shed tears at the death of fishes which they have kept and loved. And these observations, which will to most hearers seem wonderful, seem to have a further confirmation from Martial, Lib. iv. Epigr. 30, who writes thus:—

"Piscator, fuge, ne nocens," etc.

"Angler, wouldst thou be guiltless? then forbear,
For these are sacred fishes that swim here,
Who know their sovereign, and will lick his hand,
Than which none 's greater in the world's command;
Nay, more, th' have names, and when they called are,
Do to their several owners' call repair."

All the further use that I shall make of this shall be, to advise Anglers to be patient, and forbear swearing, lest they be
heard and catch no fish.[50]

And so I shall proceed next to tell you, it is certain, that
certain fields near Leominster, a town in Herefordshire, are
observed to make the sheep that graze upon them more fat
than the next, and also to bear finer wool; that is to say, that
that year in which they feed in such a particular pasture
they shall yield finer wool than they did that year before
they came to feed in it, and coarser again if they shall return
to their former pasture; and again return to a finer wool,
being fed in the fine-wool ground. Which I tell you, that
you may the better believe that I am certain, if I catch a
Trout in one meadow, he shall be white and faint, and very
like to be lousy; and as certainly, if I catch a Trout in the
next meadow, he shall be strong, and red, and lusty, and
much better meat. Trust me, Scholar, I have caught many a
Trout in a particular meadow, that the very shape and the
enamelled color of him hath been such as hath joyed me to
look on him; and I have then with much pleasure concluded
with Solomon, "Everything is beautiful in his season" (Eccles. iii. 11).

I should by promise speak next of the Salmon; but I will, by your favor, say a little of the Umber or Grayling; which is so like a Trout for his shape and feeding, that I desire I may exercise your patience with a short discourse on him; and then the next shall be of the Salmon.

THE FOURTH DAY.

CHAP. VI.—*Observations of the* UMBER *or* GRAYLING,[51]
and Directions how to fish for them.

PISCATOR.

THE Umber and Grayling are thought by some to differ, as the Herring and Pilcher do. But though they may do so in other nations, I think those in England differ nothing but in their names. Aldrovandus says, they be of a Trout kind; and Gesner says that, in his country, which is Switzerland, he is accounted the choicest of all fish. And in Italy he is, in the month of May, so highly valued, that he is sold then at a much higher rate than any other fish. The French, which call the Chub *Un Vilain,* call the Umber of the Lake Leman *Un Umble Chevalier;* and they value the Umber or Grayling so highly, that they say he feeds on gold; and say that many have been caught out of their famous river of Loire, out of whose bellies grains of gold have been often taken. And some think that he feeds on water-thyme, and smells of it at his first taking out of the water; and they may think so with as good reason as we do that our Smelts smell like violets at their being first caught, which I think is a truth. Aldrovandus says, the Salmon, the Grayling, and Trout, and all fish that live in clear and sharp streams, are made by their mother Nature of such exact shape and pleasant colors, purposely to invite us to a joy and contentedness in feasting with her.

Whether this is a truth or not, it is not my purpose to dispute; but 't is certain, all that write of the Umber declare him to be very medicinable. And Gesner says, that the fat of an Umber or Grayling being set, with a little honey, a day or two in the sun, in a little glass, is very excellent against redness or swarthiness, or anything that breeds in the eyes. Salvian[52] takes him to be called Umber from his swift swimming, or gliding out of sight more like a shadow or a ghost than a fish. Much more might be said both of his smell and taste: but I shall only tell you, that St. Ambrose, the glorious Bishop of Milan, who lived when the Church kept fasting-days, calls him the Flower-fish, or Flower of Fishes, and that he was so far in love with him, that he would not let him pass without the honor of a long discourse; but I must; and pass on to tell you how to take this dainty fish.

First, note, that he grows not to the bigness of a Trout; for the biggest of them do not usually exceed eighteen inches. He lives in such rivers as the Trout does, and is usually taken with the same baits as the Trout is, and after the same manner, for he will bite both at the minnow, or worm, or fly: though he bites not often at the minnow, and is very game-

some at the fly, and much simpler, and therefore bolder than a Trout; for he will rise twenty times at a fly, if you miss him, and yet rise again. He has been taken with a fly made of the red feathers of a Parakita, a strange outlandish bird; and he will rise at a fly not unlike a gnat or a small moth, or, indeed, at most flies that are not too big. He is a fish that lurks close all winter, but is very pleasant and jolly after mid-April, and in May, and in the hot months: he is of a very fine shape; his flesh is white, his teeth—those little ones that he has—are in his throat, yet he has so tender a mouth that he is oftener lost after an Angler has hooked him than any other fish. Though there be many of these fishes in the delicate river Dove, and in Trent, and some other smaller rivers, as that which runs by Salisbury, yet he is not so general a fish as the Trout, nor to me so good to eat or to angle for. And so I shall take my leave of him, and now come to some observations of the Salmon, and how to catch him.

THE FOURTH DAY

CHAP. VII.—*Observations of the* SALMON, *with Directions how to fish for him.*

PISCATOR.

THE Salmon is accounted the King of fresh-water fish, and is ever bred in rivers relating to the sea; yet so high, or far from it, as admits of no tincture of salt, or brackishness. He is said to breed or cast his spawn, in most rivers, in the month of August: some say that then they dig a hole or grave in a safe place in the gravel, and there place their eggs or spawn, after the melter has done his natural office, and then hide it most cunningly, and cover it over with gravel and stones; and then leave it to their Creator's protection, who, by a gentle heat which He infuses into that cold element, makes it brood and beget life in the spawn, and to become Samlets early in the spring next following.

The Salmons having spent their appointed time, and done this natural duty, in the fresh waters, they then haste to the sea before winter, both the melter and spawner: but if they be stopped by flood-gates or weirs, or lost in the fresh waters, then those so left behind by degrees grow sick, and lean, and unseasonable, and kipper; that is to say, have bony gristles grow out of their lower chaps, not unlike a hawk's beak, which hinder their feeding; and, in time, such fish so left behind pine away and die. 'T is observed that he may live thus one year from the sea; but he then grows insipid, and tasteless, and loses both his blood and strength, and pines and dies the second year. And 't is noted, that those little Salmons called Skeggers, which abound in many rivers relating to the sea, are bred by such sick Salmons that might not go to the sea, and that though they abound, yet they never thrive to any considerable bigness.

But if the old Salmon gets to the sea, then that gristle which shows him to be kipper wears away, or is cast off, as the eagle is said to cast his bill, and he recovers his strength, and comes next summer to the same river, if it be possible, to enjoy the former pleasures that there possessed him: for, as one has wittily observed, he has, like some persons of honor and riches, which have both their winter and summer houses, the fresh rivers for summer, and the salt water for winter, to spend his life in; which is not, as Sir Francis Bacon hath observed in his "History of Life and Death," above ten years. And it is to be observed, that though the Salmon does grow big in the sea, yet he grows not fat but in fresh rivers; and it is observed, that the farther they get from the sea, they be both the fatter and better.

Next I shall tell you, that though they make very hard shift to get out of the fresh rivers into the sea, yet they will make harder shift to get out of the salt into the fresh rivers, to spawn, or possess the pleasures that they have formerly found in them: to which end, they will force themselves through flood-gates, or over weirs, or hedges, or stops in the water, even to a height beyond common belief. Gesner speaks of such places as are known to be above eight feet high above water. And our Camden mentions in his Britannia the like wonder to be in Pembrokeshire, where the river Tivy falls into the sea; and that the fall is so downright, and so high, that the people stand and wonder at the strength and sleight by which they see the Salmon use to get out of the sea into the said river: and the manner and height of the place is so notable, that it is known far by the name of the Salmon-Leap. Concerning which take this also out of Michael Drayton, my honest old friend, as he tells it you in his "Polyolbion."

> "And when the Salmon seeks a fresher stream to find,
> Which hither from the sea comes yearly by his kind;
> As he towards season grows, and stems the wat'ry tract
> Where Tivy, falling down, makes an high cataract,
> Forced by the rising rocks that there her course oppose,
> As though within her bounds they meant her to enclose,—
> Here, when the laboring fish does at the foot arrive,
> And finds that by his strength he does but vainly strive;
> His tail takes in his mouth, and, bending like a bow
> That's to full compass drawn, aloft himself doth throw,
> Then springing at his height, as doth a little wand,
> That, bended end to end, and started from man's hand,
> Far off itself doth cast; so does the Salmon vault:
> And if at first he fail, his second summersault
> He instantly essays; and, from his nimble ring
> Still yerking, never leaves until himself he fling
> Above the opposing stream."

This Michael Drayton tells you of this leap or summersault of the Salmon.

And, next, I shall tell you, that it is observed by Gesner and others, that there is no better Salmon than in England; and that, though some of our northern counties have as fat and as large as the river Thames, yet none are of so excellent a taste.

And as I have told you that Sir Francis Bacon observes, the age of a Salmon exceeds not ten years, so let me next tell you, that his growth is very sudden: it is said, that, after he is got into the sea, he becomes, from a Samlet not so big as a Gudgeon, to be a Salmon, in as short a time as a gosling becomes to be a goose. Much of this has been observed, by tying a ribbon, or some known tape or thread, in the tail of some young Salmons, which have been taken in weirs as they have swimmed towards the salt water, and then by taking a part of them again, with the known mark, at the same place, at their return from the sea, which is usually about six months after; and the like experiment hath been tried upon young swallows, who have, after six months' absence, been observed to return to the same chimney, there to make their nests and habitations for the summer following: which has inclined many to think, that every Salmon usually returns to the same river in which it was bred, as young pigeons taken out of the same dove-cote have also been observed to do.

And you are yet to observe further, that the he-Salmon is usually bigger than the Spawner; and that he is more kipper, and less able to endure a winter in the fresh water, than she is: yet she is, at that time of looking less kipper and better, as watery, and as bad meat.

And yet you are to observe, that as there is no general rule without an exception, so there are some few rivers in this nation that have Trouts and Salmons in season in winter; as 't is certain there be in the river Wye in Monmouthshire, where they be in season, as Camden observes, from September till April. But, my Scholar, the observation of this and many other things, I must in manners omit, because they will prove too large for our narrow compass of time; and therefore I shall next fall upon my direction how to fish for this SALMON.

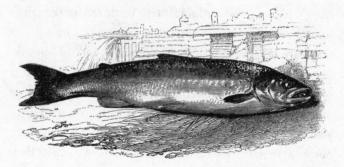

And for that: first you shall observe, that usually he stays not long in a place, as Trouts will, but, as I said, covets still to go nearer the spring-head; and that he does not as the Trout, and many other fish, lie near the water-side, or banks, or roots of trees, but swims in the deep and broad parts of the water, and usually in the middle, and near the ground, and that there you are to fish for him; and that he is to be caught as the Trout is, with a worm, a minnow, which some call a Penk, or with a fly.

And you are to observe, that he is very seldom observed to bite at a minnow, yet sometimes he will, and not usually at a fly, but more usually at a worm, and then most usually at a Lob or garden-worm, which should be well scoured, that is to say, kept seven or eight days in moss before you fish with them: and if you double your time of eight into sixteen, twenty, or more days, it is still the better; for the worms will still be clearer, tougher, and more lively, and continue so longer upon your hook. And they may be kept longer by keeping them cool and in fresh moss; and some advise to put camphor into it.

Note also, that many use to fish for a Salmon with a ring of wire on the top of their rod, through which the line may run to as great a length as is needful when he is hooked. And to that end, some use a wheel about the middle of their rod, or near their hand, which is to be observed better by seeing one of them, than by a large demonstration of words.

And now I shall tell you that which may be called a secret. I have been a-fishing with old Oliver Henley, now with God, a noted fisher both for Trout and Salmon, and have observed that he would usually take three or four worms out of his bag, and put them into a little box in his pocket, where he would usually let them continue half an hour or more before he would bait his hook with them; I have asked him his reason, and he has replied, "He did but pick the best out to be in readiness against he baited his hook the next time:" but he has been observed, both by others and myself, to catch more fish than I or any other body that has ever gone a-fishing with him could do, and especially Salmons. And I have been told lately, by one of his most intimate and secret friends, that the box in which he put those worms was anointed with a drop, or two or three, of the oil of ivy-berries, made by expression or infusion; and told, that by the worms remaining in that box an hour, or a like time, they had incorporated a kind of smell that was irresistibly attractive, enough to force any fish within the smell of them to bite. This I heard not long since from a friend, but have not tried it; yet I grant it probable, and refer my reader to Sir Francis Bacon's "Natural History," where he proves fishes may hear, and, doubtless, can more probably smell; and I am certain Gesner says the Otter can smell in the water, and I know not but that fish may do so too. 'T is left for a lover of angling, or any that desires to improve that art, to try this conclusion.

I shall also impart two other experiments, but not tried by myself, which I will deliver in the same words that they were given me by an excellent angler and a very friend, in writing: he told me the latter was too good to be told, but in a learned language, lest it should be made common.

"Take the stinking oil drawn out of Polypody of the oak by a retort, mixed with turpentine and hive-honey, and anoint your bait therewith, and it will doubtless draw the fish to it."

The other is this: "Vulnera Hederæ grandissimæ inflicta sudant Balsamun oleo gelato, albicantique persimile, odoris verò longè suavissimi."

'T is supremely sweet to any fish, and yet assafœtida may do the like.

But in these things I have no great faith, yet grant it probable; and have had from some chemical men, namely, from Sir George Hastings and others, an affirmation of them to be very advantageous: but no more of these, especially not in this place.

I might here, before I take my leave of the Salmon, tell you, that there is more than one sort of them, as namely, a Tecon, and another called in some places a Samlet, or by some, a Skegger: but these and others, which I forbear to name, may be fish of another kind, and differ, as we know a Herring and a Pilcher do; which, I think, are as different as the rivers in which they breed, and must by me be left to the disquisitions of men of more leisure, and of greater abilities than I profess myself to have.

And lastly, I am to borrow so much of your promised patience, as to tell you that the Trout or Salmon, being in season, have at their first taking out of the water, which continues during life, their bodies adorned, the one with such red spots, and the other with such black or blackish spots, as give them such an addition of natural beauty as, I think, was never given to any woman by the artificial paint or patches in which they so much pride themselves in this age. And so I shall leave them both, and proceed to some observations on the Pike.

THE FOURTH DAY.

CHAP. VIII.—*Observations of the* LUCE *or* PIKE, *with*
Directions how to fish for him.

PISCATOR.

THE mighty Luce or Pike is taken to be the Tyrant, as the Salmon is the King, of the fresh waters. 'T is not to be doubted but that they are bred, some by generation, and some not: as namely, of a weed called Pickerel-weed, unless learned Gesner be much mistaken; for he says, this weed and other glutinous matter, with the help of the sun's heat in some particular months, and some ponds apted for it by nature, do become Pikes. But doubtless divers Pikes are bred after this manner, or are brought into some ponds some such other ways as are past man's finding out, of which we have daily testimonies.

Sir Francis Bacon, in his "History of Life and Death," observes the Pike to be the longest-lived of any fresh-water fish, and yet he computes it to be not usually above forty years; and others think it to be not above ten years: and yet Gesner mentions a Pike taken in Swedeland in the year 1449, with a ring about his neck, declaring he was put into that pond by Frederick the Second, more than two hundred years before he was last taken, as by the inscription in that ring, being Greek, was interpreted by the then Bishop of Worms. But of this no more, but that it is observed that the old or very great Pikes have in them more of state than goodness; the smaller or middle-sized Pikes being by the most and choicest palates observed to be the best meat: and, contrary, the Eel is observed to be the better for age and bigness.

All Pikes that live long prove chargeable to their keepers, because their life is maintained by the death of so many other fish, even those of their own kind; which has made him by some writers to be called the Tyrant of the Rivers, or the Fresh-Water-Wolf, by reason of his bold, greedy, devouring disposition; which is so keen, as Gesner relates, a man going to a pond, where it seems a Pike had devoured all the fish, to water his mule, had a Pike bit his mule by the lips; to which the Pike hung so fast, that the mule drew him out of the water, and by that accident the owner of the mule angled out the Pike. And the same Gesner observes, that a maid in Poland had a Pike bit her by the foot as she was washing clothes in a pond. And I have heard the like of a woman in Killingworth Pond, not far from Coventry. But I have been assured by my friend Mr. Seagrave, of whom I spake to you formerly, that keeps tame Otters, that he hath known a Pike, in extreme hunger, fight with one of his Otters for a Carp that the Otter had caught, and was then bringing out of the water. I have told you who relate these things, and tell you they are persons of credit; and shall conclude this observation by telling you what a wise man has observed: "It is a hard thing to persuade the belly, because it has no ears."

But if these relations be disbelieved, it is too evident to be doubted that a Pike will devour a fish of his own kind,

PISCATOR'S LESSON

that shall be bigger than his belly or throat will receive, and swallow a part of him, and let the other part remain in his mouth till the swallowed part be digested, and then swallow that other part that was in his mouth, and so put it over by degrees; which is not unlike the ox, and some other beasts, taking their meat, not out of their mouth immediately into their belly, but first into some place betwixt, and then chew it, or digest it by degrees after, which is called chewing the cud. And doubtless Pikes will bite when they are not hungry, but, as some think, even for very anger, when a tempting bait comes near to them.

And it is observed that the Pike will eat venomous things, as some kind of frogs are, and yet live without being harmed by them; for, as some say, he has in him a natural balsam, or antidote against all poison: and he has a strange heat, that, though it appear to us to be cold, can yet digest, or put over, any fish-flesh, by degrees, without being sick. And others observe, that he never eats the venomous frog till he have first killed her, and then—as ducks are observed to do to frogs in spawning-time, at which time some frogs are observed to be venomous—so thoroughly washed her, by tumbling her up and down in the water, that he may devour her without danger. And Gesner affirms that a Polonian gentleman did faithfully assure him he had seen two young geese at one time in the belly of a Pike. And doubtless a Pike, in his height of hunger, will bite at and devour a dog that swims in a pond; and there have been examples of it, or the like; for, as I told you, "The belly has no ears when hunger comes upon it."

The Pike is also observed to be a solitary, melancholy, and a bold fish: melancholy, because he always swims or rests himself alone, and never swims in shoals or with company, as Roach and Dace, and most other fish do: and bold, because he fears not a shadow, or to see or be seen of anybody, as the Trout and Chub and all other fish do.

And it is observed by Gesner, that the jaw-bones and hearts and galls of Pikes are very medicinable for several diseases; or to stop blood, to abate fevers, to cure agues, to oppose or expel the infection of the plague, and to be many ways medicinable and useful for the good of mankind: but he observes, that the biting of a Pike is venomous and hard to be cured.

And it is observed, that the Pike is a fish that breeds but once a year, and that other fish, as namely Loaches, do breed oftener, as we are certain tame pigeons do almost every month; and yet the hawk, a bird of prey, as the Pike is of fish, breeds but once in twelve months. And you are to note, that his time of breeding, or spawning, is usually about the end of February, or somewhat later, in March, as the weather proves colder or warmer, and to note that his manner of breeding is thus: a he and a she Pike will usually go together out of a river into some ditch or creek, and that there the spawner casts her eggs, and the melter hovers over her all that time that she is casting her spawn, but touches her not.

I might say more of this, but it might be thought curiosity or worse, and shall therefore forbear it, and take up so much of your attention as to tell you that the best of pikes are noted to be in rivers; next, those in great ponds, or meres; and the worst, in small ponds.

But before I proceed further, I am to tell you that there is a great antipathy betwixt the Pike and some frogs: and this may appear to the reader of Dubravius,[53] a Bishop in Bohemia, who, in his book "Of Fish and Fish-Ponds," relates what he says he saw with his own eyes, and could not forbear to tell the reader. Which was:—

"As he and the Bishop Thurzo were walking by a large pond in Bohemia, they saw a Frog, when the Pike lay very sleepily and quiet by the shore-side, leap upon his head; and the Frog having expressed malice or anger by his swollen cheeks and staring eyes, did stretch out his legs and embraced the Pike's head, and presently reached them to his eyes, tearing with them and his teeth those tender parts: the Pike, moved with anguish, moves up and down the water, and rubs himself against weeds, and whatever he thought might quit him of his enemy: but all in vain, for the Frog did continue to ride triumphantly, and to bite and torment the Pike, till his strength failed: and then the Frog sunk with the Pike to the bottom of the water: then presently the Frog appeared again at the top and croaked, and seemed to rejoice like a conqueror, after which he presently retired to his secret hole. The Bishop, that had beheld the battle, called his fisherman to fetch his nets, and by all means to get the Pike, that they might declare what had happened: and the Pike was drawn forth, and both his eyes eaten out; at which when they began to wonder, the fisherman wished them to forbear, and assured them he was certain that Pikes were often so served."

I told this, which is to be read in the sixth chapter of the first book of Dubravius, unto a friend, who replied, "It was as improbable as to have the mouse scratch out the cat's eyes." But he did not consider that there be Fishing-Frogs, which the Dalmations call the Water-Devil, of which I might tell you as wonderful a story: but I shall tell you, that 't is not to be doubted but that there be some Frogs so fearful of the Water-Snake, that, when they swim in a place in which they fear to meet with him, they then get a reed across into their mouths, which, if they two meet by accident, secures the Frog from the strength and malice of the snake; and note, that the Frog usually swims the fastest of the two.

And let me tell you, that as there be Water and Land Frogs, so there be Land and Water Snakes. Concerning which, take this observation, that the Land-Snake breeds and hatches her eggs, which become young snakes, in some old dunghill, or a like hot place: but the Water-Snake, which is not venomous, and, as I have been assured by a great observer of such secrets, does not hatch, but breed her young alive; which she does not then forsake, but bides with them, and in case of danger will take them all into her mouth, and swim away from any apprehended danger, and then let them out again when she thinks all danger to be past: these be accidents that we anglers sometimes see, and often talk of.

But whither am I going? I had almost lost myself by remembering the discourse of Dubravius. I will therefore stop

here, and tell you according to my promise how to catch
this PIKE.

His feeding is usually of fish or frogs, and sometimes a
weed of his own called Pickerel-weed. Of which I told you
some think some Pikes are bred; for they have observed,
that where none have been put into ponds, yet they have
there found many; and that there has been plenty of that
weed in those ponds, and that that weed both breeds and
feeds them; but whether those Pikes so bred will ever breed
by generation as the others do, I shall leave to the disquisitions of men of more curiosity and leisure than I profess
myself to have; and shall proceed to tell you that you may
fish for a Pike, either with a ledger or a walking bait. And
you are to note, that I call that a ledger-bait which is fixed
or made to rest in one certain place when you shall be absent from it; and I call that a walking-bait which you take
with you, and have ever in motion. Concerning which two,
I shall give you this direction; that your Ledger-bait is best
to be a living bait, though a dead one may catch, whether it

be a fish or a frog; and that you may make them live the longer, you may, or indeed you must, take this course.

First, for your live-bait. Of fish, a Roach or Dace is, I think, best and most tempting, and a Perch is the longest lived on a hook, and having cut off his fin on his back, which may be done without hurting him, you must take your knife, which cannot be too sharp, and betwixt the head and the fin on the back, cut or make an incision, or such a scar, as you may put the arming wire of your hook into it, with as little bruising or hurting the fish as art and diligence will enable you to do; and so carrying your arming-wire along his back, unto or near the tail of your fish, betwixt the skin and the body of it, draw out that wire or arming of your hook at another scar near to his tail: then tie him about it with thread, but no harder than of necessity to prevent hurting the fish. And the better to avoid hurting the fish, some have a kind of probe to open the way, for the more easy entrance and passage of your wire or arming; but as for these, time, and a little experience, will teach you better than I can by words; therefore I will for the present say no more of this, but come next to give you some directions how to bait your hook with a Frog.

VEN. But, good Master, did you not say even now, that some Frogs were venomous, and is it not dangerous to touch them?

PISC. Yes, but I will give you some rules or cautions concerning them: and first, you are to note, that there are two kinds of Frogs; that is to say, if I may so express myself, a Flesh and a Fish Frog. By Flesh-frogs, I mean frogs that breed and live on the land; and of these there be several sorts also, and of several colors, some being speckled, some greenish, some blackish or brown: the Green-frog, which is a small one, is by Topsell taken to be venomous; and so is the Padock or Frog-padock, which usually keeps or breeds on the land, and is very large, and bony, and big, especially the she-frog of that kind; yet these will sometimes come into the water, but it is not often: and the Land-frogs are some of them observed by him to breed by laying eggs; and others to breed of the slime and dust of the earth, and that in winter they turn to slime again, and that the next summer that very slime returns to be a living creature; this is the opinion of Pliny. And Cardanus[54] undertakes to give a reason for the raining of frogs: but if it were in my power, it should rain none but Water-frogs, for those, I think, are not venomous, especially the right Water-frog, which, about February or March, breeds in ditches by slime, and blackish eggs in that slime: about which time of breeding, the he and she frogs are observed to use divers summersaults, and to croak and make a noise, which the Land-frog or Padock-frog never does. Now of these Water-frogs, if you intend to fish with a frog for a Pike, you are to choose the yellowest that you can get, for that the Pike ever likes best. And thus use your frog, that he may continue long alive.

Put your hook into his mouth, which you may easily do from the middle of April till August; and then the frog's mouth grows up, and he continues so for at least six months without eating, but is sustained, none but He whose Name is Wonderful knows how: I say, put your hook, I mean the arming-wire, through his mouth, and out at his gills, and then with a fine needle and silk sew the upper part of his leg with only one stitch to the arming-wire of your hook, or tie the frog's leg above the upper joint to the armed wire: and in so doing, use him as though you loved him, that is, harm him as little as you may possibly, that he may live the longer.

And now, having given you this direction for the baiting your Ledger-hook with a live fish or frog, my next must be to tell you how your hook thus baited must or may be used: and it is thus. Having fastened your hook to a line, which, if it be not fourteen yards long, should not be less than twelve, you are to fasten that line to any bough near to a hole where a Pike is, or is likely to lie, or to have a haunt; and then wind your line on any forked stick, all your line, except half a yard of it, or rather more; and split that forked stick with such a nick or notch at one end of it as may keep the line from any more of it ravelling from about the stick that so much of it as you intend. And choose your forked stick to be of that bigness as may keep the fish or frog from pulling the forked stick under the water till the Pike bites, and then the Pike having pulled the line forth of the cleft or nick of that stick in which it was gently fastened, he will have line enough to go to his hold and pouch the bait. And if you would have this Ledger-bait to keep at a fixed place, undisturbed by wind or other accidents, which may drive it to the shore-side,—for you are to note, that it is likeliest to catch a Pike in the midst of the water,—then hang a small plummet of lead, a stone, or piece of tile, or a turf, in a string, and cast it into the water, with the forked stick, to hang upon the ground, to be a kind of anchor to keep the forked stick from moving out of your intended place till the Pike come. This I take to be a very good way to use so many Ledger-baits as you intend to make trial of.

Or if you bait your hooks thus with live fish or frogs, and in a windy day, fasten them thus to a bough or bundle of straw, and by the help of that wind can get them to move across a pond or mere, you are like to stand still on the shore and see sport presently if there be any store of Pikes: or these live-baits may make sport, being tied about the body or wings of a goose or duck, and she chased over a pond. And the like may be done with turning three or four live-baits, thus fastened to bladders, or boughs, or bottles of hay or flags, to swim down a river, whilst you walk quietly alone on the shore, and are still in expectation of sport. The rest must be taught you by practice, for time will not allow me to say more of this kind of fishing with live-baits.

And for your dead-bait for a Pike, for that you may be taught by one day's going a-fishing with me, or any other body that fishes for him; for the baiting your hook with a dead Gudgeon or a Roach, and moving it up and down the water, is too easy a thing to take up any time to direct you to do it: and yet, because I cut you short in that, I will commute for it by telling you that that was told me for a secret. It is this.

Dissolve gum of ivy in oil of spike, and therewith anoint your dead-bait for a Pike; and then cast it into a likely place, and when it has lain a short time at the bottom, draw it towards the top of the water, and so up the stream: and it is more than likely that you have a Pike follow with more than common eagerness.

And some affirm, that any bait anointed with the marrow of the thigh-bone of an Hern is a great temptation to any fish.

These have not been tried by me, but told me by a friend of note, that pretended to do me a courtesy. But if this direction to catch a Pike thus do you no good, yet I am certain this direction how to roast him when he is caught is choicely good, for I have tried it; and it is somewhat the better for not being common: but with my direction you must take this caution, that your Pike must not be a small one, that is, it must be more than half a yard, and should be bigger.

First, open your Pike at the gills, and, if need be, cut also a little slit towards the belly. Out of these take his guts; and keep his liver, which you are to shred very small with thyme, sweet marjoram, and a little winter-savory; to these put some pickled oysters, and some anchovies, two or three; both these last whole, for the anchovies will melt, and the oysters should not; to these you must add also a pound of sweet butter, which you are to mix with the herbs that are shred, and let them all be well salted. If the Pike be more than a yard long, then you may put into these herbs more than a pound, or if he be less, then less butter will suffice. These being thus mixed, with a blade or two of mace, must be put into the Pike's belly, and then his belly so sewed up as to keep all the butter in his belly if it be possible; if not, then as much of it as you possibly can: but take not off the scales. Then you are to thrust the spit through his mouth, out at his tail; and then take four, or five, or six split sticks, or very thin laths, and a convenient quantity of tape or filleting; these laths are to be tied round about the Pike's body from his head to his tail, and the tape tied somewhat thick to prevent his breaking or falling off from the spit. Let him be roasted very leisurely, and often basted with claret-wine, and anchovies, and butter, mixed together; and also with what moisture falls from him into the pan. When you have roasted him sufficiently, you are to hold under him, when you unwind or cut the tape that ties him, such a dish as you purpose to eat him out of; and let him fall into it with the sauce that is roasted in his belly; and by this means the Pike will be kept unbroken and complete. Then, to the sauce which was within, and also that sauce in the pan, you are to add a fit quantity of the best butter, and to squeeze the juice of three or four oranges: lastly, you may either put into the Pike, with the oysters, two cloves of garlic, and take it whole out, when the Pike is cut off the spit; or to give the sauce a haut-gout, let the dish into which you let the Pike fall be rubbed with it. The using or not using of this garlic is left to your discretion.   M. B.

This dish of meat is too good for any but anglers, or very honest men; and I trust you will prove both, and therefore I have trusted you with this secret.

Let me next tell you, that Gesner tells us there are no Pikes in Spain, and that the largest are in the Lake Thrasymene in Italy; and the next, if not equal to them, are the Pikes of England; and that in England, Lincolnshire boasted to have the biggest. Just so doth Sussex boast of four sorts of fish; namely, an Arundel Mullet, a Chichester Lobster, a Shelsey Cockle, and an Amerly Trout.

But I will take up no more of your time with this relation, but proceed to give you some observations of the Carp, and how to angle for him, and to dress him:—but not till he is caught.

THE FOURTH DAY.

CHAP. IX.—*Observations of the* CARP, *with Directions how to fish for him.*

THE Carp is the Queen of Rivers: a stately, a good, and a very subtle fish, that was not at first bred, nor hath been long, in England, but is now naturalized. It is said, they were brought hither by one Mr. Mascal, a gentleman that then lived at Plumsted in Sussex, a county that abounds more with this fish than any in this nation.

You may remember that I told you, Gesner says there are no Pikes in Spain; and, doubtless, there was a time, about a hundred or a few more years ago, when there were no Carps in England, as may seem to be affirmed by Sir Richard Baker, in whose Chronicle you may find these verses:—

> "Hops and Turkeys, Carps and Beer,
> Came into England all in a year."[55]

And doubtless, as of sea-fish the Herring dies soonest out of the water, and of fresh-water fish the Trout, so, except the Eel, the Carp endures most hardness, and lives longest out of his own proper element: and therefore the report of the Carp's being brought out of a foreign country into this nation is the more probable.

Carps and Loaches are observed to breed several months in one year, which Pikes and most other fish do not. And this is partly proved by tame and wild rabbits, as also by some ducks, which will lay eggs nine of the twelve months; and yet there be other ducks that lay not longer than about one month. And it is the rather to be believed, because you shall scarce or never take a male Carp without a melt, or a female without a roe or spawn, and for the most part very much; and especially all the summer season: and it is observed, that they breed more naturally in ponds than in running waters, if they breed there at all; and that those that live in rivers are taken by men of the best palates to be much the better meat.

And it is observed, that in some ponds Carps will not breed, especially in cold ponds; but where they will breed, they breed innumerably: Aristotle and Pliny say, six times in a year, if there be no Pikes nor Perch to devour their spawn when it is cast upon grass, or flags, or weeds, where it lies ten or twelve days before it be enlivened.

The Carp, if he have water-room and good feed, will grow to a very great bigness and length; I have heard, to be much above a yard long. 'T is said by Jovius,[56] who hath writ of fishes, that in the Lake Lurian, in Italy, Carps have thriven to be more than fifty pounds' weight; which is the more probable, for as the bear is conceived and born suddenly, and being born is but short lived, so, on the contrary, the elephant is said to be two years in his dam's belly, some think he is ten years in it, and being born grows in bigness twenty years; and 't is observed too that he lives to the age

of a hundred years. And 't is also observed, that the crocodile is very long-lived, and more than that, that all that long
life he thrives in bigness: and so I think some Carps do, especially in some places; though I never saw one above
twenty-three inches, which was a great and goodly fish; but
have been assured there are of a far greater size, and in England too.

Now, as the increase of Carps is wonderful for their number, so there is not a reason found out, I think, by any, why
they should breed in some ponds and not in others of the
same nature for soil and all other circumstances. And as
their breeding, so are their decays also very mysterious: I
have both read it, and been told by a gentleman of tried
honesty, that he has known sixty or more large Carps put
into several ponds near to a house, where by reason of the
stakes in the ponds, and the owner's constant being near to
them, it was impossible they should be stolen away from
him: and that when he has, after three or four years, emp-
tied the pond, and expected an increase from them by
breeding young ones,—for that they might do so, he had, as
the rule is, put in three melters for one spawner,—he has, I
say, after three or four years, found neither a young nor old
Carp remaining. And the like I have known of one that has
almost watched the pond, and at a like distance of time, at
the fishing of a pond, found of seventy or eighty large Carps
not above five or six: and that he had forborne longer to fish
the said pond, but that he saw, in a hot day in summer, a
large Carp swim near the top of the water with a frog upon
his head; and that he upon that occasion caused his pond to

be let dry: and I say, of seventy or eighty Carps, only found five or six in the said pond, and those very sick and lean, and with every one a frog sticking so fast on the head of the said Carps, that the frog would not be got off without extreme force or killing. And the gentleman that did affirm this to me told me he saw it; and did declare his belief to be, and I also believe the same, that he thought the other Carps that were so strangely lost were so killed by frogs, and then devoured.

And a person of honor now living in Worcestershire assured me he had seen a necklace or collar of tadpoles hang like a chain or necklace of beads about a Pike's neck, and to kill him: whether it were for meat or malice must be to me a question.

But I am fallen into this discourse by accident; of which I might say more, but it has proved longer than I intended, and possibly may not to you be considerable: I shall therefore give you three or four more short observations of the Carp, and then fall upon some directions how you shall fish for him.

The age of Carps is by Sir Francis Bacon, in his "History of Life and Death," observed to be but ten years, yet others think they live longer. Gesner says, a Carp has been known to live in the Palatinate above a hundred years: but most conclude, that, contrary to the Pike or Luce, all Carps are the better for age and bigness. The tongues of Carps are noted to be choice and costly meat, especially to them that buy them: but Gesner says, Carps have no tongue like other fish, but a piece of flesh-like fish in their mouth like to a tongue, and should be called a palate: but it is certain it is choicely good, and that the Carp is to be reckoned amongst those leather-mouthed fish which I told you have their teeth in their throat; and for that reason he is very seldom lost by breaking his hold, if your hook be once stuck into his chaps.

I told you that Sir Francis Bacon thinks that the Carp lives but ten years; but Janus Dubravius has writ a book "Of Fish and Fish-Ponds," in which he says that Carps begin to spawn at the age of three years, and continue to do so till thirty: he says also, that in the time of their breeding, which is in summer, when the sun hath warmed both the earth and water, and so apted them also for generation, that then three or four male Carps will follow a female; and that then, she putting on a seeming coyness, they force her through weeds and flags, where she lets fall her eggs or spawn, which sticks fast to the weeds, and then they let fall their melt upon it, and so it becomes in a short time to be a living fish: and, as I told you, it is thought the Carp does this several months in the year; and most believe that most fish breed after this manner, except the Eel. And it has been observed, that when the spawner has weakened herself by doing that natural office, that two or three melters have helped her from off the weeds by bearing her up on both sides, and guarding her into the deep. And you may note, that, though this may seem a curiosity not worth observing, yet others have judged it worth their time and costs to make glass hives, and order them in such a manner as to see how bees have bred and made their honeycombs, and how they have obeyed their king and governed their commonwealth. But it is thought that all Carps are not bred by generation, but that some breed other ways, as some Pikes do.

The physicians make the galls and stones in the heads of Carps to be very medicinable. But 't is not to be doubted but that in Italy they make great profit of the spawn of Carps, by selling it to the Jews, who make it into red caviare, the Jews not being by their law admitted to eat of caviare made of the Sturgeon, that being a fish that wants scales, and, as may appear in Levit, xi. 10, by them reputed to be unclean.

Much more might be said out of him, and out of Aristotle, which Dubravius often quotes in his Discourse of Fishes; but it might rather perplex than satisfy you; and therefore I shall rather choose to direct you how to catch, than spend more time in discoursing either of the nature or the breeding of this CARP,

or of any more circumstances concerning him: but yet I shall remember you of what I told you before, that he is a very subtle fish, and hard to be caught.

And my first direction is, that, if you will fish for a Carp, you must put on a very large measure of patience; especially to fish for a River-Carp: I have known a very good fisher angle diligently four or six hours in a day, for three or four days together, for a River-Carp, and not have a bite. And you are to note that, in some ponds, it is as hard to catch a Carp as in a river; that is to say, where they have store of feed, and the water is of a clayish color: but you are to remember, that I have told you there is no rule without an exception; and therefore, being possessed with that hope and patience, which I wish to all fishers, especially to the Carp-Angler, I shall tell you with what bait to fish for him. But first you are to know, that it must be either early or late; and let me tell you, that in hot weather, for he will seldom bite in cold, you cannot be too early or too late at it. And some have been so curious as to say, the 10th of April is a fatal day for Carps.

The Carp bites either at worms or at paste; and of worms I think the bluish marsh or meadow worm is best; but possibly another worm, not too big, may do as well, and so may a green gentle: and as for pastes, there are almost as many sorts as there are medicines for the toothache; but doubtless sweet pastes are best; I mean pastes made with honey or with sugar: which, that you may the better beguile this crafty fish, should be thrown into the pond or place in which you fish for him some hours, or longer, before you undertake your trial of skill with the angle-rod: and, doubt-less, if it be thrown into the water a day or two before, at several times and in small pellets, you are the likelier when you fish for the Carp to obtain your desired sport. Or in a large pond, to draw them to any certain place, that they may the better and with more hope be fished for, you are to throw into it, in some certain place, either grains, or blood mixed with cow-dung or with bran; or any garbage, as chicken's guts, or the like; and then some of your small sweet pellets with which you purpose to angle: and these small pellets being a few of them also thrown in as you are angling, will be the better.

And your paste must be thus made: take the flesh of a rabbit or cat cut small, and bean-flour; and if that may not be easily got, get other flour, and then mix these together, and put to them either sugar, or honey, which I think bet-ter; and then beat these together in a mortar, or sometimes work them in your hands, your hands being very clean; and then make it into a ball, or two, or three, as you like best for your use; but you must work or pound it so long in the mor-tar, as to make it so tough as to hang upon your hook with-out washing from it, yet not too hard: or that you may the better keep it on your hook, you may knead with your paste a little, and not much, white or yellowish wool.

And if you would have this paste keep all the year for any other fish, then mix with it virgin-wax and clarified honey, and work them together with your hands before the fire; then make these into balls, and they will keep all the year.

And if you fish for a Carp with gentles, then put upon

your hook a small piece of scarlet about this bigness ☐, it being soaked in, or anointed with oil of peter, called by some oil of the rock: and if your gentles be put, two or three days before, into a box or horn anointed with honey, and so put upon your hook as to preserve them to be living, you are as like to kill this crafty fish this way as any other: but still as you are fishing, chew a little white or brown bread in your mouth, and cast it into the pond about the place where your float swims. Other baits there be; but these, with diligence and patient watchfulness, will do it better than any that I have ever practised or heard of: and yet I shall tell you, that the crumbs of white bread and honey made into a paste is a good bait for a Carp; and you know it is more easily made. And having said thus much of the Carp, my next discourse shall be of the Bream, which shall not prove so tedious: and therefore I desire the continuance of your attention.

But first I will tell you how to make this Carp, that is so curious to be caught, so curious a dish of meat, as shall make him worth all your labor and patience; and though it is not without some trouble and charges, yet it will recompense both.

Take a Carp, alive if possible, scour him, and rub him clean with water and salt, but scale him not: then open him, and put him with his blood and his liver, which you must save when you open him, into a small pot or kettle; then take sweet-marjoram, thyme, and parsley, of each half a handful; a sprig of rosemary, and another of savory; bind them into two or three small bundles, and put them to your Carp, with four or five whole onions, twenty pickled oysters, and three anchovies. Then pour upon your Carp as much claret-wine as will only cover him; and season your claret well with salt, cloves, and mace, and the rinds of oranges and lemons. That done, cover your pot and set it on a quick fire, till it be sufficiently boiled: then take out the Carp, and lay it with the broth into the dish, and pour upon it a quarter of a pound of the best fresh butter, melted and beaten with half a dozen spoonfuls of the broth, the yolks of two or three eggs, and some of the herbs shred: garnish your dish with lemons, and so serve it up, and much good do you!   Dr. T.

THE FOURTH DAY.

Chap. X.—*Observations of the* BREAM, *and Directions to catch him.*

Piscator.

THE Bream, being at a full growth, is a large and stately fish. He will breed both in rivers and ponds; but loves best to live in ponds, and where, if he likes the water and air, he will grow not only to be very large, but as fat as a hog. He is by Gesner taken to be more pleasant, or sweet, than wholesome: this fish is long in growing, but breeds exceedingly in a water that pleases him; yea, in many ponds so fast as to over-store them, and starve the other fish.

He is very broad, with a forked tail, and his scales set in excellent order: he hath large eyes, and a narrow sucking mouth; he hath two sets of teeth, and a lozenge-like bone, a bone to help his grinding. The melter is observed to have two large melts, and the female two large bags of eggs or spawn.

Gesner reports, that in Poland a certain and a great number of large Breams were put into a pond, which in the next following winter were frozen up into one entire ice, and not one drop of water remaining, nor one of these fish to be found, though they were diligently searched for; and yet the next spring, when the ice was thawed, and the weather warm, and fresh water got into the pond, he affirms they all appeared again. This Gesner affirms, and I quote my author, because it seems almost as incredible as the resurrection to an atheist. But it may win something in point of believing it, to him that considers the breeding or renovation of the silk-worm, and of many insects. And that is considerable which Sir Francis Bacon observes in his "History of Life and Death," fol. 20, that there be some herbs that die and spring every year, and some endure longer.

But though some do not, yet the French esteem this fish highly, and to that end have this proverb: "He that hath Breams in his pond is able to bid his friend welcome." And it is noted, that the best part of a Bream is his belly and head.

Some say, that Breams and Roaches will mix their eggs and melt together, and so there is in many places a bastard breed of Breams, that never come to be either large or good, but very numerous.

The baits good to catch this BREAM

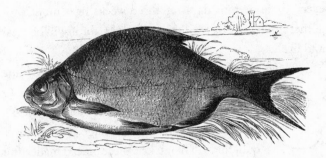

are many. First, paste made of brown bread and honey, gentles, or the brood of wasps that be young, and then not unlike gentles, and should be hardened in an oven, or dried on
a tile before the fire to make them tough: or there is at the
root of docks or flags, or rushes in watery places, a worm
not unlike a maggot, at which Tench will bite freely. Or he
will bite at a grasshopper with his legs nipped off, in June
and July; or at several flies, under water, which may be
found on flags that grow near to the water-side. I doubt not
but that there be many other baits that are good, but I will
turn them all into this most excellent one, either for a Carp
or Bream, in any river or mere: it was given to me by a most
honest and excellent Angler, and, hoping you will prove
both, I will impart it to you.

   1. Let your bait be as big a red-worm as you can find,
without a knot: get a pint or quart of them in an evening in
garden-walks, or chalky commons, after a shower of rain;
and put them with clean moss well washed and picked, and
the water squeezed out of the moss as dry as you can, into
an earthen pot or pipkin set dry, and change the moss fresh

every three or four days for three weeks or a month together; then your bait will be at the best, for it will be clear
and lively.

2. Having thus prepared your baits, get your tackling
ready and fitted for this sport. Take three long
angling-rods, and as many and more silk, or silk
and hair, lines, and as many large swan or goose
quill floats. Then take a piece of lead made after
this manner, and fasten them to the low-ends of your lines.
Then fasten your link-hook also to the lead, and let there be
about a foot or ten inches between the lead and the hook;
but be sure the lead be heavy enough to sink the float or
quill a little under the water, and not the quill to bear up the
lead, for the lead must lie on the ground. Note that your
link next the hook may be smaller than the rest of your line,
if you dare adventure, for fear of taking the Pike or Pearch,
who will assuredly visit your hooks, till they be taken out, as
I will show you afterwards, before either Carp or Bream
will come near to bite. Note also, that when the worm is
well baited, it will crawl up and down, as far as the lead will
give leave, which much enticeth the fish to bite without
suspicion.

3. Having thus prepared your baits, and fitted your tackling, repair to the river, where you have seen them to swim
in skuls or shoals in the summertime in a hot afternoon,
about three or four of the clock; and watch their going forth
of their deep holes and returning, which you may well discern, for they return about four of the clock, most of them
seeking food at the bottom, yet one or two will lie on the

top of the water, rolling and tumbling themselves whilst the rest are under him at the bottom; and so you shall perceive him to keep sentinel: then mark where he plays most, and stays longest, which commonly is in the broadest and deepest place of the river, and there, or near thereabouts, at a clear bottom and a convenient landing-place, take one of your angles ready fitted as aforesaid, and sound the bottom, which should be about eight or ten feet deep; two yards from the bank is best. Then consider with yourself whether that water will rise or fall by the next morning, by reason of any water-mills near, and according to your discretion take the depth of the place where you mean after to cast your ground-bait, and to fish, to half an inch; that the lead lying on or near the ground-bait, the top of the float may only appear upright half an inch above the water.

Thus you having found and fitted for the place and depth thereof, then go home and prepare your ground-bait; which is, next to the fruit of your labors, to be regarded.

THE GROUND-BAIT.

You shall take a peck, or a peck and a half, according to the greatness of the stream, and deepness of the water, where you mean to angle, of sweet gross-ground barley-malt, and boil it in a kettle; one or two warms is enough: then strain it through a bag into a tub, the liquor whereof hath often done my horse much good; and when the bag and malt is near cold, take it down to the water-side about eight or nine of the clock in the evening, and not before:

cast in two parts of your ground bait, squeezed hard between both your hands; it will sink presently to the bottom, and be sure it may rest in the very place where you mean to angle: if the stream run hard, or move a little, cast your malt in handfuls a little the higher, upwards the stream. You may, between your hands, close the malt so fast in handfuls, that the water will hardly part it with the fall.

Your ground thus baited, and tackling fitted, leave your bag with the rest of your tackling and ground-bait near the sporting-place all night; and in the morning, about three or four of the clock, visit the water-side, but not too near, for they have a cunning watchman, and are watchful themselves too.

Then gently take one of your three rods, and bait your hook, casting it over your ground-bait; and gently and secretly draw it to you, till the lead rests about the middle of the ground-bait.

Then take a second rod and cast in about a yard above, and your third a yard below the first rod, and stay the rods in the ground; but go yourself so far from the water-side, that you perceive nothing but the top of the floats, which you must watch most diligently. Then, when you have a bite, you shall perceive the top of your float to sink suddenly into the water; yet nevertheless be not too hasty to run to your rods, until you see that the line goes clear away; then creep to the water-side, and give as much line as possibly you can: if it be a good Carp or Bream, they will go to the farther side of the river, then strike gently, and hold your rod at a bent a little while; but if you both pull together, you are sure to lose your game, for either your line, or hook, or hold, will break: and after you have overcome them, they will make noble sport, and are very shy to be landed. The Carp is far stronger and more mettlesome than the Bream.

Much more is to be observed in this kind of fish and fishing, but it is far fitter for experience and discourse than paper. Only thus much is necessary for you to know, and to be mindful and careful of; that if the Pike or Pearch do breed in that river, they will be sure to bite first, and must first be taken. And for the most part they are very large; and will repair to your ground-bait, not that they will eat of it, but will feed and sport themselves amongst the young fry that gather about and hover over the bait.

The way to discern the Pike and to take him, if you mistrust your Bream-hook,—for I have taken a Pike a yard long several times at my Bream-hooks, and sometimes he hath had the luck to share my line,—may be thus:—

Take a small Bleak, or Roach, or Gudgeon, and bait it; and set it alive among your rods two foot deep from the cork, with a little red-worm on the point of the hook; then take a few crumbs of white bread, or some of the ground-bait, and sprinkle it gently amongst your rods. If Mr. Pike be there, then the little fish will skip out of the water at his appearance, but the live-set bait is sure to be taken.

Thus continue your sport from four in the morning till eight, and if it be a gloomy, windy day, they will bite all day long. But this is too long to stand to your rods at one place, and it will spoil your evening sport that day, which is this.

About four of the clock in the afternoon repair to your

baited place; and as soon as you come to the water-side, cast in one half of the rest of your ground-bait, and stand off: then, whilst the fish are gathering together, for there they will most certainly come for their supper, you may take a pipe of tobacco; and then in with your three rods as in the morning. You will find excellent sport that evening till eight of the clock: then cast in the residue of your ground-bait, and next morning by four of the clock visit them again for four hours, which is the best sport of all; and after that, let them rest till you and your friends have a mind to more sport.

From St. James's-tide until Bartholomew-tide is the best; when they have had all the summer's food, they are the fattest.

Observe lastly, that after three or four days' fishing together, your game will be very shy and wary, and you shall hardly get above a bite or two at a baiting; then your only way is to desist from your sport about two or three days: and in the mean time, on the place you late baited, and again intend to bait, you shall take a turf of green but short grass, as big or bigger than a round trencher; to the top of this turf, on the green side, you shall, with a needle and green thread, fasten one by one as many little red-worms as will near cover all the turf. Then take a round board or trencher, make a hole in the middle thereof, and through the turf, placed on the board or trencher, with a string or cord as long as is fitting, tied to a pole, let it down to the bottom of the water for the fish to feed upon without disturbance about two or three days; and after that you have drawn it away, you may fall to, and enjoy your former recreation.   B. A.

THE FOURTH DAY.

CHAP. XI.—*Observations of the* TENCH, *and Advice how to angle for him.*

PISCATOR.

THE Tench, the physician of fishes, is observed to love ponds better than rivers, and to love pits better than either; yet Camden observes there is a river in Dorsetshire that abounds with Tenches, but doubtless they retire to the most deep and quiet places in it.

This fish hath very large fins, very small and smooth scales, a red circle about his eyes, which are big and of a gold color, and from either angle of his mouth there hangs down a little barb. In every Tench's head there are two little stones, which foreign physicians make great use of; but he is not commended for wholesome meat, though there be very much use made of them, for outward applications.

Rondeletius says, that at his being at Rome he saw a great cure done by applying a Tench to the feet of a very sick man. This, he says, was done after an unusual manner by certain Jews. And it is observed, that many of those people have many secrets, yet unknown to Christians; secrets that have never yet been written, but have been since the days of their Solomon, who knew the nature of all things, even from the cedar to the shrub, delivered by tradition from the father to the son, and so from generation to generation without writing; or, unless it were casually, without the least communicating them to any other nation or tribe: for to do that, they account a profanation. And yet it is thought that they, or some spirit worse than they, first told us, that lice swallowed alive were a certain cure for the yellow-jaundice. This and many other medicines were discovered by them, or by revelation; for doubtless we attained them not by study.

Well, this fish, besides his eating, is very useful, both dead and alive, for the good of mankind. But I will meddle no more with that; my honest humble art teaches no such boldness: there are too many foolish meddlers in physic and divinity, that think themselves fit to meddle with hidden secrets, and so bring destruction to their followers. But I 'll not meddle with them, any farther than to wish them wiser; and shall tell you next, for I hope I may be so bold, that the Tench is the physician of fishes; for the Pike especially, and that the Pike, being either sick or hurt, is cured by the touch of the Tench. And it is observed, that the tyrant Pike will not be a wolf to his physician, but forbears to devour him though he be never so hungry.

This fish, that carries a natural balsam in him to cure both himself and others, loves yet to feed in very foul water, and amongst weeds. And yet I am sure he eats pleasantly, and doubtless you will think so too, if you taste him. And I shall therefore proceed to give you some few, and but a few, directions how to catch this TENCH,

of which I have given you these observations.

He will bite at a paste made of brown bread and honey, or at a marsh-worm, or a lob-worm; he inclines very much to any paste with which tar is mixed, and he will bite also at a smaller worm, with his head nipped off, and a cod-worm put on the hook before that worm; and I doubt not but that he will also in the three hot months, for in the nine colder he stirs not much, bite at a flag-worm, or at a green gentle, but can positively say no more of the Tench, he being a fish that I have not often angled for, but I wish my honest Scholar may, and be ever fortunate when he fishes.

THE FOURTH DAY.

CHAP. XII.—*Observations of the* PEARCH, *and Directions how to fish for him.*

PISCATOR.

THE Pearch is a very good and a very bold-biting fish. He is one of the fishes of prey that, like the Pike and Trout, carries his teeth in his mouth, which is very large; and he dare venture to kill and devour several other kinds of fish. He has a hooked, or hog-back, which is armed with sharp and stiff bristles, and all his skin armed or covered over with thick, dry, hard scales; and hath, which few other fish have, two fins on his back. He is so bold that he will invade one of his own kind, which the Pike will not do so willingly; and you may therefore easily believe him to be a bold biter.

The Pearch is of great esteem in Italy, saith Aldrovandus; and especially the least are there esteemed a dainty dish. And Gesner prefers the Pearch and Pike above the Trout, or any fresh-water fish: he says the Germans have this proverb, "More wholesome than a Pearch of Rhine:" and he says the River-Pearch is so wholesome, that physicians allow him to be eaten by wounded men, or by men in fevers, or by women in child-bed.

He spawns but once a year, and is by physicians held very nutritive; yet, by many, to be hard of digestion. They

abound more in the river Po and in England, says Rondeletius, than other parts, and have in their brain a stone,
which is, in foreign parts, sold by apothecaries, being there
noted to be very medicinable against the stone in the reins.
These be a part of the commendations which some philosophical brains have bestowed upon the fresh-water Pearch:
yet they commend the Sea-Pearch, which is known by having but one fin on his back, of which, they say, we English
see but a few, to be a much better fish.

The Pearch grows slowly, yet will grow, as I have been
credibly informed, to be almost two foot long; for an honest informer told me, such a one was not long since taken
by Sir Abraham Williams, a gentleman of worth, and a
Brother of the Angle, that yet lives, and I wish he may. This
was a deep-bodied fish, and doubtless durst have devoured
a Pike of half his own length; for I have told you he is a bold
fish, such a one as, but for extreme hunger, the Pike will not
devour: for to affright the Pike, and save himself, the Pearch
will set up his fins, much like as a turkey-cock will sometimes set up his tail.

But, my Scholar, the Pearch is not only valiant to defend
himself, but he is, as I said, a bold-biting fish, yet he will not
bite at all seasons of the year; he is very abstemious in winter, yet will bite then in the midst of the day, if it be warm:
and note, that all fish bite best about the midst of a warm
day in winter, and he hath been observed by some not usually to bite till the mulberry-tree buds; that is to say, till extreme frosts be past the spring: for when the mulberry-tree

blossoms, many gardeners observe their forward fruit to be past the danger of frosts; and some have made the like observation of the Pearch's biting.

But bite the Pearch will, and that very boldly; and as one has wittily observed, if there be twenty or forty in a hole, they may be, at one standing, all catched one after another; they being, as he says, like the wicked of the world, not afraid, though their fellows and companions perish in their sight. And you may observe, that they are not like the solitary Pike; but love to accompany one another, and march together in troops.

And the baits for this bold fish

are not many: I mean, he will bite as well at some or at any of these three, as at any or all others whatsoever,—a worm, a minnow, or a little frog, of which you may find many in hay-time: and of worms the dunghill-worm, called a Brandling, I take to be best, being well scoured in moss or fennel; or he will bite at a worm that lies under cow-dung,

with a bluish head. And if you rove for a Pearch with a minnow, then it is best to be alive, you sticking your hook
through his back fin; or a minnow with a hook in his upper
lip, and letting him swim up and down, about mid-water or
a little lower, and you still keeping him to about that depth
by a cork, which ought not to be a very little one: and the
like way you are to fish for the Pearch, with a small frog,
your hook being fastened through the skin of his leg, towards the upper part of it: and lastly, I will give you but this
advice, that you give the Pearch time enough when he bites,
for there was scarce ever any Angler that has given him too
much. And now I think best to rest myself, for I have almost
spent my spirits with talking so long.

Ven. Nay, good Master, one fish more, for you see it rains
still, and you know our Angles are like money put to usury;
they may thrive, though we sit still and do nothing but talk
and enjoy one another. Come, come, the other fish, good
Master.

Pisc. But, Scholar, have you nothing to mix with this discourse, which now grows both tedious and tiresome? Shall
I have nothing from you, that seem to have both a good
memory and a cheerful spirit?

Ven. Yes, Master, I will speak you a copy of verses that
were made by Doctor Donne, and made to show the world
that he could make soft and smooth verses, when he
thought smoothness worth his labor; and I love them the
better, because they allude to rivers, and fish, and fishing.
They be these:—

"Come, live with me, and be my love,
And we will some new pleasures prove
Of golden sands, and crystal brooks,
With silken lines and silver hooks.

"There will the river whispering run,
Warmed by the eyes more than the sun;
And there the enamel'd fish will stay,
Begging themselves they may betray.

"When thou wilt swim in that live bath,
Each fish, which every channel hath,
Most amorously to thee will swim,
Gladder to catch thee than thou him.

"If thou to be so seen be'st loath,
By sun or moon, thou dark'nest both;
And if mine eyes have leave to see,
I need not their light, having thee.

"Let others freeze with angling-reeds,
And cut their legs with shells and weeds;
Or treacherously poor fish beset
With strangling snares, or windowy net:

"Let coarse, bold hands from slimy nest
The bedded fish in banks outwrest;
Let curious traitors sleave silk flies,
To 'witch poor fishes' wandering eyes:

"For thee, thou need'st no such deceit,
For thou thyself art thine own bait:
That fish that is not catch't thereby
Is wiser far, alas! than I."

PISC. Well remembered, honest Scholar! I thank you for these choice verses, which I have heard formerly, but had quite forgot till they were recovered by your happy memory. Well, being I have now rested myself a little, I will make you some requital, by telling you some observations of the Eel, for it rains still; and because, as you say, our angles are as money put to use, that thrives when we play, therefore we'll sit still and enjoy ourselves a little longer under this honey-suckle hedge.

THE FOURTH DAY.

CHAP. XIII.—*Observations of the* EEL, *and other Fish that want scales, and how to fish for them.*

PISCATOR.

IT is agreed by most men, that the Eel is a most dainty fish: the Romans have esteemed her the Helena of their feasts, and some the queen of palate-pleasure. But most men differ about their breeding: some say they breed by generation as other fish do; and others, that they breed, as some worms do, of mud; as rats and mice, and many other living creatures, are bred in Egypt by the sun's heat when it shines upon the overflowing of the river Nilus; or out of the putrefaction of the earth, and divers other ways. Those that deny them to breed by generation as other fish do, ask, If any man ever saw an Eel to have a spawn or melt? And they are answered, that they may be as certain of their breeding as if they had seen them spawn: for they say, that they are certain that Eels have all parts fit for generation, like other fish, but so small as not to be easily discerned, by reason of their fatness, but that discerned they may be, and that the he and the she Eel may be distinguished by their fins. And Rondeletius says, he has seen Eels cling together like dew-worms.

And others say, that Eels, growing old, breed other Eels out of the corruption of their own age, which, Sir Francis

Bacon says, exceeds not ten years. And others say, that as pearls are made of glutinous dew-drops, which are condensed by the sun's heat in those countries, so Eels are bred of a particular dew, falling in the months of May or June on the banks of some particular ponds or rivers, apted by nature for that end; which in a few days are by the sun's heat turned into Eels: and some of the ancients have called the Eels that are thus bred the offspring of Jove. I have seen in the beginning of July, in a river not far from Canterbury, some parts of it covered over with young Eels, about the thickness of a straw; and these Eels did lie on the top of that water, as thick as motes are said to be in the sun: and I have heard the like of other rivers, as namely in Severn, where they are called Yelvers; and in a pond or mere near unto Staffordshire, where, about a set time in summer, such small Eels abound so much, that many of the poorer sort of people, that inhabit near to it, take such Eels out of this mere with sieves or sheets, and make a kind of Eel-cake of them, and eat it like as bread. And Gesner quotes Venerable Bede[57] to say, that in England there is an island called Ely, by reason of the innumerable number of Eels that breed in it. But that Eels may be bred as some worms, and some kind of bees and wasps are, either of dew, or out of the corruption of the earth, seems to be made probable by the barnacles and young goslings bred by the sun's heat and the rotten planks of an old ship, and hatched of trees; both which are related for truths by Du Bartas and Lobel,[58] and also by our learned Camden, and laborious Gerard[59] in his Herbal.

It is said by Rondeletius, that those Eels that are bred in rivers that relate to or be nearer to the sea, never return to the fresh waters, as the Salmon does always desire to do, when they have once tasted the salt-water; and I do the more easily believe this, because I am certain that powdered beef is a most excellent bait to catch an Eel. And though Sir Francis Bacon will allow the Eel's life to be but ten years, yet he, in his "History of Life and Death," mentions a Lamprey belonging to the Roman Emperor to be made tame, and so kept for almost threescore years: and that such useful and pleasant observations were made of this Lamprey, that Crassus the orator, who kept her, lamented her death. And we read in Doctor Hakewill, that Hortensius was seen to weep at the death of a Lamprey that he had kept long, and loved exceedingly.

It is granted by all, or most men, that Eels, for about six months, that is to say, the six cold months of the year, stir not up and down, neither in the rivers, nor in the pools in which they usually are, but get into the soft earth or mud; and there many of them together bed themselves, and live without feeding upon anything, as I have told you some swallows have been observed to do in hollow trees for those cold six months: and this the Eel and swallow do, as not being able to endure winter weather; for Gesner quotes Albertus to say, that in the year 1125, that year's winter being more cold than usually, Eels did by nature's instinct get out of the water into a stack of hay in a meadow upon dry ground, and there bedded themselves; but yet at last a frost killed them. And our Camden relates, that in Lancashire fishes were digged out of the earth with spades, where no water was near to the place. I shall say little more of the Eel, but that, as it is observed he is impatient of cold, so it hath been observed that, in warm weather, an Eel has been known to live five days out of the water.

And lastly, let me tell you that some curious searchers into the natures of fish observe that there be several sorts or kinds of Eels: as the Silver Eel, and Green or greenish Eel, with which the river of Thames abounds, and those are called Grigs; and a blackish Eel, whose head is more flat and bigger than ordinary Eels; and also an Eel whose fins are reddish, and but seldom taken in this nation, and yet taken sometimes. These several kinds of Eels are, say some, diversely bred; as namely, out of the corruption of the earth, and some by dew, and other ways, as I have said to you: and yet it is affirmed by some for a certain, that the Silver Eel is bred by generation; but not by spawning as other fish do, but that her brood come alive from her, being then little live Eels no bigger nor longer than a pin: and I have had too many testimonies of this to doubt the truth of it myself; and if I thought it needful I might prove it, but I think it is needless.

And this Eel, of which I have said so much to you, may be caught with divers kinds of baits: as namely, with pow-dered beef; with a lob or garden worm; with a minnow; or gut of a hen, chicken, or the guts of any fish; or with almost almost anything, for he is a greedy fish. But the Eel may be caught, especially, with a little, a very little Lamprey, which some call a Pride, and may in the hot months be found many of them in the river Thames, and in many mud-heaps in other rivers; yea, almost as usually as one finds worms in a dunghill.

Next note, that the Eel seldom stirs in the day, but then hides himself; and therefore he is usually caught by night, with one of these baits of which I have spoken, and may be then caught by laying hooks, which you are to fasten to the bank, or twigs of a tree; or by throwing a string cross the stream with many hooks at it, and those baited with the aforesaid baits; and a clod, or plummet, or stone, thrown into the river with this line, that so you may in the morning find it near to some fixed place, and then take it up with a drag-hook or otherwise. But these things are, indeed, too common to be spoken of, and an hour's fishing with any Angler will teach you better both for these and many other common things in the practical part of Angling, than a week's discourse. I shall therefore conclude this direction for taking the Eel, by telling you that, in a warm day in summer, I have taken many a good Eel by *snigling*, and have been much pleased with that sport.

And because you that are but a young Angler know not what snigling is, I will now teach it to you. You remember I told you that Eels do not usually stir in the daytime, for then they hide themselves under some covert, or under boards or planks about flood-gates, or weirs, or mills, or in holes in the river-banks: so that you, observing your time in a warm day, when the water is lowest, may take a strong, small hook, tied to a strong line, or to a string about a yard long; and then into one of these holes, or between any boards about a mill, or under any great stone or plank, or any place where you think an Eel may hide or shelter herself, you may, and with the help of a short stick, put in your bait, but leisurely, and as far as you may conveniently: and it is scarce to be doubted but that, if there be an Eel within the sight of it, the Eel will bite instantly, and as certainly gorge it: and you need not doubt to have him, if you pull him not out of the hole too quickly, but pull him out by degrees; for he, lying folded double in his hole, will, with the help of his tail, break all, unless you give him time to be wearied with pulling, and so get him out by degrees, not pulling too hard.

And to commute for your patient hearing this long direction, I shall next tell you how to make this EEL a most excellent dish of meat.[60]

First, wash him in water and salt; then pull off his skin below his vent or navel, and not much further: having done that, take out his guts as clean as you can, but wash him not:

then give him three or four scotches with a knife; and then put into his belly and those scotches sweet herbs, an anchovy, and a little nutmeg grated or cut very small; and your herbs and anchovies must also be cut very small, and mixed with good butter and salt: having done this, then pull his skin over him all but his head, which you are to cut off, to the end you may tie his skin about that part where his head grew, and it must be so tied as to keep all his moisture within his skin: and having done this, tie him with tape or packthread to a spit, and roast him leisurely, and baste him with water and salt till his skin breaks, and then with butter: and having roasted him enough, let what was put into his belly, and what he drips, be his sauce.   S. F.

When I go to dress an Eel thus, I wish he were as long and big as that which was caught in Peterborough River in the year 1667, which was a yard and three quarters long. If you will not believe me, then go and see at one of the coffee-houses in King Street in Westminster.

But now let me tell you, that though the Eel thus dressed be not only excellent good, but more harmless than any other way, yet it is certain that physicians account the Eel dangerous meat; I will advise you therefore, as Solomon says of honey (Prov. xxv. 16), "Hast thou found it, eat no more than is sufficient, lest thou surfeit, for it is not good to eat much honey." And let me add this, that the uncharitable Italian bids us "give Eels, and no wine, to our enemies."

And I will beg a little more of your attention to tell you, that Aldrovandus and divers physicians commend the Eel very much for medicine, though not for meat. But let me tell you one observation; that the Eel is never out of season, as Trouts and most fish are at set times; at least most Eels are not.

I might here speak of many other fish whose shape and nature are much like the Eel, and frequent both the sea and fresh rivers; as namely, the Lamprel, the Lamprey, and the Lamperne; as also of the mighty Conger, taken often in Severn about Gloucester: and might also tell in what high esteem many of them are for the curiosity of their taste. But these are not so proper to be talked of by me, because they make us Anglers no sport; therefore I will let them alone, as the Jews do, to whom they are forbidden by their law.

And, Scholar, there is also a FLOUNDER, a sea-fish, which will wander very far into fresh rivers, and there lose himself, and dwell, and thrive to a hand's breadth, and almost twice so long,—a fish without scales, and most excellent meat,— and a fish that affords much sport to the Angler, with any small worm, but especially a little bluish worm, gotten out of marsh-ground or meadows, which should be well scoured. But this, though it be most excellent meat, yet it wants scales, and is, as I told you, therefore an abomination to the Jews.

But, Scholar, there is a fish that they in Lancashire boast very much of, called a CHAR, taken there, and I think there only, in a mere called Winander-Mere; a mere, says Camden, that is the largest in this nation, being ten miles in length, and, some say, as smooth in the bottom as if it were paved with polished marble. This fish never exceeds fifteen or sixteen inches in length, and 't is spotted like a Trout, and has scarce a bone but on the back. But this, though I do not know whether it make the Angler sport, yet I would have you take notice of it, because it is a rarity, and of so high esteem with persons of great note.

Nor would I have you ignorant of a rare fish called a GUINIAD, of which I shall tell you what Camden and others speak. The river Dee, which runs by Chester, springs in Merionethshire; and, as it runs toward Chester, it runs through Pemble-Mere, which is a large water: and it is observed that, though the river Dee abounds with Salmon, and Pemble-Mere with the Guiniad, yet there is never any Salmon caught in the mere, nor a Guiniad in the river. And now my next observation shall be of the Barbel.

THE FOURTH DAY.

CHAP. XIV.—*Observations of the* BARBEL, *and Directions how to fish for him.*

PISCATOR.

THE Barbel is so called, says Gesner, by reason of his barb or wattels at his mouth, which are under his nose or chaps. He is one of those leather-mouthed fishes that I told you of, that does very seldom break his hold if he be once hooked: but he is so strong, that he will often break both rod and line, if he proves to be a big one.

But the Barbel, though he be of a fine shape, and looks big, yet he is not accounted the best fish to eat, neither for his wholesomeness nor his taste: but the male is reputed much better than the female, whose spawn is very hurtful, as I will presently declare to you.

They flock together like sheep, and are at the worst in April, about which time they spawn, but quickly grow to be in season. He is able to live in the strongest swifts of the water, and in summer they love the shallowest and sharpest streams; and love to lurk under weeds, and to feed on gravel against a rising ground, and will root and dig in the sands with his nose like a hog, and there nests himself: yet sometimes he retires to deep and swift bridges, or flood-gates, or weirs, where he will nest himself amongst piles, or in hollow places, and take such hold of moss or weeds, that, be the water never so swift, it is not able to force him from the place that he contends for. This is his constant custom in summer, when he and most living creatures sport themselves in the sun; but at the approach of winter, then he forsakes the swift streams and shallow waters, and by degrees retires to those parts of the river that are quiet and deeper: in which places, and I think about that time, he spawns; and, as I have formerly told you, with the help of the melter, hides his spawn or eggs in holes, which they both dig in the gravel: and then they mutually labor to cover it with the same sand, to prevent it from being devoured by other fish.

There be such store of this fish in the river Danube, that Rondeletius says they may in some places of it, and in some months in the year, be taken by those that dwell near to the river, with their hands, eight or ten load at a time. He says, they begin to be good in May, and that they cease to be so in August, but it is found to be otherwise in this nation: but thus far we agree with him, that the spawn of a Barbel, if it be not poison, as he says, yet that it is dangerous meat, and especially in the month of May; which is so certain, that

Gesner and Gasius[61] declare it had an ill effect upon them, even to the endangering of their lives.

This fish is of a fine cast and handsome shape, with small scales, which are placed after a most exact and curious manner, and, as I told you, may be rather said not to be ill, than to be good meat. The Chub and he have, I think, both lost part of their credit by ill cookery, they being reputed the worst or coarsest of fresh-water fish. But the BARBEL

affords an Angler choice sport, being a lusty and a cunning fish; so lusty and cunning as to endanger the breaking of the Angler's line, by running his head forcibly towards any covert, or hole, or bank; and then striking at the line, to break it off with his tail, as is observed by Plutarch, in his book "De Industria Animalium;" and also so cunning to nibble and suck off your worm close to the hook, and yet avoid the letting the hook come into his mouth.

The Barbel is also curious for his baits, that is to say, that they be clean and sweet; that is to say, to have your worms

well scoured, and not kept in sour and musty moss, for he is
a curious feeder: but at a well-scoured Lob-worm he will
bite as boldly as at any bait, and specially if, the night or two
before you fish for him, you shall bait the places where you
intend to fish for him with big worms cut into pieces: and
note, that none did ever over-bait the place, nor fish too
early or too late for a Barbel. And the Barbel will bite also
at gentles, which not being too much scoured, but green, are
a choice bait for him; and so is cheese, which is not to be
too hard, but kept a day or two in a wet linen cloth to make
it tough: with this you may also bait the water a day or two
before you fish for the Barbel, and be much the likelier to
catch store: and if the cheese were laid in clarified honey a
short time before, as namely, an hour or two, you were still
the likelier to catch fish. Some have directed to cut the
cheese into thin pieces, and toast it, and then tie it on the
hook with fine silk: and some advise to fish for the Barbel
with sheep's tallow and soft cheese beaten or worked into a
paste, and that it is choicely good in August, and I believe
it: but doubtless the Lob-worm well scoured, and the gentle not too much scoured, and cheese ordered as I have directed, are baits enough, and I think will serve in any
month; though I shall commend any Angler that tries con-
clusions, and is industrious to improve the art. And now,
my honest Scholar, the long shower and my tedious discourse are both ended together: and I shall give you but this
observation, that when you fish for a Barbel your rod and
line be both long, and of good strength; for, as I told you,
you will find him a heavy and a dogged fish to be dealt

withal, yet he seldom or never breaks his hold if he be once stricken. And if you would know more of fishing for the Umber or Barbel, get into favor with Doctor Sheldon,[62] whose skill is above others; and of that the poor that dwell about him have a comfortable experience.

And now let's go and see what interest the Trouts will pay us for letting our Angle-rods lie so long, and so quietly, in the water, for their use. Come, Scholar, which will you take up?

Ven. Which you think fit, Master.

Pisc. Why, you shall take up that; for I am certain, by viewing the line, it has a fish at it. Look you, Scholar! Well done! Come now, take up the other too; well! Now you may tell my brother Peter at night, that you have caught a leash of Trouts this day. And now let's move toward our lodging, and drink a draught of red-cow's milk as we go, and give pretty Maudlin and her honest mother a brace of Trouts for their supper.

Ven. Master, I like your motion very well; and I think it is now about milking-time, and yonder they be at it.

Pisc. God speed you, good woman! I thank you both for our songs last night: I and my companion have had such fortune a-fishing this day, that we resolve to give you and Maudlin a brace of Trouts for supper, and we will now taste a draught of your red-cow's milk.

Milkw. Marry, and that you shall with all my heart, and I will be still your debtor when you come this way: if you will but speak the word I will make you a good syllabub, of new verjuice, and then you may sit down in a hay-cock and eat it; and Maudlin shall sit by and sing you the good old song of the "Hunting in Chevy Chace," or some other good ballad, for she hath store of them. Maudlin, my honest Maudlin, hath a notable memory, and she thinks nothing too good for you, because you be such honest men.

VEN. We thank you, and intend once in a month to call upon you again, and give you a little warning, and so good night. Good night, Maudlin. And now, good Master, let's lose no time; but tell me somewhat more of fishing, and, if you please, first something of fishing for a Gudgeon.

PISC. I will, honest Scholar.

THE FOURTH DAY.

CHAP. XV.—*Observations of the* GUDGEON, *the* RUFFE, *and the* BLEAK, *and how to fish for them.*

PISCATOR.

THE GUDGEON is reputed a fish of excellent taste, and to be very wholesome: he is of a fine shape, of a silver color, and beautified with black spots both on his body and

tail. He breeds two or three times in the year, and always in summer. He is commended for a fish of excellent nourishment: the Germans call him Groundling, by reason of his feeding on the ground; and he there feasts himself in sharp streams, and on the gravel. He and the Barbel both feed so, and do not hunt for flies at any time, as most other fishes do: he is an excellent fish to enter a young Angler, being easy to be taken with a small red-worm, on or very near to the ground. He is one of those leather-mouthed fish that has his teeth in his throat, and will hardly be lost from off the hook if he be once strucken. They be usually scattered up and down every river in the shallows, in the heat of summer; but in autumn, when the weeds begin to grow sour or rot, and the weather colder, then they gather together, and get into the deeper parts of the water; and are to be fished for there, with your hook always touching the ground, if you fish for him with a float, or with a cork. But many will fish for the Gudgeon by hand, with a running-line upon the ground, without a cork, as a Trout is fished for, and it is an excellent way, if you have a gentle rod and as gentle a hand.

There is also another fish called a POPE, and by some a RUFFE; a fish that is not known to be in some rivers: he is

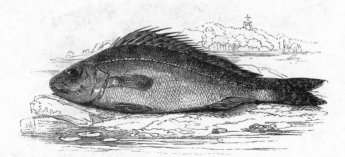

much like the Pearch for his shape, and taken to be better than the Pearch, but will not grow to be bigger than a Gudgeon: he is an excellent fish, no fish that swims is of a pleasanter taste, and he is also excellent to enter a young Angler, for he is a greedy biter, and they will usually lie, abundance of them together, in one reserved place, where the water is deep, and runs quietly; and an easy Angler, if he has found where they lie, may catch forty or fifty, or sometimes twice so many, at a standing.

You must fish for him with a small red worm, and if you bait the ground with earth, it is excellent.

There is also a Bleak, or Fresh-water Sprat, a fish that is ever in motion, and therefore called by some the River-Swallow; for just as you shall observe the Swallow to be, most evenings in summer, ever in motion, making short and quick turns when he flies to catch flies in the air, by which he lives, so does the Bleak at the top of the water. Ausonius would have him called BLEAK, from his whitish

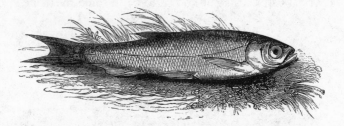

color: his black is of a pleasant sad or sea-water-green, his belly white and shining as the mountain snow. And, doubt-less, though he have the fortune, which virtue has in poor people, to be neglected, yet the Bleak ought to be much val-ued, though we want Allamot-salt, and the skill that the Italians have to turn them into Anchovies. This fish may be caught with a Pater-noster line; that is, six or eight very small hooks tied along the line, one half a foot above the other: I have seen five caught thus at one time, and the bait has been gentles, than which none is better.

Or this fish may be caught with a fine small artificial fly,

which is to be of a very sad brown color, and very small, and
the hook answerable. There is no better sport than whip-
ping for Bleaks in a boat, or on a bank in the swift water in
a summer's evening, with a hazel top about five or six foot
long, and a line twice the length of the rod. I have heard Sir
Henry Wotton say, that there be many that in Italy will
catch swallows so, or especially martins, this bird-angler
standing on the top of a steeple to do it, and with a line twice
so long as I have spoken of: and let me tell you, Scholar, that
both Martins and Bleaks be most excellent meat.

And let me tell you, that I have known a Hern that did
constantly frequent one place caught with a hook baited
with a big minnow or a small gudgeon. The line and hook
must be strong, and tied to some loose staff, so big as she
cannot fly away with it,—a line not exceeding two yards.

THE FOURTH DAY.

CHAP. XVI.—*Is of nothing, or that which is nothing worth.*

PISCATOR.

M
Y purpose was to give you some directions concerning Roach and Dace, and some other inferior fish,
which make the Angler excellent sport, for you know there
is more pleasure in hunting the hare than in eating her: but
I will forbear at this time to say any more, because you see
yonder come our Brother Peter and honest Coridon. But I
will promise you, that, as you and I fish and walk to-
morrow towards London, if I have now forgotten anything
that I can then remember, I will not keep it from you.

Well met, Gentlemen; this is lucky that we meet so just
together at this very door. Come, Hostess, where are you?
Is supper ready? Come, first give us drink, and be as quick
as you can, for I believe we are all very hungry. Well,
Brother Peter and Coridon, to you both! come, drink, and
then tell me what luck of fish: we two have caught but ten
Trouts, of which my Scholar caught three; look, here's
eight, and a brace we gave away: we have had a most pleasant day for fishing and talking, and are returned home both
weary and hungry; and now meat and rest will be pleasant.

PET. And Coridon and I have had not an unpleasant day,
and yet I have caught but five Trouts; for indeed we went to
a good honest ale-house, and there we played at shovel-

board half the day; all the time that it rained we were there, and as merry as they that fished. And I am glad we are now with a dry house over our heads; for, hark! how it rains and blows. Come, Hostess, give us more ale, and our supper with what haste you may: and when we have supped let us have your song, Piscator, and the catch that your Scholar promised us, or else Coridon will be dogged.

Pisc. Nay, I will not be worse than my word; you shall not want my song, and I hope I shall be perfect in it.

Ven. And I hope the like for my catch, which I have ready too: and therefore let 's go merrily to supper, and then have a gentle touch at singing and drinking; but the last with moderation.

Cor. Come, now for your song, for we have fed heartily. Come, Hostess, lay a few more sticks on the fire, and now sing when you will.

Pisc. Well then here 's to you, Coridon; and now for my song.

> "O, the gallant fisher's life,
> It is the best of any;
> 'T is full of pleasure, void of strife,
> And 't is beloved by many:
>> Other joys
>> Are but toys,
>> Only this
>> Lawful is;
>> For our skill
>> Breeds no ill,
> But content and pleasure.

"In a morning up we rise,
Ere Aurora's peeping:
Drink a cup to wash our eyes,
Leave the sluggard sleeping:
    Then we go
    To and fro,
    With our knacks
    At our backs,
    To such streams
    As the Thames,
If we have the leisure.

"When we please to walk abroad
For our recreation,
In the fields is our abode,
Full of delectation:
    Where in a brook
    With a hook,
    Or a lake,
    Fish we take;
    There we sit,
    For a bit,
Till we fish entangle.

"We have gentles in a horn,
We have paste and worms too:
We can watch both night and morn
Suffer rain and storms too.
    None do here
    Use to swear,
    Oaths do fray
    Fish away;
    We sit still,
    And watch our quill;
Fishers must not wrangle.

"If the sun's excessive heat
Make our bodies swelter,
To an osier-hedge we get
For a friendly shelter;
        Where in a dike
        Pearch or Pike,
        Roach or Dace,
        We do chase,
        Bleak or Gudgeon
        Without grudging;
We are still contented.

"Or we sometimes pass an hour
Under a green willow;
That defends us from a shower,
Making earth our pillow;
        Where we may
        Think and pray,
        Before death
        Stops our breath.
        Other joys
        Are but toys,
And to be lamented."

                                    JO. CHALKHILL.

VEN. Well sung, Master! This day's fortune and pleasure, and this night's company and song, do all make me more and more in love with Angling. Gentlemen, my Master left me alone for an hour this day; and I verily believe he retired himself from talking with me, that he might be so perfect in this song; was it not, Master?

PISC. Yes, indeed, for it is many years since I learned it;

and having forgotten a part of it, I was forced to patch it up by the help of mine own invention, who am not excellent at poetry, as my part of the song may testify: but of that I will say no more, lest you should think I mean by discommending it to beg your commendations of it. And therefore, without replications, let's hear your catch, Scholar; which I hope will be a good one, for you are both musical and have a good fancy to boot.

VEN. Marry, and that you shall; and as freely as I would have my honest Master tell me some more secrets of fish and fishing as we walk and fish towards London to-morrow. But, Master, first let me tell you that, that very hour which you were absent from me, I sat down under a willow-tree by the water-side, and considered what you had told me of the owner of that pleasant meadow in which you then left me: that he had a plentiful estate, and not a heart to think so; that he had at this time many lawsuits depending, and that they both damped his mirth, and took up so much of his time and thoughts, that he himself had not leisure to take the sweet content that I, who pretended no title to them, took in his fields: for I could there sit quietly; and, looking on the water, see some fishes sport themselves in the silver streams, others leaping at flies of several shapes and colors; looking on the hills, I could behold them spotted with woods and groves; looking down the meadows, could see here a boy gathering lilies and lady-smocks, and there a girl cropping culverkeyes and cowslips, all to make garlands suitable to this present month of May. These, and

A. H. Tourrier

THE ANGLER'S SONG

many other field-flowers, so perfumed the air, that I
thought that very meadow like that field in Sicily, of which
Diodorus speaks, where the perfumes arising from the
place make all dogs that hunt in it to fall off, and to lose
their hottest scent. I say, as I thus sat, joying in my own
happy condition, and pitying this poor rich man that owned
this and many other pleasant groves and meadows about
me, I did thankfully remember what my Saviour said, that
the meek possess the earth; or rather, they enjoy what the
other possess and enjoy not: for Anglers, and meek, quiet-
spirited men, are free from those high, those restless
thoughts, which corrode the sweets of life; and they, and
they only, can say, as the poet has happily expressed it:—

> "Hail! blest estate of lowliness!
> Happy enjoyments of such minds,
> As, rich in self-contentedness,
> Can, like the reeds in roughest winds,
>   By yielding make that blow but small
>   At which proud oaks and cedars fall."

There came also into my mind at that time certain verses
in praise of a mean estate and an humble mind; they were
written by Phineas Fletcher,[63] an excellent Divine, and an
excellent Angler, and the author of excellent Piscatory
Eclogues, in which you shall see the picture of this good
man's mind; and I wish mine to be like it.

> "No empty hopes, no courtly fears, him fright,
> No begging wants his middle-fortune bite,

But sweet content exiles both misery and spite.
His certain life, that never can deceive him,
    Is full of thousand sweets, and rich content;
The smooth-leaved beeches in the field receive him
    With coolest shade, till noontide's heat be spent :
His life is neither tossed in boisterous seas,
Or the vexatious world, or lost in slothful ease:
Pleased and full blest he lives, when he his God can please.

"His bed, more safe than soft, yields quiet sleeps,
    While by his side his faithful spouse hath place;
His little son into his bosom creeps,
    The lively picture of his father's face.
His humble house or poor state ne'er torment him;
Less he could like, if less his God had lent him;
And when he dies, green turfs do for a tomb content him."

Gentlemen, these were a part of the thoughts that then possessed me. And I there made a conversion of a piece of an old catch, and added more to it, fitting them to be sung by us Anglers. Come, Master, you can sing well; you must sing a part of it as it is in this paper.

Pet. I marry, Sir, this is music indeed! This has cheered my heart, and made me to remember six verses in praise of Music, which I will speak to you instantly.

"Music! miraculous rhetoric! that speak'st sense
Without a tongue, excelling eloquence;
With what ease might thy errors be excused,
Wert thou as truly loved as thou 'rt abused!
But thou dull souls neglect, and some reprove thee,
I cannot hate thee, 'cause the Angels love thee."

VEN. And the repetition of these last verses of music have called to my memory what Mr. Edmund Waller, a lover of the angle, says of Love and Music.

> "Whilst I listen to thy voice,
>   Chloris, I feel my heart decay;
> That powerful voice
>   Calls my fleeting soul away:
> O, suppress that magic sound,
> Which destroys without a wound!
>
> "Peace, Chloris, peace; or singing die,
> That together you and I
>   To heaven may go:
>   For all we know
> Of what the blessed do above
> Is, that they sing, and that they love."

PISC. Well remembered, Brother Peter; these verses came seasonably, and we thank you heartily. Come, we will all join together, my Host and all, and sing my Scholar's Catch over again, and then each man drink the t'other cup and to bed, and thank God we have a dry house over our heads.

PISC. Well now, Good night to everybody.
PET. And so say I.
VEN. And so say I.
COR. Good night to you all; and I thank you.

PISC. Good morrow, Brother Peter! and the like to you, honest Coridon. Come, my Hostess says there is seven shillings to pay: let's each man drink a pot for his morning's draught, and lay down his two shillings; that so my Hostess may not have occasion to repent herself of being so diligent, and using us so kindly.

PET. The motion is liked by everybody, and so, Hostess, here 's your money: we Anglers are all beholden to you; it will not be long ere I 'll see you again. And now, Brother Piscator, I wish you and my Brother, your Scholar, a fair day and good fortune. Come, Coridon, this is our way.

THE FIFTH DAY.

VENATOR.

GOOD Master, as we go now towards London, be still so courteous as to give me more instructions, for I have several boxes in my memory, in which I will keep them all very safe; there shall not one of them be lost.

PISC. Well, Scholar, that I will: and I will hide nothing from you that I can remember, and can think may help you forward towards a perfection in this art. And because we have so much time, and I have said so little of Roach and Dace, I will give you some directions concerning them.

Some say the Roach is so called from *rutilus,* which, they say, signifies red fins. He is a fish of no great reputation for his dainty taste; and his spawn is accounted much better than any other part of him. And you may take notice, that, as the Carp is accounted the water-fox for his cunning, so the Roach is accounted the water-sheep for his simplicity or foolishness. It is noted that the Roach and Dace recover strength, and grow in season in a fortnight after spawning: the Barbel and Chub in a month; the Trout in four months; and the Salmon in the like time, if he gets into the sea, and after into fresh water.

Roaches be accounted much better in the river than in a pond, though ponds usually breed the biggest. But there is a kind of bastard small Roach that breeds in ponds, with a very forked tail, and of a very small size, which some say is bred by the Bream and right Roach, and some ponds are stored with these beyond belief; and knowing men that know their difference call them Ruds: they differ from the true Roach as much as a Herring from a Pilchard. And these bastard breed of Roach are now scattered in many rivers, but I think not in the Thames, which I believe affords the largest and fattest in this nation, especially below London Bridge. The Roach is a leather-mouthed fish, and has a kind of saw-like teeth in his throat. And lastly, let me tell you, the Roach makes an Angler excellent sport, especially the great Roaches about London, where I think there be the best Roach-Anglers; and I think the best Trout-Anglers be in Derbyshire, for the waters there are clear to an extremity.

Next, let me tell you, you shall fish for this Roach in

winter with paste or gentles; in April, with worms or cadis; in the very hot months, with little white snails, or with flies under water, for he seldom takes them at the top, though the Dace will. In many of the hot months, Roaches may also be caught thus: take a May-fly or Ant-fly, sink him with a little lead to the bottom near to the piles or posts of a bridge, or near to any posts of a weir, I mean any deep place where Roaches lie quietly, and then pull your fly up very leisurely, and usually a Roach will follow your bait to the very top of the water, and gaze on it there, and run at it and take it lest the fly should fly away from him.

I have seen this done at Windsor and Henley Bridge, and great store of Roach taken; and sometimes a Dace or Chub. And in August you may fish for them with a paste made only of the crumbs of bread, which should be of pure fine man-chet; and that paste must be so tempered betwixt your hands till it be both soft and tough too: a very little water, and time and labor, and clean hands, will make it a most excellent paste. But when you fish with it, you must have a small hook, a quick eye, and a nimble hand, or the bait is lost and the fish too; if one may lose that which he never had. With this paste you may, as I said, take both the Roach and the DACE or DARE,

for they be much of a kind, in matter of feeding, cunning, goodness, and usually in size. And therefore take this general direction for some other baits which may concern you to take notice of. They will bite almost at any fly, but especially at Ant-flies; concerning which take this direction, for it is very good.

Take the blackish Ant-fly out of the mole-hill or ant-hill, in which place you shall find them in the month of June; or, if that be too early in the year, then doubtless you may find them in July, August, and most of September. Gather them alive, with both their wings, and then put them into a glass that will hold a quart or a pottle: but first put into the glass a handful, or more, of the moist earth out of which you gather them, and as much of the roots of the grass of the said hillock; and then put in the flies gently, that they lose not their wings: lay a clod of earth over it, and then so many as are put into the glass without bruising will live there a month or more, and be always in a readiness for you to fish with: but if you would have them keep longer, then get any great earthen pot, or barrel of three or four gallons, which is better, then wash your barrel with water and honey; and having put into it a quantity of earth and grass-roots, then put in your flies, and cover it, and they will live a quarter of a year. These, in any stream and clear water, are a deadly bait for Roach or Dace, or for a Chub; and your rule is, to fish not less than a handful from the bottom.

I shall next tell you a winter-bait for a Roach, a Dace, or Chub; and it is choicely good. About All-hallontide, and so till frost comes, when you see men ploughing up heath-

ground, or sandy ground, or greenswards, then follow the
plough, and you shall find a white worm as big as two mag-
gots, and it hath a red head; you may observe in what
ground most are, for there the crows will be very watchful
and follow the plough very close; it is all soft, and full of
whitish guts: a worm that is in Norfolk, and some other
counties, called a Grub, and is bred of the spawn or eggs of
a beetle, which she leaves in holes that she digs in the
ground under cow or horse dung, and there rests all winter,
and in March or April comes to be, first a red, and then a
black beetle: gather a thousand or two of these, and put
them, with a peck or two of their own earth, into some tub
or firkin, and cover and keep them so warm that the frost or
cold air or winds kill them not: these you may keep all winter, and kill fish with them at any time; and if you put some
of them into a little earth and honey a day before you use
them, you will find them an excellent bait for Bream, Carp,
or indeed for almost any fish.

And after this manner you may also keep gentles all winter, which are a good bait then, and much the better for
being lively and tough. Or you may breed and keep gentles
thus: take a piece of beast's liver, and with a cross-stick hang
it in some corner over a pot or barrel, half full of dry clay;
and as the gentles grow big, they will fall into the barrel, and
scour themselves, and be always ready for use whensoever
you incline to fish; and these gentles may be thus created till
after Michaelmas. But if you desire to keep gentles to fish
with all the year, then get a dead cat or a kite, and let it be
fly-blown; and when the gentles begin to be alive and to

stir, then bury it and them in soft, moist earth, but as free from frost as you can, and these you may dig up at any time when you intend to use them: these will last till March, and about that time turn to be flies.

But if you be nice to foul your fingers, which good Anglers seldom are, then take this bait: get a handful of well-made malt, and put it into a dish of water, and then wash and rub it betwixt your hands till you make it clean, and as free from husks as you can; then put that water from it, and put a small quantity of fresh water to it, and set it in something that is fit for that purpose over the fire, where it is not to boil apace, but leisurely and very softly, until it become somewhat soft, which you may try by feeling it betwixt your finger and thumb; and when it is soft, then put your water from it: and then take a sharp knife, and, turning the sprout-end of the corn upward, with the point of your knife take the back part of the husk off from it, and yet leaving a kind of inward husk on the corn, or else it is marred; and then cut off that sprouted end, I mean a little of it, that the white may appear, and so pull off the husk on the cloven side, as I directed you; and then cutting off a very little of the other end, that so your hook may enter; and, if your hook be small and good, you will find this to be a very choice bait, either for winter or summer, you sometimes casting a little of it into the place where your float swims.

And to take the Roach and Dace, a good bait is the young brood of wasps or bees, if you dip their heads in blood; especially good for Bream, if they be baked or hardened in their husks in an oven, after the bread is taken out of it; or hardened on a fire-shovel: and so also is the thick blood of sheep, being half dried on a trencher, that so you may cut it into such pieces as may best fit the size of your hook; and a little salt keeps it from growing black, and makes it not the worse, but better: this is taken to be a choice bait if rightly ordered.

There be several oils of a strong smell that I have been told of, and to be excellent to tempt fish to bite, of which I could say much. But I remember I once carried a small bottle from Sir George Hastings to Sir Henry Wotton, they were both chemical men, as a great present: it was sent, and received, and used, with great confidence; and yet, upon inquiry, I found it did not answer the expectation of Sir Henry; which, with the help of this and other circumstances, makes me have little belief in such things as many men talk of. Not but that I think fishes both smell and hear, as I have expressed in my former discourse: but there is a mysterious knack, which though it be much easier than the philosopher's stone, yet is not attainable by common capacities, or else lies locked up in the brain or breast of some chemical man, that, like the Rosicrucians, will not yet reveal it. But let me nevertheless tell you, that camphor, put with moss into your worm-bag with your worms, makes them, if many Anglers be not very much mistaken, a tempting bait, and the Angler more fortunate. But I stepped by chance into this discourse of oils, and fishes smelling; and though there might be more said, both of it and of baits for Roach and Dace, and other float-fish, yet I will forbear it at this time, and tell you in the next place how you are to prepare your tackling: concerning which, I will, for sport-sake, give you an old rhyme out of an old fish-book, which will prove a part, and but a part, of what you are to provide.

> "My rod and my line, my float and my lead,
>   My hook and my plummet, my whetstone and knife,
> My basket, my baits both living and dead,
>   My net and my meat, for that is the chief:
> Then I must have thread, and hairs green and small,
> With mine Angling-purse, and so you have all."

But you must have all these tackling, and twice so many more, with which, if you mean to be a fisher, you must store yourself; and to that purpose I will go with you either to Mr. Margrave,[64] who dwells amongst the booksellers in St. Paul's Church-yard, or to Mr. John Stubbs, near to the Swan in Golding Lane; they be both honest men, and will fit an Angler with what tackling he lacks.*

VEN. Then, good Master, let it be at——, for he is nearest to my dwelling, and I pray let 's meet there the 9th of May next about two of the clock; and I'll want nothing that a fisher should be furnished with.

PISC. Well, and I 'll not fail you, God willing, at the time and place appointed.

VEN. I thank you, good Master, and I will not fail you. And, good Master, tell me what baits more you remember, for it will not now be long ere we shall be at Tottenham

---

*I have heard that the tackling hath been priced at fifty pounds, in the Inventory of an Angler.

High Cross; and when we come thither I will make you some requital of your pains, by repeating as choice a copy of verses as any we have heard since we met together; and that is a proud word, for we have heard very good ones.

PISC. Well, Scholar, and I shall be then right glad to hear them. And I will, as we walk, tell you whatsoever comes in my mind, that I think may be worth your hearing. You may make another choice bait thus: Take a handful or two of the best and biggest wheat you can get; boil it in a little milk, like as frumity is boiled; boil it so till it be soft, and then fry it very leisurely with honey and a little beaten saffron dissolved in milk; and you will find this a choice bait, and good I think for any fish, especially for Roach, Dace, Chub, or Grayling: I know not but that it may be as good for a River-Carp, and especially if the ground be a little baited with it.

And you may also note, that the spawn of most fish is a very tempting bait, being a little hardened on a warm tile, and cut into fit pieces. Nay, mulberries and those blackberries which grow upon briers be good baits for Chubs or Carps: with these many have been taken in ponds, and in some rivers where such trees have grown near the water, and the fruit customarily dropped into it. And there be a hundred other baits, more than can be well named; which, by constant baiting the water, will become a tempting bait for any fish in it.

You are also to know, that there be divers kinds of CADIS, or CASE-WORMS, that are to be found in this nation in several distinct counties, and in several little brooks that relate to bigger rivers: as namely, one Cadis called a Piper, whose husk or case is a piece of reed about an inch long, or longer, and as big about as the compass of a two-pence. These worms being kept three or four days in a woollen bag with sand at the bottom of it, and the bag wet once a day, will in three or four days turn to be yellow; and these be a choice bait for the Chub or Chavender, or indeed for any great fish, for it is a large bait.

There is also a lesser Cadis-worm, called a Cock-spur, being in fashion like the spur of a cock, sharp at one end, and the case or house in which this dwells is made of small husks, and gravel, and slime, most curiously made of these, even so as to be wondered at; but not to be made by man, no more than a kingfisher's nest can, which is made of little fishes' bones, and have such a geometrical interweaving and connection, as the like is not to be done by the art of man. This kind of Cadis is a choice bait for any float-fish; it is much less than the Piper-Cadis, and to be so ordered; and these may be so preserved, ten, fifteen, or twenty days, or it may be longer.

There is also another Cadis, called by some a Straw-worm, and by some a Ruff-coat; whose house or case is made of little pieces of bents, and rushes, and straws, and water-weeds, and I know not what; which are so knit together with condensed slime, that they stick about her husk or case, not unlike the bristles of a hedgehog. These three Cadises are commonly taken in the beginning of summer; and are good, indeed, to take any kind of fish, with float or otherwise. I might tell you of many more, which as these do early, so those have their time also of turning to be flies later in summer; but I might lose myself and tire you by such a discourse. I shall, therefore, but remember you, that to know these and their several kinds, and to what flies every particular Cadis turns, and then how to use them, first as they be Cadis, and after as they be flies, is an art, and an art that every one that professes to be an Angler has not leisure to search after; and, if he had, is not capable of learning.

I'll tell you, Scholar, several countries have several kinds of Cadises, that indeed differ as much as dogs do: that is to say, as much as a very cur and a greyhound do. These be usually bred in the very little rills or ditches that run into bigger rivers; and, I think, a more proper bait for those very rivers than any other. I know not, or of what, this Cadis receives life, or what colored fly it turns to; but doubtless they are the death of many Trouts: and this is one killing way.

Take one, or more if need be, of these large yellow Cadis: pull off his head, and with it pull out his black gut; put the body, as little bruised as is possible, on a very little hook, armed on with a red hair, which will show like the Cadis-head; and a very little thin lead, so put upon the shank of the hook that it may sink presently. Throw this bait, thus ordered, which will look very yellow, into any great still hole where a Trout is, and he will presently venture his life for it, 't is not to be doubted, if you be not espied; and that the bait first touch the water, before the line: and this will do best in the deepest, stillest water.

Next let me tell you, I have been much pleased to walk quietly by a brook with a little stick in my hand, with which I might easily take these and consider the curiosity of their composure: and if you shall ever like to do so, then note that your stick must be a little hazel or willow, cleft, or have a nick at one end of it, by which means you may with ease take many of them in that nick out of the water, before you have any occasion to use them. These, my honest Scholar, are some observations told to you as they now come suddenly into my memory, of which you may make some use: but for the practical part, it is that that makes an Angler: it is diligence, and observation, and practice, and an ambition to be the best in the art, that must do it. I will tell you, Scholar, I once heard one say, "I envy not him that eats better meat than I do, nor him that is richer, or that wears better clothes than I do: I envy nobody but him, and him only, that catches more fish than I do." And such a man is like to prove an Angler; and this noble emulation I wish to you and all young Anglers.

THE FIFTH DAY.

CHAP. XVIII.—*Of the* MINNOW *or* PENK, *of the* LOACH,
and of the BULL-HEAD, *or* MILLER'S-THUMB.

THERE be also three or four other little fish that I had almost forgot, that all are without scales; and may, for excellency of meat, be compared to any fish of greatest value and largest size. They be usually full of eggs or spawn all the months of summer; for they breed often, as 't is observed mice and many of the smaller four-footed creatures of the earth do; and as those, so these come quickly to their full growth and perfection. And it is needful that they breed both often and numerously; for they be, besides other accidents of ruin, both a prey and baits for other fish. And first I shall tell you of the MINNOW or PENK.

The Minnow hath, when he is in perfect season and not sick, which is only presently after spawning,—a kind of dappled or waved color, like to a panther, on his sides, inclining to a greenish and sky-color, his belly being milk-white, and his back almost black or blackish. He is a sharp biter at a small worm, and in hot weather makes excellent sport for young Anglers, or boys, or women that love that recreation. And in the spring they make of them excellent Minnow-Tansies; for, being washed well in salt, and their heads and tails cut off, and their guts taken out, and not washed after,—they prove excellent for that use; that is, being fried with yolks of eggs, the flowers of cowslips, and of primroses, and a little tansy; thus used they make a dainty dish of meat.

The LOACH is, as I told you, a most dainty fish: he breeds and feeds in little and clear swift brooks, or rills, and lives there upon the gravel, and in the sharpest streams: he grows not to be above a finger long, and no thicker than is suitable to that length. This Loach is not unlike the shape of the Eel: he has a beard or wattles like a Barbel. He has two fins at his sides, four at his belly, and one at his tail; he is dappled with many black or brown spots; his mouth is Barbel-like under his nose. This fish is usually full of eggs or spawn, and is by Gesner, and other learned physicians, commended for great nourishment, and to be very grateful both to the palate and stomach of sick persons. He is to be fished for with a very small worm at the bottom; for he very seldom or never rises above the gravel, on which, I told you, he usually gets his living.

The MILLER'S-THUMB or BULL-HEAD, is a fish of no pleasing shape. He is by Gesner compared to the Sea-toad-fish, for his similitude and shape. It has a head, big and flat, much greater than suitable to his body; a mouth very wide and usually gaping. He is without teeth, but his lips are very rough, much like to a file. He hath two fins near to his gills, which be roundish or crested; two fins also under the belly; two on the back; one below the vent; and the fin of his tail is round. Nature hath painted the body of this fish with whitish, blackish, brownish spots. They be usually full of eggs or spawn all the summer, I mean the females; and those eggs swell their vents almost into the form of a dug. They begin to spawn about April, and, as I told you, spawn several months in the summer. And in the winter, the Min-

now, and Loach, and Bull-Head dwell in the mud, as the
Eel doth, or we know not where; no more than we know
where the cuckoo and swallow, and other half-year birds,
which first appear to us in April, spend their six cold, winter, melancholy months. This Bull-Head does usually dwell
and hide himself in holes, or amongst stones, in clear water:
and in very hot days will lie a long time very still, and sun
himself, and will be easy to be seen upon any flat stone, or
any gravel; at which time he will suffer an Angler to put a
hook baited with a small worm very near unto his very
mouth: and he never refuses to bite, nor indeed to be caught
with the worst of Anglers. Matthiolus[65] commends him
much more for his taste and nourishment than for his shape
or beauty.

There is also a little fish called a Sticklebag: a fish without scales, but hath his body fenced with several prickles. I
know not where he dwells in winter, nor what he is good for
in summer, but only to make sport for boys and women-
anglers, and to feed other fish that be fish of prey, as Trouts
in particular, who will bite at him as at a Penk; and better,
if your hook be rightly baited with him: for he may be so
baited as, his tail turning like the sail of a windmill, will
make him turn more quick than any Penk or Minnow can.
For note, that the nimble turning of that, or the Minnow, is
the perfection of Minnow fishing. To which end, if you put
your hook into his mouth, and out at his tail; and then, having first tied him with white thread a little above his tail,
and placed him after such a manner on your hook as he is
like to turn, then sew up his mouth to your line, and he is

like to turn quick, and tempt any Trout: but if he does not turn quick, then turn his tail a little more or less towards the inner part, or towards the side of the hook; or put the Minnow or Sticklebag a little more crooked or more straight on your hook, until it will turn both true and fast: and then doubt not but to tempt any great Trout that lies in a swift stream. And the Loach that I told you of will do the like: no bait is more tempting, provided the Loach be not too big.

And now, Scholar, with the help of this fine morning, and your patient attention, I have said all that my present memory will afford me concerning most of the several fish that are usually fished for in fresh waters.

VEN. But, Master, you have, by your former civility, made me hope that you will make good your promise, and say something of the several rivers that be of most note in this nation; and also of fish-ponds, and the ordering of them: and do it, I pray, good Master, for I love any discourse of rivers, and fish and fishing: the time spent in such discourse passes away very pleasantly.

THE FIFTH DAY.

CHAP. XIX.[66]—*Of several Rivers, and some Observations of Fish.*

PISCATOR.

WELL, Scholar, since the ways and weather do both favor us, and that we yet see not Tottenham Cross, you shall see my willingness to satisfy your desire. And, first, for the rivers of this nation: there be, as you may note out of Doctor Heylin's Geography and others, in number three hundred and twenty-five; but those of chiefest note he reckons and describes as followeth.

1. The chief is THAMISIS, compounded of two rivers, Thame and Isis; whereof the former, rising somewhat beyond Thame in Buckinghamshire, and the latter near Cirencester in Gloucestershire, meet together about

junction is the Thamisis, or Thames. Hence it flieth betwixt Berks, Buckinghamshire, Middlesex, Surrey, Kent, and Essex, and so weddeth himself to the Kentish Medway in the very jaws of the ocean. This glorious river feeleth the violence and benefit of the sea more than any river in Europe; ebbing and flowing twice a day more than sixty miles: about whose banks are so many fair towns, and princely palaces, that a German poet thus truly spake:—

"Tot campos, et.

"We saw so many woods and princely bowers,
Sweet fields, brave palaces, and stately towers,
So many gardens, dressed with curious care,
That Thames with royal Tiber may compare."

2. The second river of note is SABRINA or SEVERN. It hath its beginning in Plinlimmon Hill in Montgomeryshire, and his end seven miles from Bristol; washing, in the mean space, the walls of Shrewsbury, Worcester, and Gloucester, and divers other places and palaces of note.

3. TRENT, so called from thirty kind of fishes that are found in it, or for that it receiveth thirty lesser rivers; who, having his fountain in Staffordshire, and gliding through the counties of Nottingham, Lincoln, Leicester, and York, augmenteth the turbulent current of Humber, the most violent stream of all the isle. This Humber is not, to say truth, a distinct river, having a spring-head of his own, but it is rather the mouth, or æstuarium, of divers rivers here con-

fluent and meeting together: namely, your Derwent, and especially of Ouse and Trent; and (as the Danow, having received into its channel the rivers Dravus, Savus, Tibiscus, and divers others) changeth his name into this of Humberabus, as the old geographers call it.

4. MEDWAY, a Kentish river, famous for harboring the royal navy.

5. TWEED, the northeast bound of England, on whose northern banks is seated the strong and impregnable town of Berwick.

6. TYNE, famous for Newcastle, and her inexhaustible coal-pits. These, and the rest of principal note, are thus comprehended in one of Mr. Drayton's Sonnets.

"Our floods' queen, Thames, for ships and swans is crowned;
  And stately Severn for her shore is praised;
The crystal Trent for fords and fish renowned;
  And Avon's fame to Albion's cliffs is raised.
Carlegion-Chester vaunts her holy Dee;
  York many wonders of her Ouse can tell;
The Peak her Dove, whose banks so fertile be,
  And Kent will say her Medway doth excel.
Cotswold commends her Isis to the Thame;
  Our northern borders boast of Tweed's fair flood;
Our western parts extol their Willy's fame,
  And the old Lea brags of the Danish blood."

These observations are out of learned Dr. Heylin, and my old deceased friend, Michael Drayton; and because you say you love such discourses as these of rivers and fish and fishing, I love you the better, and love the more to impart them to you: nevertheless, Scholar, if I should begin but to name the several sorts of strange fish that are usually taken in many of those rivers that run into the sea, I might beget wonder in you, or unbelief, or both: and yet I will venture to tell you a real truth concerning one lately dissected by Dr. Wharton,[67] a man of great learning and experience, and of equal freedom to communicate it; one that loves me and my art; one to whom I have been beholden for many of the choicest observations that I have imparted to you. This good man, that dares do anything rather than tell an untruth, did, I say, tell me he lately dissected one strange fish, and he thus described it to me.

"The fish was almost a yard broad, and twice that length; his mouth wide enough to receive or take into it the head of a man; his stomach seven or eight inches broad. He is of a slow motion, and usually lies or lurks close in the mud, and has a movable string on his head about a span, or near unto a quarter of a yard long, by the moving of which, which is his natural bait, when he lies close and unseen in the mud, he draws other smaller fish so close to him that he can suck them into his mouth, and so devours and digests them."

And, Scholar, do not wonder at this, for, besides the credit of the relator, you are to note, many of these, and fishes which are of the like and more unusual shapes, are very often taken on the mouths of our sea-rivers, and on the sea-shore. And this will be no wonder to any that have travelled Egypt; where 't is known the famous river Nilus does not only breed fishes that yet want names, but, by the over-flowing of that river, and the help of the sun's heat on the fat slime which that river leaves on the banks, when it falls back into its natural channel, such strange fish and beasts are also bred, that no man can give a name to, as Grotius, in his "Sophom," and others, have observed.

But whither am I strayed in this discourse? I will end it by telling you, that at the mouth of some of these rivers of ours Herrings are so plentiful, as namely, near to Yarmouth in Norfolk, and in the West-country Pilchers so very plentiful, as you will wonder to read what our learned Camden relates of them in his "Britannia," pp. 178, 186.

Well, Scholar, I will stop here, and tell you what by reading and conference I have observed concerning fish ponds.

THE FIFTH DAY.

CHAP. XX.[68]—*Of Fish-Ponds, and how to order them.*

PISCATOR.

DOCTOR Lebault,[69] the learned Frenchman, in his large discourse of *Maison Rustique*, gives this direction for making of fish-ponds. I shall refer you to him to read it at large; but I think I shall contract it, and yet make it as useful.

He adviseth, that when you have drained the ground, and made the earth firm where the head of the pond must be, that you must then, in that place, drive in two or three rows of oak or elm piles, which should be scorched in the fire, or half burnt, before they be driven into the earth; for being thus used it preserves them much longer from rotting. And having done so, lay fagots or bavins of smaller wood betwixt them; and then earth betwixt and above them: and then, having first very well rammed them and the earth, use another pile in like manner as the first were: and note, that the second pile is to be of or about the height that you intend to make your sluice or flood-gate, or the vent that you intend shall convey the overflowings of your pond, in any flood that shall endanger the breaking of the pond-dam.

Then he advises that you plant willows or owlers about it, or both: and then cast in bavins in some places not far from the side, and in the most sandy places, for fish both to spawn upon, and to defend them and the young fry from the many fish, and also from vermin, that lie at watch to destroy them; especially the spawn of the Carp and Tench, when 't is left to the mercy of ducks or vermin.

He, and Dubravius, and all others, advise, that you make choice of such a place for your pond, that it may be refreshed with a little rill, or with rain-water running or falling into it; by which fish are more inclined both to breed, and are also refreshed and fed the better, and do prove to be of a much sweeter and more pleasant taste.

To which end it is observed, that such pools as be large, and have most gravel, and shallows where fish may sport themselves, do afford fish of the purest taste. And note, that in all pools it is best for fish to have some retiring-place; as namely, hollow banks, or shelves, or roots of trees, to keep them from danger; and, when they think fit, from the extreme heat of summer; as also from the extremity of cold in winter. And note, that if many trees be growing about your pond, the leaves thereof falling into the water make it nauseous to the fish, and the fish to be so to the eater of it.

'T is noted that the Tench and Eel love mud, and the Carp loves gravelly ground, and in the hot months to feed on grass. You are to cleanse your pond, if you intend either profit or pleasure, once every three or four years, especially some ponds, and then let it lie dry six or twelve months, both to kill the water-weeds, as water-lilies, candocks, reate, and bulrushes, that breed there: and also, that as these die for want of water, so grass may grow in the pond's bottom, which Carps will eat greedily in all the hot months if

the pond be clean. The letting your pond dry and sowing
oats in the bottom is also good, for the fish feed the faster:
and, being some time let dry, you may observe what kind of
fish either increases or thrives best in that water; for they
differ much both in their breeding and feeding.

Lebault also advises, that if your ponds be not very large
and roomy, that you often feed your fish by throwing into
them chippings of bread, curds, grains, or the entrails of
chickens, or of any fowl or beast that you kill to feed yourselves; for these afford fish a great relief. He says that frogs
and ducks do much harm, and devour both the spawn and
the young fry of all fish, especially of the Carp; and I have,
besides experience, many testimonies of it. But Lebault al-
lows water-frogs to be good meat, especially in some
months, if they be fat; but you are to note, that he is a
Frenchman, and we English will hardly believe him,
though we know frogs are usually eaten in his country;
however, he advises to destroy them and kingfishers out of
your ponds. And he advises not to suffer much shooting at
wild-fowl; for that, he says, affrightens, and harms, and destroys, the fish.

Note, that Carps and Tench thrive and breed best when
no other fish is put with them into the same pond; for all
other fish devour their spawn, or at least the greatest part of
it. And note, that clods of grass thrown into any pond feed
any Carps in summer; and that garden-earth and parsley
thrown into a pond recovers and refreshes the sick fish. And
note, that when you store your pond, you are to put into it
two or three melters for one spawner, if you put them into

a breeding-pond; but if into a nurse-pond, or feeding-pond, in which they will not breed, then no care is to be taken whether there be most male or female Carps.

It is observed that the best ponds to breed Carps are those that be stony or sandy, and are warm and free from wind; and that are not deep, but have willow-trees, and grass on their sides, over which the water does sometimes flow: and note, that Carps do more usually breed in marle-pits, or pits that have clean clay-bottoms, or in new ponds, or ponds that lie dry a winter-season, than in old ponds that be full of mud and weeds.

Well, Scholar, I have told you the substance of all that either observation or discourse, or a diligent survey of Dubravius and Lebault hath told me: not that they, in their long discourses, have not said more; but the most of the rest are so common observations, as if a man should tell a good arithmetician, that twice two is four. I will therefore put an end to this discourse, and we will here sit down and rest us.

THE FIFTH DAY.

CHAP. XXI.—*Directions for making of a Line, and for the coloring of both Rod and Line.*

PISCATOR.

WELL, Scholar, I have held you too long about these cadis, and smaller fish, and rivers, and fish-ponds; and my spirits are almost spent, and so I doubt is your patience; but being we are now almost at Tottenham, where I first met you, and where we are to part, I will lose no time, but give you a little direction how to make and order your lines, and to color the hair of which you make your lines, for that is very needful to be known of an Angler; and also how to paint your rod, especially your top; for a right-grown top is a choice commodity, and should be preserved from the water soaking into it, which makes it in wet weather to be heavy, and fish ill-favoredly, and not true; and also it rots quickly for want of painting: and I think a good top is worth preserving, or I had not taken care to keep a top above twenty years.

But first for your line.[70] First, note, that you are to take care that your hair be round and clear, and free from galls, or scabs, or frets; for a well-chosen, even, clear, round hair, of a kind of glass-color, will prove as strong as three uneven, scabby hairs, that are ill-chosen, and full of galls or uneven-ness. You shall seldom find a black hair but it is round, but many white are flat and uneven; therefore if you get a lock of right, round, clear, glass-color hair, make much of it.

And for making your line, observe this rule: first let your hair be clean washed ere you go about to twist it; and then choose not only the clearest hair for it, but hairs that be of an equal bigness, for such do usually stretch all together, and break all together, which hairs of an unequal bigness never do, but break singly, and so deceive the Angler that trusts to them.

When you have twisted your links, lay them in water for a quarter of an hour at least, and then twist them over again before you tie them into a line; for those that do not so, shall usually find their line to have a hair or two shrink, and be shorter than the rest at the first fishing with it; which is so much of the strength of the line lost for want of first water-ing it and then re-twisting it; and this is most visible in a seven-hair line, one of those which hath always a black hair in the middle.

And for dyeing of your hairs, do it thus. Take a pint of strong ale, half a pound of soot, and a little quantity of the juice of walnut-tree leaves, and an equal quantity of alum; put these together into a pot, pan, or pipkin, and boil them half an hour; and having so done, let it cool; and being cold, put your hair into it, and there let it lie: it will turn your hair to be a kind of water or glass-color, or greenish; and the longer you let it lie, the deeper colored it will be. You might be taught to make many other colors, but it is to little purpose; for doubtless the water-color or glass-colored hair is the most choice and most useful for an Angler; but let it not be too green.

But if you desire to color hair greener, then do it thus. Take a quart of small ale, half a pound of alum; then put these into a pan or pipkin, and your hair into it with them; then put it upon a fire, and let it boil softly for half an hour; and then take out your hair, and let it dry; and, having so done, then take a pottle of water, and put into it two handfuls of marigolds, and cover it with a tile, or what you think fit, and set it again on the fire, where it is to boil again softly for half an hour, about which time the scum will turn yellow; then put into it half a pound of copperas, beaten small, and with it the hair that you intend to color; then let the hair be boiled softly till half the liquor be wasted; and then let it cool three or four hours, with your hair in it: and you are to observe, that the more copperas you put into it, the greener it will be; but doubtless the pale green is best. But if you desire yellow hair, which is only good when the weeds rot, then put in the more marigolds; and abate most of the copperas, or leave it quite out, and take a little verdigris instead of it. This for coloring your hair.

And as for painting your rod, which must be in oil, you must first make a size with glue and water boiled together until the glue be dissolved, and the size of a lye-color; then strike your size upon the wood with a bristle, or a brush, or pencil, whilst it is hot. That being quite dry, take white lead, and a little red lead, and a little coal-black, so much as all together will make an ash-color; grind these all together with linseed oil; let it be thick, and lay it thin upon the wood with a brush or pencil: this do for the ground of any color to lie upon wood.

For a green: Take pink and verdigris, and grind them together in linseed-oil, as thin as you can well grind it; then lay it smoothly on with your brush, and drive it thin: once doing, for the most part, will serve, if you lay it well; and if twice, be sure your first color be thoroughly dry before you lay on a second.

Well, Scholar, having now taught you to paint your rod, and we having still a mile to Tottenham-High-Cross, I will, as we walk towards it, in the cool shade of this sweet honeysuckle hedge, mention to you some of the thoughts and joys that have possessed my soul since we two met together. And these thoughts shall be told you, that you also may join with me in thankfulness, to "the Giver of every good and perfect gift," for our happiness. And, that our present happiness may appear to be the greater, and we the more thankful for it, I will beg you to consider with me, how many do, even at this very time, lie under the torment of the stone, the gout, and toothache; and this we are free from. And every misery that I miss is a new mercy; and therefore let us be thankful. There have been, since we met, others that have met disasters of broken limbs; some have been blasted, others thunder-strucken; and we have been freed from these, and all those many other miseries that threaten human nature: let us therefore rejoice and be thankful. Nay, which is a far greater mercy, we are free from the unsupportable burden of an accusing, tormenting conscience,—a misery that none can bear: and therefore let us praise Him for His preventing grace, and say, Every misery that I miss is a new mercy. Nay, let me tell you, there be many that have forty times our estates, that would give the greatest part of it to be healthful and cheerful like us; who, with the expense of a little money have eat and drank, and laughed, and angled, and sung, and slept securely; and rose next day, and cast away care, and sung, and laughed, and angled again; which are blessings rich men cannot purchase with all their money. Let me tell you, Scholar, I have a rich neighbor, that is always so busy that he has no leisure to laugh: the whole business of his life is to get money, and more money, that he may still get more and more money; he is still drudging on, and says, that Solomon says, "The diligent hand maketh rich;" and it is true indeed: but he considers not that 't is not in the power of riches to make a man happy; for it was wisely said, by a man of great observation, "That there be as many miseries beyond riches, as on this side them." And yet God deliver us from pinching poverty; and grant that, having a competency, we may be content and thankful. Let not us repine, or so much as think the gifts of God unequally dealt, if we see another abound with riches; when, as God knows, the cares that are the keys that keep those riches, hang often so heavily at the rich man's girdle, that they clog him with weary days, and restless nights, even when others sleep quietly. We see but the outside of the rich man's happiness: few consider him to be like the silkworm, that, when she seems to play, is, at the very same time, spinning her own bowels, and consuming herself. And this many rich men do; loading themselves with corroding cares, to keep what they have, probably, unconscionably got. Let us, therefore, be thankful for health and a competence, and above all, for a quiet conscience.

Let me tell you, Scholar, that Diogenes walked on a day, with his friend, to see a country-fair; where he saw ribbons, and looking-glasses, and nut-crackers, and fiddles, and hobby-horses, and many other gimcracks; and having observed them, and all the other finnimbruns that make a complete country-fair, he said to his friend, "Lord! How many things are there in this world, of which Diogenes hath no need!" And truly it is so, or might be so, with very many who vex and toil themselves to get what they have no need of. Can any man charge God, that he hath not given him enough to make his life happy? No, doubtless; for nature is content with a little. And yet you shall hardly meet with a man that complains not of some want; though he, indeed, wants nothing but his will, it may be, nothing but his will of his poor neighbor, for not worshipping, or not flattering him: and thus, when we might be happy and quiet, we create trouble to ourselves. I have heard of a man that was angry with himself because he was no taller; and of a woman that broke her looking-glass because it would not show her face to be as young and handsome as her next neighbor's was. And I knew another, to whom God had given health, and plenty; but a wife, that nature had made peevish, and her husband's riches had made purse-proud, and must, because she was rich, and for no other virtue, sit in the highest pew in the church; which being denied her, she engaged her husband into a contention for it; and, at last, into a lawsuit with a dogged neighbor, who was as rich as he, and had a wife as peevish and purse-proud as the other: and this lawsuit begot higher oppositions, and actionable words, and more vexations and lawsuits; for you must remember, that both were rich, and must therefore have their wills. Well, this wilful, purse-proud lawsuit lasted during the life of the first husband; after which his wife vexed and chid, and chid and vexed, till she also chid and vexed herself into her grave: and so the wealth of these poor rich people was curst into a punishment: because they wanted meek and thankful hearts; for those only can make us happy. I knew a man that had health and riches, and several houses, all beautiful and ready furnished, and would often trouble himself and family to be removing from one house to another; and being asked by a friend, why he removed so often from one house to another, replied, "It was to find content in some one of them." But his friend, knowing his temper, told him, "If he would find content in any of his houses, he must leave himself behind him; for content will never dwell but in a meek and quiet soul." And this may appear, if we read and consider what our Saviour says in St.

Matthew's Gospel: for he there says, "Blessed be the merciful, for they shall obtain mercy. Blessed be the pure in heart, for they shall see God. Blessed be the poor in spirit, for theirs is the kingdom of heaven. And, Blessed be the meek, for they shall possess the earth." Not that the meek shall not also obtain mercy, and see God, and be comforted, and at last come to the kingdom of heaven; but in the mean time he, and he only, possesses the earth as he goes toward that kingdom of heaven, by being humble and cheerful, and content with what his good God has allotted him. He has no turbulent, repining, vexatious thoughts, that he deserves better; nor is vexed when he sees others possessed of more honor, or more riches than his wise God has allotted for his share; but he possesses what he has with a meek and contented quietness; such a quietness as makes his very dreams pleasing both to God and himself.

My honest Scholar, all this is told to incline you to thankfulness; and to incline you the more, let me tell you, that though the prophet David was guilty of murder and adultery, and many other of the most deadly sins, yet he was said to be a man after God's own heart, because he abounded more with thankfulness than any other that is mentioned in Holy Scripture, as may appear in his book of Psalms; where there is such a commixture of his confessing of his sins and unworthiness, and such thankfulness for God's pardon and mercies, as did make him to be accounted, even by God himself, to be a man after his own heart: and let us in that, labor to be as like him as we can; let not the blessings we receive daily from God make us not to value, or not praise Him, because they be common: let not us forget to praise Him for the innocent mirth and pleasure we have met with since we met together. What would a blind man give to see the pleasant rivers, and meadows, and flowers, and fountains, that we have met with since we met together? I have been told, that if a man that was born blind could obtain to have his sight for but only one hour during his whole life, and should, at the first opening of his eyes, fix his sight upon the sun when it was in his full glory, either at the rising or setting of it, he would be so transported and amazed, and so admire the glory of it, that he would not willingly turn his eyes from that first ravishing object, to behold all the other various beauties this world could present to him. And this, and many other like blessings, we enjoy daily. And for most of them, because they be so common, most men forget to pay their praises; but let not us; because it is a sacrifice so pleasing to Him that made that sun, and us, and still protects us, and gives us flowers, and showers, and stomachs, and meat, and content, and leisure to go a-fishing.

Well, Scholar, I have almost tired myself, and, I fear, more than almost tired you. But I now see Tottenham High-Cross; and our short walk thither shall put a period to my too long discourse; in which my meaning was, and is, to plant that in your mind, with which I labor to possess my own soul, that is, a meek and thankful heart. And to that end I have showed you, that riches without them do not make any man happy. But let me tell you, that riches with them remove many fears and cares; and therefore my advice is, that you endeavor to be honestly rich, or contentedly poor; but be sure that your riches be justly got, or you spoil all. For it is well said by Caussin,[71] "He that loses his conscience has nothing left that is worth keeping." Therefore be sure you look to that. And, in the next place, look to your health: and if you have it, praise God, and value it next to a good conscience; for health is the second blessing that we mortals are capable of; a blessing that money cannot buy; and therefore value it, and be thankful for it. As for money, which may be said to be the third blessing, neglect it not: but note, that there is no necessity of being rich; for, I told you, there be as many miseries beyond riches as on this side them: and, if you have a competence, enjoy it with a meek, cheerful, thankful heart. I will tell you, Scholar, I have heard a grave divine say,[72] that God has two dwellings; one in heaven, and the other in a meek and thankful heart: which Almighty God grant to me, and to my honest Scholar! And so you are welcome to Tottenham High-Cross.

VEN. Well, Master, I thank you for all your good directions; but for none more than this last of thankfulness, which I hope I shall never forget. And pray now let's rest ourselves in this sweet shady arbor, which Nature herself has woven with her own fine fingers; 't is such a contexture of woodbines, sweetbrier, jessamine, and myrtle, and so interwoven as will secure us both from the sun's violent heat, and from the approaching shower. And, being sat down, I will requite a part of your courtesies with a bottle of sack, milk, oranges, and sugar, which, all put together, make a drink like nectar; indeed, too good for anybody but us An-

glers. And so, Master, here is a full glass to you of that
liquor; and when you have pledged me, I will repeat the
verses which I promised you. It is a copy printed amongst
some of Sir Henry Wotton's, and doubtless made either by
him or by a lover of Angling. Come, Master, now drink a
glass to me, and then I will pledge you, and fall to my repetition; it is a description of such country recreations as I
have enjoyed since I had the happiness to fall into your
company.

"Quivering fears, heart-tearing cares,
Anxious sighs, untimely tears,
    Fly, fly to courts,
    Fly to fond worldlings' sports,
Where strained sardonic smiles are glozing still,
And Grief is forced to laugh against her will:
    Where mirth's but mummery,
    And sorrows only real be.

"Fly, from our country pastimes, fly,
Sad troops of human misery.
    Come, serene looks,
    Clear as the crystal brooks,
Or the pure azured heaven, that smiles to see
The rich attendance of our poverty:
    Peace and a secure mind,
    Which all men seek, we only find.

"Abused mortals, did you know
Where joy, heart's-ease, and comforts grow,
    You'd scorn proud towers,
    And seek them in these bowers;

Where winds, sometimes, our woods perhaps may shake.
But blust'ring care could never tempest make;
    Nor murmurs e'er come nigh us,
    Saving of fountains that glide by us.

"Here's no fantastic masque, nor dance,
But of our kids that frisk and prance;
    Nor wars are seen,
    Unless upon the green
Two harmless lambs are butting one the other,
Which done, both bleating run each to his mother:
    And wounds are never found,
    Save what the ploughshare gives the ground.

"Here are no entrapping baits
To hasten too, too hasty fates,
    Unless it be
    The fond credulity
Of silly fish, which, worldling like, still look
Upon the bait, but never on the hook:
    Nor envy, 'less among
    The birds, for prize of their sweet song.

"Go, let the diving negro seek
For gems hid in some forlorn creek:
    We all pearls scorn,
    Save what the dewy morn
Congeals upon each little spire of grass,
Which careless shepherds beat down as they pass:
    And gold ne'er here appears,
    Save what the yellow Ceres bears.

"Blest silent groves! O may you be
Forever mirth's best nursery!

May pure contents
Forever pitch their tents
Upon these downs, these meads, these rocks, these mountains,
And peace still slumber by these purling fountains:
Which we may every year
Meet when we come a-fishing here."

Pisc. Trust me, Scholar, I thank you heartily for these
verses: they be choicely good, and doubtless made by a lover
of Angling. Come, now, drink a glass to me, and I will requite you with another very good copy: it is a Farewell to
the Vanities of the World, and some say, written by Sir
Harry Wotton, who I told you was an excellent Angler. But
let them be writ by whom they will, he that writ them had
a brave soul, and must needs be possessed with happy
thoughts at the time of their composure.

"Farewell, ye gilded follies, pleasing troubles!
Farewell, ye honored rags, ye glorious bubbles!
Fame's but a hollow echo; Gold, pure clay;
Honor, the darling but of one short day;
Beauty, th' eye's idol, but a damasked skin;
State, but a golden prison, to live in
And torture free-born minds; embroidered trains,
Merely but pageants for proud swelling veins;
And blood allied to greatness is alone
Inherited, not purchased, nor our own.
Fame, Honor, Beauty, State, Train, Blood, and Birth
Are but the fading blossoms of the earth.

"I would be great,—but that the sun doth still
Level his rays against the rising hill:

I would be high,—but see the proudest oak
Most subject to the rending thunder-stroke:
I would be rich,—but see men, too unkind,
Dig in the bowels of the richest mind:
I would be wise,—but that I often see
The fox suspected, whilst the ass goes free:
I would be fair,—but see the fair and proud,
Like the bright sun, oft setting in a cloud:
I would be poor,—but know the humble grass
Still trampled on by each unworthy ass:
Rich, hated; Wise, suspected; Scorned if poor;
Great, feared; Fair, tempted; High, still envied more:
   I have wished all; but now I wish for neither;
   Great, High, Rich, Wise, nor Fair; Poor I'll be rather.

"Would the World now adopt me for her heir,
Would Beauty's queen entitle me the fair,—
Fame speak me Fortune's minion;—could I vie
Angels with India; with a speaking eye
Command bare heads, bowed knees, strike justice dumb
As well as blind and lame; or give a tongue
To stones by epitaphs; be called great master
In the loose rhymes of every poetaster;—
Could I be more than any man that lives,
Great, fair, rich, wise, all in superlatives:
Yet I more freely would these gifts resign,
Than ever Fortune would have made them mine;
   And hold one minute of this holy leisure
   Beyond the riches of this empty pleasure.

"Welcome, pure thoughts! Welcome, ye silent groves!
These guests, these courts, my soul most dearly loves.
Now the winged people of the sky shall sing
My cheerful anthems to the gladsome spring:

A prayer-book now shall be my looking-glass,
In which I will adore sweet Virtue's face.
Here dwell no hateful looks, no palace-cares,
No broken vows dwell here, nor pale-faced fears:
Then here I'll sit, and sigh my hot love's folly,
And learn t' affect an holy melancholy:
    And if Contentment be a stranger, then
    I'll ne'er look for it, but in heaven again."

VEN. Well, Master, these verses be worthy to keep a room in every man's memory. I thank you for them; and I thank you for your many instructions, which, God willing, I will not forget. And as St. Austin, in his Confessions, Book IV. Chap. 3, commemorates the kindness of his friend Verecundus, for lending him and his companion a country-house, because there they rested and enjoyed themselves free from the troubles of the world; so, having had the like advantage, both by your conversation and the Art you have taught me, I ought ever to do the like; for indeed, your company and discourse have been so useful and pleasant, that I may truly say, I have only lived since I enjoyed them and turned Angler, and not before. Nevertheless, here I must part with you, here in this now sad place, where I was so happy as first to meet you: but I shall long for the 9th of May, for then I hope again to enjoy your beloved company at the appointed time and place. And now I wish for some somniferous potion, that might force me to sleep away the intermitted time, which will pass away with me as tediously as it does with men in sorrow; nevertheless I will make it as short as I can, by my hopes and wishes. And my good Master, I will not forget the doctrine which you told me Socrates taught his scholars, that they should not think to be honored so much for being philosophers, as to honor philosophy by their virtuous lives. You advised me to the like concerning Angling, and I will endeavor to do so, and to live like those many worthy men, of which you made mention in the former part of your discourse. This is my firm resolution. And as a pious man advised his friend, that, to beget mortification, he should frequent churches, and view monuments, and charnel-houses, and then and there consider, how many dead bones Time had piled up at the gates of Death: so when I would beget content, and increase confidence in the power, and wisdom, and providence of Almighty God, I will walk the meadows by some gliding stream, and there contemplate the lilies that take no care, and those very many other various little living creatures, that are not only created, but fed, man knows not how, by the goodness of the God of nature, and therefore trust in him. This is my purpose; and so, "Let everything that hath breath praise the Lord:" and let the blessing of St. Peter's Master be with mine.

Pisc. And upon all that are lovers of virtue, and dare trust in his providence, and be quiet, and go a-Angling.

Study to be quiet.—1 Thes. iv. 11.

THE
COMPLETE ANGLER:

OR, THE

CONTEMPLATIVE MAN'S RECREATION.

PART II.

BEING
INSTRUCTIONS HOW TO ANGLE FOR A
TROUT OR GRAYLING IN A CLEAR STREAM.

CHARLES COTTON

Qui mihi non credit, faciat licet ipse periclum
Et fuerit scriptis æquior ille meis.

To my most worthy Father and Friend, Mr. Izaak
Walton, *the Elder.*

Sir:

Being you were pleased, some years past, to grant me
your free leave to do what I have here attempted, and observing you never retract any promise, when made in favor
even of your meanest friends, I accordingly expect to see
these following particular directions for the taking of a
trout to wait upon your better and more general rules for all
sorts of angling: and, though mine be neither so perfect, so
well digested, nor indeed so handsomely couched, as they
might have been, in so long a time as since your leave was
granted, yet I dare affirm them to be generally true; and
they had appeared too in something a neater dress, but that
I was surprised with the sudden news of a sudden new edition of your *Complete Angler;* so that, having but a little
more than ten days' time to turn me in, and rub up my
memory, for, in truth, I have not, in all this long time,
though I have often thought on 't, and almost as often resolved to go presently about it, I was forced upon the instant to scribble what I here present you; which I have also
endeavored to accommodate to your own method. And, if
mine be clear enough for the honest Brothers of the Angle
readily to understand, which is the only thing I aim at, then
I have my end, and shall need to make no further apology:

a writing of this kind not requiring, if I were master of any such thing, any eloquence to set it off or recommend it; so that if you, in your better judgment, or kindness rather, can allow it passable, for a thing of this nature, you will then do me honor, if the *Cipher,* fixed and carved in the front of my little fishing-house, may be here explained: and to permit me to attend you in public, who, in private, have ever been, am, and ever resolve to be, sir,

Your most affectionate son and servant,

Charles Cotton .../

Beresford,
10th of March, 167⅚

To my most honored Friend, CHARLES COTTON, *Esq.*

SIR:

You now see I have returned you your very pleasant and useful discourse of the Art of Fly-fishing, printed just as it was sent me: for I have been so obedient to your desires, as to endure all the praises you have ventured to fix upon me in it. And when I have thanked you for them, as the effects of an undissembled love, then let me tell you, sir, that I will really endeavor to live up to the character you have given of me; if there were no other reason, yet for this alone, that you, that love me so well, and always think what you speak, may not, for my sake, suffer by a mistake in your judgment.

And, sir, I have ventured to fill a part of your margin, by way of paraphrase, for the reader's clearer understanding the situation, both of your Fishing-house, and the pleasantness of that you dwell in. And I have ventured also to give him a copy of verses that you were pleased to send me, now some years past; in which he may see a good picture of both; and so much of your own mind, too, as will make any reader that is blest with a generous soul to love you the better. I confess, that for doing this you may justly judge me too bold: if you do, I will say so too; and so far commute for my offence, that, though I be more than a hundred miles from you, and in the eighty-third year of my age, yet I will forget both, and next month begin a pilgrimage to beg your pardon; for I would die in your favor; and till then will live, sir,

Your most affectionate father and friend,

London,
April 29th, 1676.

The subjoined fac-simile of Walton's handwriting, and a seal given him by Dr. Donne, will be interesting to the Waltonian reader.

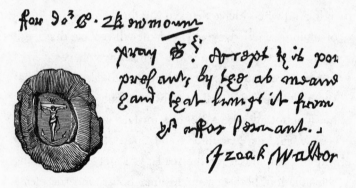

For Do^r. C. Bewmount.

pray S^r, Accept this pore presant, by the as meane hand that brings it from

Y^r. affec. servant,

Izaak Walton.

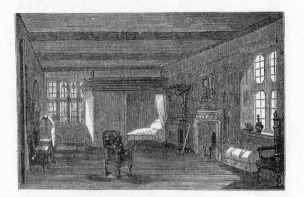

THE RETIREMENT.

IRREGULAR STANZAS,

ADDRESSED TO

MR. IZAAK WALTON.

I.

Farewell, thou busy world! and may
We never meet again:
Here I can eat, and sleep, and pray,
And do more good in one short day,
Than he, who his whole age outwears
Upon the most conspicuous theatres,
Where naught but vanity and vice do reign.

II.

Good God! how sweet are all things here!
How beautiful the fields appear!
  How cleanly do we feed and lie!
Lord! what good hours do we keep!
How quietly we sleep!
  What peace! what unanimity!
How innocent from the lewd fashion
Is all our business, all our recreation!

III.

O how happy here 's our leisure!
O how innocent our pleasure!
O ye valleys! O ye mountains!
O ye groves, and crystal fountains!
How I love at liberty,
By turns, to come and visit ye!

IV.

Dear Solitude, the soul's best friend,
   That man acquainted with himself dost make,
And all his Maker's wonders to entend,
With thee I here converse at will,
And would be glad to do so still;
   For it is thou alone that keep'st the soul awake.

V.

How calm and quite a delight
   Is it alone
To read, and meditate, and write;
   By none offended, and offending none!
To walk, ride, sit, or sleep at one's own ease,
And, pleasing a man's self, none other to displease!

VI.

O my beloved Nymph! fair Dove!
Princess of Rivers! how I love
   Upon thy flowery banks to lie,
And view thy silver stream,
When gilded by a summer's beam,
   And in it all thy wanton fry
   Playing at liberty;
And, with my angle upon them,

The all of treachery
I ever learned industriously to try.

VII.

Such streams, Rome's yellow Tiber cannot show,
The Iberian Tagus, or Ligurian Po;
The Maese, the Danube, and the Rhine,
Are puddle-water all, compared with thine;
And Loire's pure streams yet too polluted are
With thine much purer to compare;
The rapid Garonne, and the winding Seine,
Are both too mean,
Beloved Dove, with thee
To vie priority;
Nay, Thame and Isis when conjoined submit,
And lay their trophies at thy silver feet.

VIII.

O my beloved rocks, that rise
To awe the earth and brave the skies!
From some aspiring mountain's crown,
    How dearly do I love,
Giddy with pleasure, to look down,
    And from the vales to view the noble heights above!
O my beloved caves! from Dog-star's heat,
And all anxieties, my safe retreat;
What safety, privacy, what true delight,
In th' artificial night
Your gloomy entrails make,
Have I taken, do I take!
How oft, when grief has made me fly
To hide me from society,
Ev'n of my dearest friends, have I
    In your recesses' friendly shade

All my sorrows open laid,
And my most secret woes intrusted to your privacy!

IX.

Lord! would men let me alone,
What an over-happy one
  Should I think myself to be,
Might I, in this desert place,
Which most men in discourse disgrace,
  Live but undisturbed and free!
Here, in this despised recess,
  Would I, maugre Winter's cold,
And the Summer's worst excess,
  Try to live out to sixty full years old!
And all the while,
  Without an envious eye,
On any thriving under Fortune's smile
  Contented live, and then—contented die.

                            C. C.

THE FIRST DAY.

CHAPTER I.

PISCATOR JUNIOR AND VIATOR.

PISCATOR.

OU are happily overtaken, Sir. May a man be so bold as to inquire how far you travel this way?

VIATOR. Yes, sure, Sir, very freely; though it be a question I cannot very well resolve you, as not knowing myself how far it is to Ashbourn, where I intend tonight to take up my inn.

PISC. Why then, Sir, seeing I perceive you to be a stranger in these parts, I shall take upon me to inform you, that from the town you last came through, called Brailsford, it is five miles; and you are not yet above half a mile on this side.

Viat. So much! I was told it was but ten miles from Derby; and, methinks, I have rode almost so far already.

Pisc. O, Sir, find no fault with large measure of good land; which Derbyshire abounds in, as much as most counties of England.

Viat. It may be so; and good land, I confess, affords a pleasant prospect: but, by your good leave, Sir, large measure of foul way is not altogether so acceptable.

Pisc. True, Sir; but the foul way serves to justify the fertility of the soil, according to the proverb, "There is good land where there is foul way:" and is of good use to inform you of the riches of the country you are come into, and of its continual travel and traffic to the country-town you came from: which is also very observable by the fulness of its road, and the laden horses you meet everywhere upon the way.

Viat. Well, Sir, I will be content to think as well of your country as you would desire. And I shall have a good deal of reason both to think and to speak very well of you, if I may obtain the happiness of your company to the forementioned place; provided your affairs lead you that way, and that they will permit you to slack your pace, out of complacency to a traveller utterly a stranger in these parts, and who am still to wander further out of my own knowledge.

Pisc. Sir, you invite me to my own advantage, and I am ready to attend you; my way lying through that town; but

my business, that is, my home, some miles beyond it; however, I shall have time enough to lodge you in your quarters, and afterwards to perform my own journey. In the
mean time, may I be so bold as to inquire the end of your
journey?

Viat. 'T is into Lancashire, Sir, and about some business
of concern to a near relation of mine: for I assure you, I do
not use to take long journeys, as from Essex, upon the single account of pleasure.

Pisc. From thence, Sir! I do not then wonder you should
appear dissatisfied with the length of the miles, and the
foulness of the way; though I am sorry you should begin to
quarrel with them so soon: for, believe me, Sir, you will find
the miles much longer and the way much worse, before you
come to your journey's end.

Viat. Why truly, Sir, for that, I am prepared to expect the
worst; but methinks the way is mended since I had the good
fortune to fall into your good company.

Pisc. You are not obliged to my company for that: but because you are already past the worst, and the greatest part of
your way to your lodging.

Viat. I am very glad to hear it, both for the ease of myself and my horse: but especially because I may then expect
a freer enjoyment of your conversation: though the short-
ness of the way will, I fear, make me lose it the sooner.

Pisc. That, Sir, is not worth your care; and I am sure you
deserve much better, for being content with so ill company.
But we have already talked away two miles of your journey;

for, from the brook before us, that runs at the foot of this
sandy hill, you have but three miles to Ashbourn.

VIAT. I meet everywhere in this country with these little
brooks; and they look as if they were full of fish. Have they
not Trouts in them?

PISC. That is a question which is to be excused in a
stranger, as you are: otherwise, give me leave to tell you, it
would seem a kind of affront to our country, to make a
doubt of what we pretend to be famous for, next, if not before, our malt, wool, lead, and coal: for you are to understand, that we think we have as many fine rivers, rivulets,
and brooks as any country whatever; and they are all full of
Trouts, and some of them the best, it is said, by many degrees, in England.

VIAT. I was first, Sir, in love with you, and now shall be so
enamored of your country, by this account you give me of it,
as to wish myself a Derbyshire man, or at least that I might
live in it; for you must know I am a pretender to the Angle,
and, doubtless, a Trout affords the most pleasure to the Angler of any sort of fish whatever; and the best Trouts must
needs make the best sport: but this brook, and some others
I have met with upon this way, are too full of wood for that
recreation.

PISC. This, Sir! why this, and several others like it, which
you have past, and some that you are like to pass, have
scarce any name amongst us: but we can show you as fine
rivers, and as clear from wood, or any other encumbrance to
hinder an Angler, as any you ever saw; and for clear, beau-

tiful streams, Hantshire itself, by Mr. Izaak Walton's good leave, can show none such; nor I think any country in Europe.

VIAT. You go far, Sir, in the praise of your country rivers, and I perceive have read Mr. Walton's Complete Angler, by your naming of Hantshire; and I pray what is your opinion of that book?

PISC. My opinion of Mr. Walton's book is the same with every man's that understands anything of the art of Angling, that it is an excellent good one; and that the forementioned gentleman understands as much of fish, and fishing, as any man living. But I must tell you further, that I have the happiness to know his person, and to be intimately acquainted with him; and in him to know the worthiest man, and to enjoy the best and the truest friend any man ever had: nay, I shall yet acquaint you further, that he gives me leave to call him father, and I hope is not yet ashamed to own me for his adopted son.

VIAT. In earnest, Sir, I am ravished to meet with a friend of Mr. Izaak Walton's, and one that does him so much right in so good and true a character: for I must boast to you, that I have the good fortune to know him too, and came acquainted with him much after the same manner I do with you; that he was my Master who first taught me to love Angling, and then to become an Angler; and, to be plain with you, I am the very man deciphered in his book under the name of Venator; for I was wholly addicted to the Chase, till he taught me as good, a more quiet, innocent, and less dangerous diversion.

PISC. Sir, I think myself happy in your acquaintance; and before we part shall entreat leave to embrace you. You have said enough to recommend you to my best opinion; for my Father Walton will be seen twice in no man's company he does not like, and likes none but such as he believes to be very honest men; which is one of the best arguments, or at least of the best testimonies I have, that I either am, or that he thinks me, one of those, seeing I have not yet found him weary of me.

VIAT. You speak like a true friend; and, in doing so, render yourself worthy of his friendship. May I be so bold as to ask your name?

PISC. Yes surely, Sir, and if you please a much nicer question; my name is ———, and I intend to stay long enough in your company, if I find you do not dislike mine, to ask yours too. In the mean time, because we are now almost at Ashbourn, I shall freely and bluntly tell you, that I am a Brother of the Angle too; and, peradventure, can give you some instructions how to angle for a Trout in a clear river, that my Father Walton himself will not disapprove; though he did either purposely omit, or did not remember them when you and he sat discoursing under the sycamore-tree. And, being you have already told me whither your journey is intended, and that I am better acquainted with the country than you are, I will heartily and earnestly entreat you will not think of staying at this town, but go on with me six miles farther to my house, where you shall be extremely welcome; it is directly in your way; we have day enough to perform our jour-

ney, and, as you like your entertainment, you may there repose yourself a day or two, or as many more as your occa-
sions will permit, to recompense the trouble of so much a
longer journey.

Viat. Sir, you surprise me with so friendly an invitation
upon so short acquaintance: but how advantageous soever it
would be to me, and that my haste, perhaps, is not so great,
but it might dispense with such a divertisement as I
promise myself in your company, yet I cannot, in modesty,
accept your offer, and must therefore beg your pardon: I
could otherwise, I confess, be glad to wait upon you, if upon
no other account but to talk of Mr. Izaak Walton, and to receive those instructions you say you are able to give me for
the deceiving a Trout; in which art I will not deny but that
I have an ambition to be one of the greatest deceivers:
though I cannot forbear freely to tell you that I think it hard
to say much more than has been read to me upon that subject.

Pisc. Well, Sir, I grant that too; but you must know that
the variety of rivers require different ways of Angling: however, you shall have the best rules I am able to give, and I
will tell you nothing I have not made myself as certain of,
as any man can be in thirty years' experience, for so long I
have been a dabbler in that art; and that, if you please to stay
a few days, you shall in a very great measure see made good
to you. But of that hereafter: and now, Sir, if I am not mistaken, I have half overcome you; and that I may wholly conquer that modesty of yours, I will take upon me to be so

familiar as to say, you must accept my invitation; which, that you may the more easily be persuaded to do, I will tell you that my house stands upon the margin of one of the finest rivers for Trouts and Grayling in England; that I have lately built a little fishing-house[73] upon it, dedicated to Anglers, over the door of which you will see the two first letters of my Father Walton's name and mine, twisted in cipher;* that you shall lie in the same bed he has sometimes been contented with, and have such country entertainment as my friends sometimes accept; and be as welcome, too, as the best friend of them all.

VIAT. No doubt, Sir, but my Master Walton found good reason to be satisfied with his entertainment in your house; for you, who are so friendly to a mere stranger, who deserves so little, must needs be exceeding kind and free to him who deserves so much.

PISC. Believe me, no: and such as are intimately acquainted with that gentleman know him to be a man who will not endure to be treated like a stranger. So that his acceptation of my poor entertainments has ever been a pure effect of his own humility and good nature, and nothing else. But, Sir, we are now going down the Spittle Hill into the town; and therefore let me importune you suddenly to resolve, and most earnestly not to deny me.

VIAT. In truth, Sir, I am so overcome by your bounty, that I find I cannot; but must render myself wholly to be disposed by you.

---

*As in the title-page.

PISC. Why that's heartily and kindly spoken, and I as heartily thank you: and, being you have abandoned yourself to my conduct, we will only call and drink a glass on horseback at the Talbot, and away.

VIAT. I attend you. But what pretty river is this, that runs under this stone bridge? Has it a name?

PISC. Yes, 't is called Henmore, and has in it both Trout and Grayling; but you will meet with one or two better anon. And so soon as we are past through the town, I will endeavor, by such discourse as best likes you, to pass away the time till you come to your ill quarters.

VIAT. We can talk of nothing with which I shall be more delighted, than of Rivers and Angling.

PISC. Let those be the subjects then. But we are now come to the Talbot. What will you drink, Sir, ale or wine?

VIAT. Nay, I am for the country liquor, Derbyshire ale, if you please; for a man should not, methinks, come from London to drink wine in the Peak.

PISC. You are in the right: and yet, let me tell you, you may drink worse French wine in many taverns in London, than they have sometimes at this house. What, Ho! bring us a flagon of your best ale. And now, Sir, my service to you, a good health to the honest gentleman you know of; and you are welcome into the Peak.

VIAT. I thank you, Sir, and present you my service again, and to all the honest Brothers of the Angle.

PISC. I 'll pledge you, Sir: so there 's for your ale, and

farewell. Come, Sir, let us be going: for the sun grows low, and I would have you look about you as you ride; for you will see an odd country, and sights that will seem strange to you.

THE FIRST DAY.

Chapter II.

Piscator.

SO, Sir, now we have got to the top of the hill out of town, look about you, and tell me how you like the country.

VIAT. Bless me! what mountains are here! Are we not in Wales?

PISC. No, but in almost as mountainous a country; and yet these hills, though high, bleak, and craggy, breed and feed good beef and mutton above ground, and afford good store of lead within.

VIAT. They had need of all those commodities to make amends for the ill landscape: but I hope our way does not lie over any of these, for I dread a precipice.

PISC. Believe me, but it does, and down one especially, that will appear a little terrible to a stranger; though the way is passable enough, and so passable, that we, who are natives of these mountains, and acquainted with them, disdain to alight.

VIAT. I hope though, that a foreigner is privileged to use his own discretion, and that I may have the liberty to intrust my neck to the fidelity of my own feet, rather than to those of my horse; for I have no more at home.

PISC. 'T were hard else. But in the mean time, I think

THE BRIDGE

't were best, while this way is pretty even, to mend our pace, that we may be past that hill I speak of, to the end your apprehension may not be doubled for want of light to discern the easiness of the descent.

VIAT. I am willing to put forward as fast as my beast will give me leave; though I fear nothing in your company. But what pretty river is this we are going into?

PISC. Why this, Sir, is called Bentley Brook, and is full of very good Trout and Grayling; but so encumbered with wood in many places, as is troublesome to an Angler.

VIAT. Here are the prettiest rivers and the most of them in this country that ever I saw: do you know how many you have in the country?

PISC. I know them all, and they were not hard to reckon, were it worth the trouble; but the most considerable of them I will presently name you. And to begin where we now are, for you must know we are now upon the very skirts of Derbyshire; we have, first, the river Dove, that we shall come to by and by, which divides the two counties of Derby and Stafford, for many miles together; and is so called from the swiftness of its current, and that swiftness occasioned by the declivity of its course, and by being so straitened in that course betwixt the rocks; by which, and those very high ones, it is hereabout, for four or five miles, confined into a very narrow stream. A river that, from a contemptible fountain, which I can cover with my hat, by the confluence of other rivers, rivulets, brooks, and rills, is swelled,—before it falls into Trent, a little below Egginton, where it loses the name,—to such a breadth and depth as to be in most places navigable, were not the passage frequently interrupted with fords and weirs: and has as fertile banks as any river in England, none excepted. And this river, from its head, for a mile or two, is a black water,—as all the rest of the Derbyshire rivers of note originally are; for they all spring from the mosses,—but is in a few miles' travel so clarified, by the addition of several clear, and very great springs, bigger than itself, which gush out of the limestone rocks, that before it comes to my house, which is but six or seven miles from its source, you will find it one of the purest crystalline streams you have seen.

VIAT. Does Trent spring in these parts?

PISC. Yes, in these parts: not in this county, but somewhere towards the upper end of Staffordshire, I think not far from a place called Trentham; and thence runs down not far from Stafford to Wolsley Bridge, and, washing the skirts and purlieus of the Forest of Needwood, runs down to Burton in the same county: thence it comes into this where we now are, and, running by Swarkeston and Dunnington, receives Derwent at Wildon; and so to Nottingham, thence to Newark, and by Gainsborough to Kingston upon Hull, where it takes the name of Humber, and thence falls into the sea: but that the map will best inform you.

VIAT. Know you whence this river Trent derives its name?

PISC. No, indeed, and yet I have heard it often discoursed upon, when some have given its denomination from the forenamed Trentham, though that seems rather a derivative from it; others have said, 't is so called from thirty rivers that fall into it, and there lose their names; which cannot be, neither, because it carries that name from its very fountain, before any other rivers fall into it: others derive it from thirty several sorts of fish that breed there; and that is the most likely derivation: but be it how it will, it is doubtless one of the finest rivers in the world, and the most abounding with excellent Salmon, and all sorts of delicate fish.

VIAT. Pardon me, Sir, for tempting you into this digression: and then proceed to your other rivers, for I am mightily delighted with this discourse.

PISC. It was no interruption, but a very seasonable question; for Trent is not only one of our Derbyshire rivers, but the chief of them, and into which all the rest pay the tribute of their names; which I had, perhaps, forgot to insist upon, being got to the other end of the county, had you not awoke my memory. But I will now proceed; and the next river of note, for I will take them as they lie eastward from us, is the river Wye: I say of note, for we have two lesser betwixt us and it, namely, Lathkin, and Bradford; of which Lathkin is, by many degrees, the purest and most transparent stream that I ever yet saw, either at home or abroad; and breeds, 't is said, the reddest and the best Trouts in England; but neither of these are to be reputed rivers, being no better than great springs. The river Wye then has its source near unto Buxton, a town some ten miles from hence, famous for a warm bath, and which you are to ride through in your way to Manchester: a black water too at the fountain, but, by the same reason with Dove, becomes very soon a most delicate clear river, and breeds admirable Trout and Grayling, reputed by those who, by living upon its banks, are partial to it, the best of any; and this running down by Ashford, Bakewell, and Haddon, at a town a little lower called Rowsley, falls into Derwent, and there loses its name. The next in order is Derwent, a black water too, and that not only from its fountain, but quite through its progress, not having these crystal springs to wash and cleanse it, which the two forementioned have: but abounds with Trout and Grayling, such as they are, towards its source, and with Salmon below: and this river from the upper and utmost part of this county, where it springs, taking its course by Chatsworth, Darley, Matlock, Derby, Burrow-Ash, and Awberson, falls into Trent at a place called Wildon, and there loses its name. The east side of this County of Derby is bounded by little inconsiderable rivers, as Awber, Eroways, and the like, scarce worth naming, but Trouty too, and further we are not to inquire. But, Sir, I have carried you, as a man may say, by water, till we are now come to the descent of the formidable hill I told you of, at the foot of which runs the river Dove, which I cannot but love above all the rest; and therefore prepare yourself to be a little frighted.

VIAT. Sir, I see you would fortify me, that I should not shame myself; but I dare follow where you please to lead me; and I see no danger yet; for the descent, methinks, is thus far green, even, and easy.

PISC. You will like it worse presently, when you come to the brow of the hill:—and now we are there, what think you?

VIAT. What do I think? Why I think it the strangest place that ever, sure, men and horses went down; and that, if there be any safety at all, the safest way is to alight.

PISC. I think so too for you, who are mounted upon a beast not acquainted with these slippery stones: and, though I frequently ride down, I will alight too, to bear you company, and to lead you the way; and, if you please, my man shall lead your horse.

VIAT. Marry, Sir! and thank you too: for I am afraid I shall have enough to do to look to myself; and with my horse in my hand should be in a double fear, both of breaking my neck, and my horse's falling on me; for it is as steep as a penthouse.

PISC. To look down from hence it appears so, I confess; but the path winds and turns, and will not be found so troublesome.

VIAT. Would I were well down though! Hoist thee! there's one fair 'scape! these stones are so slippery I cannot stand! yet again! I think I were best lay my heels in my neck, and tumble down.

PISC. If you think your heels will defend your neck, that is the way to be soon at the bottom. But give me your hand at this broad stone, and then the worst is past.

VIAT. I thank you, Sir, I am now past it, I can go myself. What's here? the sign of a bridge? Do you use to travel with wheelbarrows in this country?

PISC. Not that I ever saw, Sir. Why do you ask that question?

VIAT. Because this bridge certainly was made for nothing else; why a mouse can hardly go over it: 't is not two fingers broad.

PISC. You are pleasant, and I am glad to see you so: but I have rid over the bridge many a dark night.

VIAT. Why, according to the French proverb, and 't is a good one among a great many of worse sense and sound that language abounds in, *Ce que Dieu garde, est bien gardé.* They whom God takes care of are in safe protection; but, let me tell you, I would not ride over it for a thousand pounds, nor fall off it for two; and yet I think I dare venture on foot, though if you were not by to laugh at me, I should do it on all four.

PISC. Well, Sir, your mirth becomes you, and I am glad to see you safe over; and now you are welcome into Stafford-shire.

VIAT. How, Staffordshire! What do I there trow? There is not a word of Staffordshire in all my direction.

PISC. You see you are betrayed into it; but it shall be in order to something that will make amends; and 't is but an ill mile or two out of your way.

VIAT. I believe all things, Sir, and doubt nothing. Is this your beloved river Dove? 'T is clear and swift, indeed, but a very little one.

PISC. You see it here at the worst; we shall come to it anon again after two miles riding, and so near as to lie upon the very banks.

VIAT. Would we were there once! But I hope we have no more of these Alps to pass over.

Pisc. No, no, Sir, only this ascent before you, which you see is not very uneasy; and then you will no more quarrel with your way.

Viat. Well, if ever I come to London, of which many a man there, if he were in my place would make a question, I will sit down and write my travels; and, like Tom Coriate,[74] print them at my own charge. Pray what do you call this hill we come down?

Pisc. We call it Hanson Toot.

Viat. Why, farewell Hanson Toot! I'll no more on thee: I'll go twenty miles about first. Puh! I sweat, that my shirt sticks to my back.

Pisc. Come, Sir, now we are up the hill, and now how do you?

Viat. Why, very well, I humbly thank you, Sir, and warm enough, I assure you. What have we here, a church! As I'm an honest man, a very pretty church! Have you churches in this country, Sir?

Pisc. You see we have: but, had you seen none, why should you make that doubt, Sir?

Viat. Why, if you will not be angry, I 'll tell you I thought myself a stage or two beyond Christendom.

Pisc. Come, come! we 'll reconcile you to our country, before we part with you; if showing you good sport with Angling will do it.

Viat. My respect to you, and that together may do much, Sir; otherwise, to be plain with you, I do not find myself much inclined that way.

Pisc. Well, Sir, your raillery upon our mountains has

brought us almost home. And look you where the same river of Dove has again met us to bid you welcome, and to invite you to a dish of Trouts to-morrow.

VIAT. Is this the same we saw at the foot of Penmen-Maure? It is a much finer river here.

PISC. It will appear yet much finer to-morrow. But look you, Sir, here appears the house, that is now like to be your inn, for want of a better.

VIAT. It appears on a sudden, but not before 't was looked for. It stands prettily, and here 's wood about it too, but so young, as appears to be of your own planting.

PISC. It is so. Will it please you to alight, Sir.—And now permit me, after all your pains and dangers, to take you in my arms, and to assure you that you are infinitely welcome.

VIAT. I thank you, Sir, and am glad with all my heart I am here; for, in downright truth, I am exceeding weary.

PISC. You will sleep so much the better: you shall presently have a light supper, and to bed. Come, Sirs, lay the cloth, and bring what you have presently, and let the gentleman's bed be made ready in the mean time, in my Father Walton's chamber. And now, Sir, here is my service to you; and once more welcome!

VIAT. I, marry, Sir, this glass of good sack has refreshed me. And I 'll make as bold with your meat, for the trout has got me a good stomach.

PISC. Come, Sir, fall to then, you see my little supper is always ready when I come home; and I 'll make no stranger of you.

Viat. That your meal is so soon ready, is a sign your servants know your certain hours, Sir. I confess I did not expect it so soon; but now 't is here, you shall see I will make myself no stranger.

Pisc. Much good do your heart! and I thank you for that friendly word. And now, Sir, my service to you in a cup of More-Lands ale; for you are now in the More-Lands, but within a spit and a stride of the Peak. Fill my friend his glass.

Viat. Believe me, you have good ale in the More-Lands: far better than that at Ashbourn.

Pisc. That it may soon be; for Ashbourn has, which is a kind of a riddle, always in it the best malt, and the worst ale in England. Come, take away, and bring us some pipes, and a bottle of ale, and go to your own suppers. Are you for this diet, Sir?

Viat. Yes, Sir, I am for one pipe of tobacco; and I perceive yours is very good by the smell.

Pisc. The best I can get in London, I assure you. But, Sir, now you have thus far complied with my designs, as to take a troublesome journey into an ill country, only to satisfy me; how long may I hope to enjoy you?

Viat. Why, truly, Sir, as long as I conveniently can; and longer, I think, you would not have me.

Pisc. Not to your inconvenience by any means, Sir, but I see you are weary, and therefore I will presently wait on you to your chamber, where take counsel of your pillow, and to-morrow resolve me. Here! take the lights, and pray follow them, Sir: here you are like to lie: and, now I have showed you your lodgings, I beseech you command anything you want; and so I wish you good rest!

VIAT. Good night, Sir!

THE SECOND DAY.

CHAPTER III.

PISCATOR.

GOOD morrow, Sir! What, up and dressed so early?

VIAT. Yes, Sir, I have been dressed this half-hour; for I rested so well, and have so great a mind either to take, or see a Trout taken, in your fine river, that I could no longer lie abed.

PISC. I am glad to see you so brisk this morning, and so eager of sport; though, I must tell you, this day proves so calm, and the sun rises so bright, as promises no great success to the Angler; but, however, we 'll try; and, one way or other, we shall, sure, do something. What will you have to your breakfast, or what will you drink this morning?

Viat. For breakfast, I never eat any, and for drink I am very indifferent; but if you please to call for a glass of ale, I 'm for you: and let it be quickly, if you please, for I long to see the little fishing-house you spoke of, and to be at my lesson.

Pisc. Well, Sir! You see the ale is come without calling; for though I do not know yours, my people know my diet; which is always one glass so soon as I am dressed, and no more till dinner; and so my servants have served you.

Viat. My thanks. And now, if you please, let us look out this fine morning.

Pisc. With all my heart; boy, take the key of my fishing-house, and carry down those two angle-rods in the hall-window, thither, with my fish-pannier, pouch, and landing-net; and stay you there till we come. Come, Sir, we 'll walk after; where, by the way, I expect you should raise all the exceptions against our country you can.

Viat. Nay, Sir, do not think me so ill-natured nor so uncivil: I only made a little bold with it last night to divert you, and was only in jest.

Pisc. You were then in as good earnest as I am now with you: but had you been really angry at it, I could not blame you; for, to say the truth, it is not very taking at first sight. But look you, Sir, now you are abroad, does not the sun shine as bright here as in Essex, Middlesex, or Kent, or any of your southern counties?

Viat. 'T is a delicate morning indeed! And I now think this a marvellous pretty place.

PISC. Whether you think so or no, you cannot oblige me more than to say so; and those of my friends who know my humor, and are so kind as to comply with it, usually flatter me that way. But look you, Sir, now you are at the brink of the hill, how do you like my river, the vale it winds through like a snake, and the situation of my little fishing-house?

VIAT. Trust me, 't is all very fine; and the house seems at this distance a neat building.

PISC. Good enough for that purpose. And here is a bowling-green too, close by it; so, though I am myself no very good bowler, I am not totally devoted to my own pleasure, but that I have also some regard to other men's. And now, Sir, you are come to the door[75]; pray walk in, and there we will sit and talk, as long as you please.

VIAT. Stay, what's here over the door? PISCATORIBUS SACRUM!* Why then I perceive I have some title here; for I am one of them, though one of the worst; and here below it is the cipher too you spoke of, and 't is prettily contrived. Has my Master Walton ever been here to see it? for it seems new built.

PISC. Yes, he saw it cut in the stone before it was set up; but never in the posture it now stands: for the house was but building when he was last here, and not raised so high as the arch of the door. And I am afraid he will not see it yet;

---

*There is, under this motto, the cipher mentioned in the title-page. And some part of the fishing-house has been described; but the pleasantness of the river, mountains, and meadows about it cannot, unless Sir Philip Sidney, or Mr. Cotton's father, were again alive to do it.

for he has lately writ me word, he doubts his coming down this summer; which, I do assure you, was the worst news he could possibly have sent me.

VIAT. Men must sometimes mind their affairs to make more room for their pleasures; and 't is odds he is as much displeased with the business that keeps him from you, as you are that he comes not. But I am the most pleased with this little house of anything I ever saw: it stands in a kind of peninsula, too, with a delicate clear river about it. I dare hardly go in, lest I should not like it so well within as without; but by your leave I 'll try. Why this is better and better, fine lights, finely wainscoted, and all exceeding neat, with a marble table and all in the middle.

PISC. Enough, Sir, enough! I have laid open to you the part where I can worst defend myself; and now you attack me there! Come, boy, set two chairs, and whilst I am taking a pipe of tobacco, which is always my breakfast, we will, if you please, talk of some other subject.

VIAT. None fitter, then, Sir, for the time and place, than those instructions you promised.

PISC. I begin to doubt, by something I discover in you, whether I am able to instruct you, or no: though, if you are really a stranger to our clear northern rivers, I still think I can; and therefore, since it is yet too early in the morning at this time of the year, to-day being but the 7th of March, to cast a fly upon the water, if you will direct me what kind of fishing for a Trout I shall read you a lecture on, I am willing and ready to obey you.

Viat. Why, Sir, if you will so far oblige me and that it may not be too troublesome to you, I would entreat you would run through the whole body of it; and I will not conceal from you, that I am so far in love with you, your courtesy, and pretty Moreland seat, as to resolve to stay with you long enough by intervals; for I will not oppress you, to hear all you can say upon that subject.

Pisc. You cannot oblige me more than by such a promise. And, therefore, without more ceremony I will begin to tell you, that my Father Walton having read to you before, it would look like a presumption in me, and peradventure would do so in any other man, to pretend to give lessons for Angling after him who, I do really believe, understands as much of it, at least, as any man in England; did I not pre-acquaint you, that I am not tempted to it by any vain opinion of myself, that I am able to give you better directions; but, having from my childhood pursued the recreation of Angling in very clear rivers,—truly I think by much, some of them at least, the clearest in this kingdom,—and the manner of Angling here with us, by reason of that exceeding clearness, being something different from the method commonly used in others, which, by being not near so bright, admit of stronger tackle, and allow a nearer approach to the stream;—I may, peradventure, give you some instructions, that may be of use even in your own rivers; and shall bring you acquainted with more flies, and show you how to make them, and with what dubbing too, than he has taken notice of in his Complete Angler.

Viat. I beseech you, Sir, do: and, if you will lend me your steel, I will light a pipe the while; for that is commonly my breakfast in a morning, too.

THE SECOND DAY.

CHAPTER IV.

PISCATOR.

WHY then, Sir, to begin methodically, as a master in any art should do,—and I will not deny but that I think myself a master in this,—I shall divide Angling for Trout or Grayling into these three ways: at the top, at the bottom, and in the middle; which three ways, though they are all of them, as I shall hereafter endeavor to make it appear, in some sort common to both those kinds of fish, yet are they not so generally and absolutely so but that they will necessarily require a distinction; which, in due place, I will also give you.

That which we call angling at the top is with a fly; at the bottom, with a ground-bait; in the middle, with a minnow, or ground-bait.

Angling at the top is of two sorts: with a quick-fly, or with an artificial-fly.

That we call angling at the bottom is also of two sorts: by the hand, or with a cork or float.

That we call angling in the middle is also of two sorts: with a minnow for a Trout, or with a ground-bait for a Grayling.

Of all which several sorts of Angling I will, if you can have the patience to hear me, give you the best account I can.

VIAT. The trouble will be yours, and mine the pleasure and the obligation. I beseech you, therefore, to proceed.

PISC. Why, then, first of Fly-fishing.

THE SECOND DAY.

CHAP. V.—*Of* FLY-FISHING.

PISCATOR.

FLY-fishing, or fishing at the top, is, as I said before, of two sorts: with a Natural, and living, Fly, or with an Artificial, and made, Fly.

First, then, Of the Natural Fly: of which we generally use but two sorts, and those but in the two months of May and June only, namely, the Green-drake and the Stone-fly; though I have made use of a third that way, called the Camlet-fly, with very good success for Grayling, but never saw it angled with by any other after this manner, my master only excepted, who died many years ago, and was one of the best Anglers that ever I knew.

These are to be angled with, with a short line, not much more than half the length of your rod, if the air be still; or with a longer, very near or all out as long as your rod, if you have any wind to carry it from you: and this way of fishing we call Daping, Dabbing, or Dibbling; wherein you are always to have your line flying before you up or down the river as the wind serves, and to angle as near as you can to the bank of the same side whereon you stand: though where you see a fish rise near you, you may guide your quick-fly over him, whether in the middle, or on the contrary side; and, if you are pretty well out of sight, either by kneeling or

the interposition of a bank or bush, you may almost be sure
to raise, and take him too, if it be presently done; the fish
will otherwise, peradventure, be removed to some other
place, if it be in the still-deeps, where he is always in motion, and roving up and down to look for prey; though in a
stream, you may always, almost, especially if there be a good
stone near, find him in the same place. Your line ought in
this case to be three good hairs next the hook; both by reason you are, in this kind of Angling, to expect the biggest
fish, and also that, wanting length to give him line after he
is struck, you must be forced to tug for 't; to which I will also
add, that, not an inch of your line being to be suffered to
touch the water in dibbling, it may be allowed to be the
stronger. I should now give you a description of those flies,
their shape and color, and then give you an account of their
breeding, and withal show you how to keep and use them;
but shall defer that to their proper place and season.

VIAT. In earnest, Sir, you discourse very rationally of this
affair, and I am glad to find myself mistaken in you; for in
plain truth I did not expect so much from you.

PISC. Nay, Sir, I can tell you a great deal more than this,
and will conceal nothing from you. But I must now come to
the second way of angling at the top, which is with an
artificial-fly, which also I will show you how to make before
I have done: but first shall acquaint you, that with this you
are to angle with a line longer, by a yard and a half or sometimes two yards, than your rod; and with both this, and the
other, in a still day, in the streams, in a breeze that curls the

water in the still-deeps, where (excepting in May and June, that the best Trouts will lie in shallow streams to watch for prey, and even then too) you are like to hit the best fish.

For the length of your rod, you are always to be governed by the breadth of the river you shall choose to angle at: and for a Trout-river, one of five or six yards long is commonly enough; and longer, though never so neatly and artificially made, it ought not to be, if you intend to fish at ease; and if otherwise, where lies the sport?

Of these, the best that ever I saw are made in Yorkshire, which are all of one piece: that is to say of several, six, eight, ten, or twelve pieces, so neatly pieced, and tied together with fine thread below, and silk above, as to make it taper, like a switch, and to ply with a true bent to your hand. And these, too, are light, being made of fir-wood for two or three lengths nearest to the hand, and of other wood nearer to the top; that a man might very easily manage the longest of them that ever I saw, with one hand. And these, when you have given over Angling for a season, being taken to pieces, and laid up in some dry place, may afterwards be set together again in their former postures, and will be as straight, sound, and good as the first hour they were made; and being laid in oil and color, according to your Master Walton's direction, will last many years.

The length of your line, to a man that knows how to handle his rod, and to cast it, is no manner of encumbrance, excepting in woody places and in landing of a fish, which every one that can afford to angle for pleasure has somebody to do for him. And the length of line is a mighty advantage to the fishing at distance; and to fish *fine,* and *far off,* is the first and principal rule for Trout-Angling.

Your line in this case should never be less, nor ever exceed two hairs next to the hook; for one (though some I know will pretend to more art than their fellows) is indeed too few, the least accident, with the finest hand, being sufficient to break it; but he that cannot kill a Trout of twenty inches long with two, in a river clear of wood and weeds, as this and some other of ours are, deserves not the name of an Angler.

Now to have your whole line as it ought to be, two of the first lengths nearest the hook should be of two hairs apiece; the next three lengths above them of three; the next three above them of four; and so of five, and six, and seven, to the very top: by which means your rod and tackle will, in a manner, be taper from your very hand to your hook; your line will fall much better and straighter, and cast your fly to any certain place to which the hand and eye shall direct it, with less weight and violence, than would otherwise circle the water and fright away the fish.

In casting your line, do it always before you, and so that your fly may first fall upon the water, and as little of your line with it as is possible; though if the wind be stiff, you will then of necessity be compelled to drown a good part of your line to keep your fly in the water: and in casting your fly, you must aim at the further, or nearer bank, as the wind serves your turn; which also will be with and against you on the same side, several times in an hour, as the river winds in its course; and you will be forced to angle up and down by turns accordingly; but are to endeavor, as much as you can, to have the wind evermore on your back. And always be sure to stand as far off the bank as your length will give you leave when you throw to the contrary side: though, when the wind will not permit you so to do, and that you are constrained to angle on the same side whereon you stand, you must then stand on the very brink of the river, and cast your fly at the utmost length of your rod and line, up or down the river as the gale serves.

It only remains, touching your line, to inquire whether your two hairs, next to the hook, are better twisted, or open. And for that I should declare that I think the open way the better, because it makes less show in the water; but that I have found an inconvenience, or two, or three, that have made me almost weary of that way: of which one is, that, without dispute, they are not so strong open as twisted; another, that they are not easily to be fastened of so exact an equal length in the arming, that the one will not cause the other to bag, by which means a man has but one hair, upon the matter, to trust to; and the last is, that these loose flying hairs are not only more apt to catch upon every twig or bent they meet with, but moreover the hook, in falling upon the water, will very often rebound, and fly back betwixt the hairs, and there stick (which, in a rough water especially, is not presently to be discerned by the Angler), so as the point of the hook shall stand reversed; by which means your fly swims backwards, makes a much greater circle in the water, and, till taken home to you and set right, will never raise any fish; or, if it should, I am sure, but by a very extraordinary chance, can hit none.

Having done with both these ways of fishing at the top, the length of your rod, and line, and all, I am next to teach you how to make a fly; and afterwards, of what dubbing you are to make the several flies I shall hereafter name to you.

In making a fly, then, which is not a Hackle, or Palmer-fly (for of those, and their several kinds, we shall have occasion to speak every month in the year), you are first to hold your hook fast betwixt the forefinger and thumb of your left hand, with the back of the shank upwards, and the point towards your fingers' ends: then take a strong small silk of the color of the fly you intend to make, wax it well with wax of the same color too: to which end you are always, by the way, to have wax of all colors about you; and draw it betwixt your finger and thumb, to the head of the shank, and then whip it twice or thrice about the bare hook, which you must know is done, both to prevent slipping, and also that the shank of the hook may not cut the hairs of your towght, which sometimes it will otherwise do. Which being done, take your line and draw it likewise betwixt your finger and thumb, holding the hook so fast, as only to suffer it to pass by, until you have the knot of your towght almost to the middle of the shank of your hook, on the inside of it; then whip your silk twice or thrice about both hook and line, as hard as the strength of the silk will permit. Which being done, strip the feather for the wings proportionable to the bigness of your fly, placing that side downwards which grew

uppermost before, upon the back of the hook, leaving so
much only as to serve for the length of the wing of the point
of the plume lying reversed from the end of the shank upwards: then whip your silk twice or thrice about the root-
end of the feather, hook, and towght. Which being done,
clip off the root-end of the feather close by the arming, and
then whip the silk fast and firm about the hook and towght,
until you come to the bend of the hook: but not further, as
you do at London, and so make a very unhandsome, and, in
plain English, a very unnatural and shapeless fly. Which
being done, cut away the end of your towght, and fasten it.
And then take your dubbing which is to make the body of
your fly, as much as you think convenient; and, holding it
lightly with your hook betwixt the finger and thumb of your
left hand, take your silk with the right, and twisting it betwixt the finger and thumb of that hand, the dubbing will
spin itself about the silk, which when it has done, whip it
about the armed-hook backward, till you come to the setting on of the wings. And then take the feather for the
wings, and divide it equally into two parts; and turn them
back towards the end of the hook, the one on the one side
and the other on the other of the shank, holding them fast
in that posture betwixt the forefinger and thumb of your
left hand. Which done, warp them so down as to stand and
slope towards the bend of the hook; and, having warped up
to the end of the shank, hold the fly fast betwixt the finger
and thumb of your left hand, and then take the silk betwixt
the finger and thumb of your right hand, and, where the

warping ends, pinch or nip it with your thumb-nail against
your finger, and strip away the remainder of your dubbing
from the silk; and then, with the bare silk, whip it once or
twice about, make the wings to stand in due order, fasten,
and cut it off: after which with the point of a needle raise
up the dubbing gently from the warp; twitch off the superfluous hairs of your dubbing; leave the wings of an equal
length,—your fly will never else swim true;—and the work
is done. And this way of making a fly, which is certainly the
best of all other, was taught me by a kinsman of mine, one
Captain Henry Jackson, a near neighbor, an admirable Fly-
Angler; by many degrees the best fly-maker that ever I yet
met with. And now that I have told you how a fly is to be
made, you shall presently see me make one, with which you
may peradventure take a Trout this morning, notwithstanding the unlikeliness of the day; for it is now nine of the
clock, and fish will begin to rise if they will rise to-day. I will
walk along by you, and look on: and, after dinner, I will proceed in my lecture of Fly-fishing.

VIAT. I confess I long to be at the river; and yet I could sit
here all day to hear you; but some of the one, and some of
the other, will do well: and I have a mighty ambition to take
a Trout in your river Dove.

PISC. I warrant you shall: I would not for more than I will
speak of but you should, seeing I have so extolled my river
to you. Nay, I will keep you here a month, but you shall have
one good day of sport before you go.

VIAT. You will find me, I doubt, too tractable that way;
for, in good earnest, if business would give me leave, and

that, if it were fit, I could find in my heart to stay with you forever.

PISC. I thank you, Sir, for that kind expression; and now let me look out my things to make this fly.

THE SECOND DAY.

CHAPTER VI.

PISCATOR.

BOY! come, give me my dubbing-bag here presently. And now, Sir, since I find you so honest a man, I will make no scruple to lay open my treasure before you.

VIAT. Did ever any one see the like! What a heap of trumpery is here! certainly never an Angler in Europe has his shop half so well furnished as you have.

PISC. You, perhaps, may think now that I rake together this trumpery, as you call it, for show only; to the end that such as see it, which are not many I assure you, may think me a great master in the art of Angling; but let me tell you here are some colors, as contemptible as they seem here, that are very hard to be got; and scarce any one of them, which, if it should be lost, I should not miss, and be concerned about the loss of it too, once in the year. But look you, Sir, amongst all these I will choose out these two colors only, of which, this is bear's hair, this darker, no great matter what: but I am sure I have killed a great deal of fish with it; and with one or both of these, you shall take Trout or Grayling this very day, notwithstanding all disadvantages, or my art shall fail me.

VIAT. You promise comfortably, and I have a great deal of reason to believe everything you say; but I wish the fly were made, that we were at it.

Pisc. That will not be long in doing; and pray observe then. You see first how I hold my hook, and thus I begin. Look you, here are my first two or three whips about the bare hook; thus I join hook and line; thus I put on my wings; thus I twirl and lap on my dubbing; thus I work it up towards the head; thus I part my wings; thus I nip my superfluous dubbing from my silk; thus fasten; thus trim and adjust my fly: and there's a fly made. And now how do you like it?

Viat. In earnest, admirably well; and it perfectly resembles a fly: but we about London make the bodies of our flies both much bigger and longer,—so long as even almost to the very beard of the hook.

Pisc. I know it very well, and had one of those flies given me by an honest gentleman, who came with my Father Walton to give me a visit; which, to tell you the truth, I hung in my parlor window to laugh at: but Sir, you know the proverb, "They who go to Rome must do as they at Rome do;" and, believe me, you must here make your flies after this fashion, or you will take no fish. Come, I will look you out a line, and you shall put it on, and try it. There, Sir, now I think you are fitted; and now beyond the farther end of the walk you shall begin. I see at that bend of the water above, the air crisps the water a little. Knit your line first here, and then go up thither, and see what you can do.

Viat. Did you see that, Sir?

Pisc. Yes, I saw the fish, and he saw you too, which made him turn short; you must fish farther off, if you intend to have any sport here; this is no New River, let me tell you!

That was a good Trout, believe me; did you touch him?

VIAT. No, I would I had, we would not have parted so! Look you, there was another! This is an excellent fly!

PISC. That fly, I am sure, would kill fish, if the day were right; but they only chew at it, I see, and will not take it. Come, Sir, let us return back to the fishing-house; this still water I see will not do our business to-day. You shall now, if you please, make a fly yourself, and try what you can do in the streams with that; and I know a Trout taken with a fly of your own making will please you better than twenty with one of mine. Give me that bag again, Sirrah. Look you, Sir, there is a hook, towght, silk, and a feather for the wings: be doing with those, and I will look you out a dubbing that I think will do.

VIAT. This is a very little hook.

PISC. That may serve to inform you, that it is for a very little fly, and you must make your wings accordingly; for as the case stands it must be a little fly, and a very little one too, that must do your business. Well said! believe me you shift your fingers very handsomely: I doubt I have taken upon me to teach my master. So, here's your dubbing now.

VIAT. This dubbing is very black.

PISC. It appears so in hand, but step to the door and hold it up betwixt your eye and the sun, and it will appear a shining red: let me tell you, never a man in England can discern the true color of a dubbing any way but that; and therefore choose always to make your flies on such a bright sunshine day as this, which also you may the better do, because it is worth nothing to fish in. Here, put it on; and be sure to

LANDING THE GRAYLING

make the body of your fly as slender as you can. Very good! Upon my word you have made a marvellous handsome fly.

Viat. I am very glad to hear it; 't is the first that ever I made of this kind in my life.

Pisc. Away, away! You are a doctor at it: but I will not commend you too much, lest I make you proud. Come, put it on, and you shall now go downward to some streams betwixt the rocks below the little foot-bridge you see there, and try your fortune. Take heed of slipping into the water as you follow me under this rock. So, now you are over, and now throw in.

Viat. This is a fine stream indeed! There's one! I have him.

Pisc. And a precious catch you have of him; pull him out! I see you have a tender hand. This is a diminutive gentleman; e'en throw him in again, and let him grow till he be more worthy your anger.

Viat. Pardon me, Sir, all 's fish that comes to the hook with me now. Another!

Pisc. And of the same standing.

Viat. I see I shall have good sport now. Another! and a Grayling. Why, you have fish here at will.

Pisc. Come, come, cross the bridge, and go down the other side, lower; where you will find finer streams, and better sport, I hope, than this. Look you, Sir, here is a fine stream now. You have length enough, stand a little farther off, let me entreat you; and do but fish this stream like an artist, and peradventure a good fish may fall to your share. How now! What, is all gone?

Viat. No, I but touched him; but that was a fish worth taking.

Pisc. Why now, let me tell you, you lost that fish by your own fault, and through your own eagerness and haste; for you are never to offer to strike a good fish, if he do not strike himself, till first you see him turn his head after he has taken your fly; and then you can never strain your tackle in the striking, if you strike with any manner of moderation. Come, throw in once again, and fish me this stream by inches; for I assure you here are very good fish: both Trout and Grayling lie here; and at that great stone on the other side, 't is ten to one a good Trout gives you the meeting.

Viat. I have him now, but he has gone down towards the bottom. I cannot see what he is, yet he should be a good fish by his weight: but he makes no great stir.

Pisc. Why then, by what you say, I dare venture to assure you 't is a Grayling, who is one of the deadest-hearted fishes in the world; and the bigger he is, the more easily taken. Look you, now you see him plain; I told you what he was. Bring hither that landing-net, Boy. And now, Sir, he is your own; and believe me a good one, sixteen inches long I warrant him: I have taken none such this year.

Viat. I never saw a Grayling before look so black.

Pisc. Did you not? Why then, let me tell you, that you never saw one before in right season; for then a Grayling is very black about his head, gills, and down his back; and has his belly of a dark gray, dappled with black spots, as you see this is; and I am apt to conclude, that from thence he derives his name of Umber. Though I must tell you this fish is past his prime, and begins to decline, and was in better season at Christmas than he is now. But move on, for it grows towards dinnertime; and there is a very great and fine stream below, under that rock, that fills the deepest pool in all the river, where you are almost sure of a good fish.

Viat. Let him come, I 'll try a fall with him. But I had thought that the Grayling had been always in season with the Trout, and had come in and gone out with him.

Pisc. O no! assure yourself a Grayling is a winter-fish; but such a one as would deceive any but such as know him very well indeed; for his flesh, even in his worst season, is so firm, and will so easily calver, that in plain truth he is very good meat at all times; but in his perfect season, which, by the way, none but an overgrown Grayling will ever be, I think him so good a fish as to be little inferior to the best Trout that ever I tasted in my life.

Viat. Here 's another skip-jack; and I have raised five or six more at least whilst you were speaking. Well, go thy way, little Dove! thou art the finest river that ever I saw, and the fullest of fish. Indeed, Sir, I like it so well, that I am afraid you will be troubled with me once a year, so long as we two live.

Pisc. I am afraid I shall not, Sir; but were you once here a May or a June, if good sport would tempt you, I should then expect you would sometimes see me; for you would then say it were a fine river indeed, if you had once seen the sport at the height.

Viat. Which I will do, if I live, and that you please to give me leave. There was one; and there another.

PISC. And all this in a strange river, and with a fly of your own making! Why, what a dangerous man are you!

VIAT. I, Sir, but who taught me? and as Damœtas says by his man Dorus, so you may say by me,—

"If my man such praises have,
What then have I, that taught the knave?"

But what have we got here? A rock springing up in the middle of the river! this is one of the oddest sights that ever I saw.

PISC. Why, Sir, from that Pike,* that you see standing up there distant from the rock, this is called Pike-Pool. And young Mr. Izaak Walton was so pleased with it, as to draw it in landscape in black and white, in a blank book I have at home; as he has done several prospects of my house also, which I keep for a memorial of his favor, and will show you, when we come up to dinner.

VIAT. Has young Master Izaak Walton been here too?

PISC. Yes, marry has he, Sir, and that again, and again too; and in France since, and at Rome, and at Venice, and I can't tell where; but I intend to ask him a great many hard questions so soon as I can see him, which will be, God willing,

---

*'T is a rock in the fashion of a spire-steeple, and almost as big. It stands in the midst of the river Dove, and not far from Mr. Cotton's house; below which place this delicate river takes a swift career betwixt many mighty rocks, much higher and bigger than St. Paul's Church, before 't was burnt. And this Dove, being opposed by one of the highest of them, has at last forced itself a way through it; and, after a mile's concealment, appears again with more glory and beauty than before that opposition, running through the most pleasant valleys and most fruitful meadows that this nation can justly boast of.

next month. In the mean time, Sir, to come to this fine
stream at the head of this great pool, you must venture over
these slippery, cobbling stones. Believe me, Sir, there you
were nimble, or else you had been down! But now you are
got over, look to yourself; for, on my word, if a fish rise here,
he is like to be such a one as will endanger your tackle. How
now!

VIAT. I think you have such command here over the
fishes, that you can raise them by your word, as they say
conjurors can do spirits, and afterward make them do what
you bid them; for here 's a Trout has taken my fly; I had
rather have lost a crown. What luck 's this! He was a lovely
fish, and turned up a side like a salmon!

PISC. O Sir, this is a war where you sometimes win, and
must sometimes expect to lose. Never concern yourself for
the loss of your fly; for ten to one I teach you to make a better. Who 's that calls?

SERVANT. Sir, will it please you to come to dinner?

PISC. We come. You hear, Sir, we are called; and now take
your choice, whether you will climb this steep hill before
you, from the top of which you will go directly into the
house, or back again over these stepping-stones, and about
by the bridge.

VIAT. Nay, sure the nearest way is best; at least my stomach tells me so; and I am now so well acquainted with your
rocks, that I fear them not.

PISC. Come, then, follow me; and so soon as we have
dined, we will down again to the little house, where I will
begin at the place I left off about fly-fishing, and read you

another lecture; for I have a great deal more to say upon that subject.

Viat. The more the better; I could never have met with a more obliging master, my first excepted; nor such sport can all the rivers about London ever afford as is to be found in this pretty river.

Pisc. You deserve to have better, both because I see you are willing to take pains, and for liking this little so well; and better I hope to show you before we part.

THE SECOND DAY.

CHAPTER VII.

VIATOR.

COME, Sir! having now well dined, and being again set in your little house, I will now challenge your promise, and entreat you to proceed in your instruction for Fly-fishing; which, that you may be the better encouraged to do, I will assure you that I have not lost, I think, one syllable of what you have told me; but very well retain all your directions both for the rod, line, and making a fly, and now desire an account of the flies themselves.

PISC. Why, Sir, I am ready to give it you, and shall have

the whole afternoon to do it in, if nobody come in to inter-
rupt us; for you must know, besides the unfitness of the day,
that the afternoons so early in March signify very little to
angling with a fly; though with a minnow, or a worm, something might, I confess, be done.

To begin then where I left off. My Father Walton tells us
but of twelve artificial-flies, to angle with at the top, and
gives their names: of which some are common with us here;
and I think I guess at most of them by his description, and
I believe they all breed, and are taken in our rivers, though
we do not make them either of the same dubbing, or fashion. And it may be in the rivers about London, which I pre-
sume he has most frequented, and where 't is likely he has
done most execution, there is not much notice taken of
many more; but we are acquainted with several others here,
though, perhaps, I may reckon some of his by other names
too; but if I do, I shall make you amends by an addition to
his catalogue. And although the forenamed great Master in
the art of Angling, for so in truth he is, tells you that no
man should in honesty catch a Trout till the middle of
March, yet I hope he will give a man leave sooner to take a
Grayling; which, as I told you, is in the dead months in his
best season; and do assure you, which I remember by a very
remarkable token, I did once take upon the sixth day of December one, and only one, of the biggest Graylings, and the
best in season, that ever I yet saw, or tasted; and do usually
take Trouts too, and with a fly, not only before the middle
of this month, but almost every year in February, unless it

be a very ill spring indeed; and have sometimes in January, so early as New-year's-tide, and in frost and snow, taken Grayling in a warm sunshine day for an hour or two about noon; and to fish for him with a grub it is then the best time of all.

I shall therefore begin my fly-fishing with that month (though I confess very few begin so soon, and that such as are so fond of the sport as to embrace all opportunities, can rarely in that month find a day fit for their purpose), and tell you that, upon my knowledge, these flies in a warm sun, for an hour or 'two in the day, are certainly taken.

JANUARY.

1. A RED BROWN, with wings of the male of a mallard, almost white; the dubbing, of the tail of a black long-coated cur, such as they commonly make muffs of; for the hair on the tail of such a dog dyes and turns to a red brown, but the hair of a smooth-coated dog of the same color will not do, because it will not dye, but retains its natural color. And this fly is taken, in a warm sun, this whole month through.

2. There is also a very little BRIGHT-DUN GNAT, as little as can possibly be made, so little as never to be fished with, with above one hair next the hook: and this is to be made of a mixed dubbing of marten's fur, and the white of a hare's-scut; with a very white and small wing. And 't is no great matter how fine you fish, for nothing will rise in this month but a Grayling; and of them I never, at this season, saw any taken with a fly, of above a foot long, in my life; but of little ones, about the bigness of a smelt, in a warm day and a

glowing sun, you may take enough with these two flies; and they are both taken the whole month through.

FEBRUARY.

1. Where the RED BROWN of the last month ends, another, almost of the same color, begins with this; saving, that the dubbing of this must be of something a blacker color, and both of them warpt on with red silk. The dubbing that should make this fly, and that is the truest color, is to be got off the black spot of a hog's ear: not that a black spot in any part of the hog will not afford the same color, but that the hair in that place is by many degrees softer, and more fit for the purpose: his wing must be as the other; and this kills all this month, and is called the LESSER RED-BROWN.

2. This month also a PLAIN HACKLE, or Palmer-fly, made with a rough black body, either of black spaniel's fur, or the whirl of an ostrich-feather, and the red hackle of a capon over all, will kill; and, if the weather be right, make very good sport.

3. Also a LESSER HACKLE with a black body also, silver-twist over that, and a red feather over all, will fill your pannier, if the month be open, and not bound up in ice, and snow, with very good fish; but in case of a frost and snow, you are to angle only with the smallest gnats, browns, and duns, you can make; and with those are only to expect Graylings no bigger than sprats.

4. In this month, upon a whirling round water, we have a GREAT HACKLE; the body black, and wrapped with a red feather of a capon untrimmed; that is, the whole length of

the hackle staring out (for we sometimes barb the Hackle-feather short all over, sometimes barb it only a little, and sometimes barb it close underneath); leaving the whole length of the feather on the top or back of the fly, which makes it swim better, and, as occasion serves, kills very great fish.

5. We make use also, in this month, of another GREAT HACKLE; the body black, and ribbed over with gold twist, and a red feather over all; which also does great execution.

6. Also a GREAT DUN, made with dun bear's hair, and the wings of the gray feather of a mallard near unto his tail; which is absolutely the best fly can be thrown upon a river this month, and with which an angler shall have admirable sport.

7. We have also this month the GREAT BLUE DUN; the dubbing of the bottom of bear's hair next to the roots, mixed with a little blue camlet; the wings of the dark gray feather of a mallard.

8. We have also this month a DARK BROWN; the dubbing of a brown hair off the flank of a brended cow, and the wings of the gray drake's feather.

And note, that these several Hackles, or Palmer-flies, are some for one water and one sky, and some for another; and, according to the change of those, we alter their size and color. And note also, that both in this, and all other months of the year, when you do not certainly know what fly is taken, or cannot see any fish to rise, you are then to put on a small Hackle, if the water be clear, or a bigger, if something dark, until you have taken one; and then, thrusting your finger through his gills, to pull out his gorge, which being opened with your knife, you will then discover what fly is taken, and may fit yourself accordingly.

For the making of a Hackle, or Palmer-fly, my Father Walton has already given you sufficient direction.

MARCH.

For this month you are to use all the same Hackles, and flies with the other; but you are to make them less.

1. We have besides for this month, a little Dun called a WHIRLING-DUN, though it is not the Whirling-Dun indeed, which is one of the best flies we have; and for this the dubbing must be of the bottom fur of a squirrel's tail, and the wing of the gray feather of a drake.

2. Also a BRIGHT BROWN; the dubbing either of the brown of a spaniel, or that of a cow's flank, with a gray wing.

3. Also a WHITISH DUN, made of the roots of camel's hair, and the wings of the gray feather of a mallard.

4. There is also for this month a fly, called the THORN-TREE FLY; the dubbing an absolute black, mixed with eight or ten hairs of Isabella-colored mohair, the body as little as can be made, and the wings of a bright mallard's feather: an admirable fly, and in great repute amongst us for a killer.

5. There is, beside this, another BLUE DUN, the dubbing of which it is made being thus to be got. Take a small-tooth comb, and with it comb the neck of a black greyhound, and the down that sticks in the teeth will be the finest blue that ever you saw. The wings of this fly can hardly be too white;

and he is taken about the tenth of this month, and lasteth till the four-and-twentieth.

6. From the tenth of this month also, till towards the end, is taken a little BLACK GNAT: the dubbing either of the fur of a black water-dog, or the down of a young black water-coot; the wings of the male of a mallard, as white as may be; the body as little as you can possibly make it, and the wings as short as his body.

7. From the sixteenth of this month also, to the end of it, we use a BRIGHT BROWN; the dubbing for which is to be had out of a skinner's lime-pits, and of the hair of an abortive calf, which the lime will turn to be so bright as to shine like gold; for the wings of this fly, the feather of a brown hen is best; which fly is also taken till the tenth of April.

APRIL.

All the same Hackles and flies that were taken in March will be taken in this month also; with this distinction only concerning the flies, that all the browns be lapped with red silk, and the duns with yellow.

1. To these a SMALL BRIGHT BROWN, made of spaniel's fur, with a light gray wing, in a bright day and a clear water, is very well taken.

2. We have too a little DARK BROWN; the dubbing of that color, and some violet camlet mixed, and the wing of a gray feather of a mallard.

3. From the sixth of this month to the tenth, we have also a fly called the VIOLET-FLY; made of a dark violet stuff, with the wings of the gray feather of a mallard.

4. About the twelfth of this month comes in the fly called the WHIRLING-DUN, which is taken every day, about the mid-time of day, all this month through, and by fits from thence to the end of June; and is commonly made of the down of a fox-cub, which is of an ash color at the roots, next the skin, and ribbed about with yellow silk; the wings of the pale gray feather of a mallard.

5. There is also a YELLOW DUN; the dubbing of camel's hair, and yellow camlet or wool, mixed, and a white-gray wing.

6. There is also, this month, another LITTLE BROWN, besides that mentioned before; made with a very slender body, the dubbing of dark brown, and violet camlet mixed, and a gray wing; which, though the direction for the making be near the other, is yet another fly; and will take when the other will not, especially in a bright day, and a clear water.

7. About the twentieth of this month comes in a fly called the HORSE-FLESH FLY; the dubbing of which is a blue mohair, with pink-colored and red tammy mixed, a light-colored wing, and a dark brown head. This fly is taken best in an evening, and kills from two hours before sunset till twilight; and is taken the month through.

MAY.

And now, Sir, that we are entering into the month of May, I think it requisite to beg not only your attention, but also your best patience; for I must now be a little tedious with you, and dwell upon this month longer than ordinary; which that you may the better endure, I must tell you, this month deserves and requires to be insisted on, forasmuch as it alone, and the next following, afford more pleasure to the Fly-Angler than all the rest. And here it is that you are to expect an account of the Green-Drake, and Stone-fly, promised you so long ago, and some others that are peculiar to this month, and part of the month following; and that, though not so great either in bulk or name, do yet stand in competition with the two before named; and so, that it is yet undecided, amongst the anglers, to which of the pretenders to the title of the May-fly it does properly and duly belong. Neither dare I, where so many of the learned in this art of Angling are got in dispute about the controversy, take upon me to determine; but I think I ought to have a vote amongst them, and according to that privilege shall give you my free opinion; and peradventure when I have told you all, you may incline to think me in the right.

VIAT. I have so great a deference to your judgment in these matters, that I must always be of your opinion; and the more you speak, the faster I grow to my attention, for I can never be weary of hearing you upon this subject.

PISC. Why that's encouragement enough; and now prepare yourself for a tedious lecture; but I will first begin with the flies of less esteem,—though almost anything will take a Trout in May,—that I may afterwards insist the longer upon those of greater note and reputation. Know, therefore, that the first fly we take notice of in this month, is called

1. The TURKEY-FLY; dubbing ravelled out of some blue stuff, and lapped about with yellow silk; the wings of a gray mallard's feather.

2. Next a GREAT HACKLE or PALMER-FLY, with a YELLOW BODY; ribbed with gold twist, and large wings of a mallard's feather dyed yellow, with a red capon's hackle over all.

3. Then a BLACK FLY; the dubbing of a black spaniel's fur, and the wings of a gray mallard's feather.

4. After that a LIGHT BROWN, with a slender body; the dubbing twirled upon small red silk, and raised with the point of a needle, that the ribs or rows of silk may appear through; the wings of the gray feather of a mallard.

5. Next a LITTLE DUN; the dubbing of a bear's dun whirled upon yellow silk, the wings of the gray feather of a mallard.

6. Then a WHITE GNAT, with a pale wing, and a black head.

7. There is also this month a fly called the PEACOCK-FLY; the body made of a whirl of a peacock's feather, with a red head, and wings of a mallard's feather.

8. We have then another very killing fly, known by the name of the DUN-CUT; the dubbing of which is a bear's dun, with a little blue and yellow mixed with it, a large dun wing, and two horns at the head, made of the hairs of a squirrel's tail.

9. The next is the COW-LADY, a little fly; the body of a peacock's feather, the wing of a red feather, or strips of the red hackle of a cock.

10. We have then the COW-DUNG FLY; the dubbing light-brown and yellow mixed, the wing the dark gray feather of a mallard. And note, that besides these above mentioned, all the same Hackles and flies, the Hackles only brighter,

and the flies smaller, that are taken in April, will also be taken this month, as also all Browns and Duns. And now I come to my Stone-Fly, and Green-Drake, which are the Matadores for Trout and Grayling; and, in their season, kill more fish in our Derbyshire rivers than all the rest, past and to come, in the whole year besides.

But first I am to tell you, that we have four several flies which contend for the title of the May-fly: namely,

The GREEN-DRAKE,
The STONE-FLY,
The BLACK-FLY, and
The LITTLE YELLOW MAY-FLY.

And all these have their champions and advocates to dispute, and plead their priority; though I do not understand why the two last named should, the first two having so manifestly the advantage, both in their beauty, and the wonderful execution they do in their season.

11. Of these, the GREEN-DRAKE comes in about the twentieth of this month, or betwixt that and the latter end, for they are sometimes sooner, and sometimes later, according to the quality of the year; but never well taken till towards the end of this month, and the beginning of June. The Stone-Fly comes much sooner, so early as the middle of April; but is never well taken till towards the middle of May, and continues to kill much longer than the Green-Drake stays with us,—so long as to the end almost of June; and indeed, so long as there are any of them to be seen upon

the water; and sometimes in an artificial fly, and late at night, or before sunrise in a morning, longer.

Now both these flies, and, I believe, many others, though I think not all, are certainly and demonstratively bred in the very rivers where they are taken: our Cadis or Cod-bait, which lie under stones in the bottom of the water, most of them turning into those two flies; and, being gathered in the husk, or crust, near the time of their maturity, are very easily known and distinguished; and are of all other the most remarkable, both for their size, as being of all other the biggest, the shortest of them being a full inch long, or more, and for the execution they do, the Trout and Grayling being much more greedy of them than of any others; and indeed, the Trout never feeds fat, nor comes into his perfect season, till these flies come in.

Of these, the Green-Drake never discloses from his husk, till he be first there grown to full maturity, body, wings, and all; and then he creeps out of his cell, but with his wings so crimped and ruffled, by being pressed together in that narrow room, that they are, for some hours, totally useless to him; by which means he is compelled either to creep upon the flags, sedges, and blades of grass, if his first rising from the bottom of the water be near the banks of the river, till the air and sun stiffen and smooth them; or, if his first appearance above water happen to be in the middle, he then lies upon the surface of the water like a ship at hull; for his feet are totally useless to him there, and he cannot creep upon the water as the Stone-fly can, until his wings have got stiffness to fly with, if by some Trout or Grayling he be

not taken in the interim, which ten to one he is; and then
his wings stand high, and closed exact upon his back, like
the butterfly, and his motion in flying is the same. His body
is, in some, of a paler, in others, of a darker yellow, for they
are not all exactly of a color; ribbed with rows of green, long,
slender, and growing sharp towards the tail, at the end of
which he has three long small whisks of a very dark color,
almost black, and his tail turns up towards his back like a
mallard; from whence, questionless, he has his name of the
Green-Drake. These, as I think I told you before, we commonly dape or dibble with; and, having gathered great store
of them into a long draw-box, with holes in the cover to
give them air, where also they will continue fresh and vig-
orous a night or more, we take them out thence by the
wings, and bait them thus upon the hook. We first take one,
for we commonly fish with two of them at a time, and,
putting the point of the hook into the thickest part of his
body under one of his wings, run it directly through, and
out at the other side, leaving him spitted cross upon the
hook; and then taking the other, put him on after the same
manner, but with his head the contrary way; in which posture they will live upon the hook, and play with their wings
for a quarter of an hour, or more; but you must have a care
to keep their wings dry, both from the water, and also that
your fingers be not wet when you take them out to bait
them; for then your bait is spoiled.

Having now told you how to angle with this fly alive, I
am now to tell you next, how to make an artificial-fly, that
will so perfectly resemble him, as to be taken in a rough

windy day when no flies can lie upon the water, nor are to be found about the banks and sides of the river, to a wonder; and with which you shall certainly kill the best Trout and Grayling in the river.

The artificial Green-Drake, then, is made upon a large hook; the dubbing, camel's hair, bright bear's hair, the soft down that is combed from a hog's bristles and yellow camlet, well mixed together; the body long, and ribbed about with green silk, or rather yellow, waxed with green wax, the whisks of the tail, of the long hairs of sables, or fitchet, and the wings of the white-gray feather of a mallard, dyed yellow; which also is to be dyed thus.

Take the root of a Barbary-tree, and shave it, and put to it woody viss, with as much alum as a walnut, and boil your feathers in it with rainwater; and they will be of a very fine yellow.

I have now done with the Green-Drake; excepting to tell you, that he is taken at all hours during his season, whilst there is any day upon the sky; and with a made-fly I once took, ten days after he was absolutely gone, in a cloudy day, after a shower, and in a whistling wind, five and thirty very great Trouts and Graylings, betwixt five and eight of the clock in the evening; and had no less than five or six flies, with three good hairs apiece, taken from me in despite of my heart, besides.

12. I should now come next to the Stone-fly, but there is another gentleman in my way, that must of necessity come in between; and that is the GRAY-DRAKE, which, in all shapes and dimensions, is perfectly the same with the other,

but quite almost of another color; being of a paler and more livid yellow and green, and ribbed with black quite down his body, with black, shining wings, and so diaphanous and tender, cobweb-like, that they are of no manner of use for daping, but come in and are taken after the Green-Drake, and in an artificial fly kill very well; which fly is thus made: the dubbing of the down of a hog's bristles, and black spaniel's fur, mixed, and ribbed down the body with black silk, the whisks of the hairs of the beard of a black cat, and the wings of the black-gray feather of a mallard.

And now I come to the Stone-Fly, but am afraid I have already wearied your patience; which if I have I beseech you freely tell me so, and I will defer the remaining instructions for Fly-Angling till some other time.

Viat. No, truly, Sir, I can never be weary of hearing you. But if you think fit, because I am afraid I am too troublesome, to refresh yourself with a glass and a pipe: you may afterwards proceed, and I shall be exceedingly pleased to hear you.

Pisc. I thank you, Sir, for that motion; for, believe me, I am dry with talking. Here, Boy! give us here a bottle, and a glass; and, Sir, my service to you, and to all our friends in the South.

Viat. Your servant, Sir, and I 'll pledge you as heartily; for the good powdered beef I eat at dinner, or something else, has made me thirsty.

THE SECOND DAY.

CHAPTER VIII.

VIATOR.

SO, Sir, I am now ready for another lesson, so soon as you please to give it me.

PISC. And I, Sir, as ready to give you the best I can. Having told you the time of the Stone-fly's coming in, and that he is bred of a cadis in the very river where he is taken, I am next to tell you, that,

13. This same STONE-FLY has not the patience to continue in his crust, or husk, till his wings be full grown; but so soon as ever they begin to put out, that he feels himself strong (at which time we call him a Jack), squeezes himself out of

prison, and crawls to the top of some stone; where, if he can find a chink that will receive him, or can creep betwixt two stones, the one lying hollow upon the other (which, by the way, we also lay so purposely to find them), he there lurks till his wings be full grown, and there is your only place to find him; and from thence doubtless he derives his name:— though, for want of such convenience, he will make shift with the hollow of a bank, or any other place where the wind cannot come to fetch him off. His body is long, and pretty thick, and as broad at the tail, almost, as in the middle: his color a very fine brown, ribbed with yellow, and much yellower on the belly than the back: he has two or three whisks also at the tag of his tail, and two little horns upon his head: his wings, when full grown, are double, and flat down his back, of the same color but rather darker than his body, and longer than it; though he makes but little use of them, for you shall rarely see him flying, though often swimming and paddling, with several feet he has under his belly, upon the water, without stirring a wing. But the Drake will mount steeple-high into the air; though he is to be found upon flags and grass too, and, indeed, everywhere high and low near the river; there being so many of them in their season, as, were they not a very inoffensive insect, would look like a plague: and these Drakes (since I forgot to tell you before, I will tell you here) are taken by the fish to that incredible degree, that, upon a calm day, you shall see the still-deeps continually all over circles by the fishes rising, who will gorge themselves with those flies, till they purge again out of their gills: and the Trouts are at that time so lusty and strong, that one of eight or ten inches long will then more struggle and tug, and more endanger your tackle, than one twice as big in winter: but pardon this digression.

This Stone-Fly, then, we dape or dibble with, as with the Drake, but with this difference: that whereas the Green-Drake is common both to stream and still, and to all hours of the day, we seldom dape with this but in the streams, for in a whistling wind a made-fly in the deep is better,—and rarely but early and late, it not being so proper for the mid-time of the day; though a great Grayling will then take it very well in a sharp stream, and here and there a Trout too, but much better towards eight, nine, ten, or eleven of the clock at night, at which time also the best fish rise, and the later the better, provided you can see your fly; and when you cannot, a made-fly will murder, which is to be made thus: the dubbing of bear's dun with a little brown and yellow camlet very well mixed; but so placed, that your fly may be more yellow on the belly and towards the tail underneath than in any other part; and you are to place two or three hairs of a black cat's beard on the top of the hook, in your arming, so as to be turned up, when you warp on your dubbing, and to stand almost upright, and staring one from another: and note that your fly is to be ribbed with yellow silk; and the wings long, and very large, of the dark gray feather of a mallard.

14. The next May-fly is the Black-Fly; made with a black

body, of the whirl of an ostrich-feather, ribbed with silver-twist, and the black hackle of a cock over all; and is a killing fly, but not to be named with either of the other.

15. The last May-fly, that is of the four pretenders, is the Little Yellow May-Fly; in shape exactly the same with the Green-Drake, but a very little one, and of as bright a yellow as can be seen; which is made of a bright yellow camlet, and the wings of a white-gray feather dyed yellow.

16. The last fly for this month, and which continues all June, though it comes in in the middle of May, is the fly called the Camlet-Fly; in shape like a moth, with fine diapered, or water-wings, and with which, as I told you before, I sometimes used to dibble; and Grayling will rise mightily at it. But the artificial fly, which is only in use amongst our Anglers, is made of a dark-brown shining camlet, ribbed over with a very small light-green silk, the wings of the double-gray feather of a mallard; and 't is a killing fly for small fish. And so much for May.

June.

From the first to the four-and-twentieth, the Green-Drake and Stone-fly are taken, as I told you before.

1. From the twelfth to the four-and-twentieth, late at night, is taken a fly, called the Owl-Fly, the dubbing of a white weasel's tail, and a white-gray wing.

2. We have then another Dun, called the Barm-Fly, from its yeasty color; the dubbing of the fur of a yellow-dun cat, and a gray wing of a mallard's feather.

3. We have also a HACKLE with a purple body, whipped about with a red capon's feather.

4. As also a GOLD-TWIST HACKLE with a purple body, whipped about with a red capon's feather.

5. To these we have, this month, a FLESH-FLY; the dubbing of a black spaniel's fur, and blue wool mixed, and a gray wing.

6. Also another LITTLE FLESH-FLY; the body made of the whirl of a peacock's feather, and the wings of the gray feather of a drake.

7. We have then the PEACOCK-FLY; the body and wing both made of the feather of that bird.

8. There is also the Flying-Ant, or ANT-FLY; the dubbing of brown and red camlet mixed, with a light gray wing.

9. We have likewise a BROWN GNAT; with a very slender body of brown and violet camlet well mixed, and a light gray wing.

10. And another little BLACK GNAT; the dubbing of black mohair, and a white-gray wing.

11. As also a GREEN GRASSHOPPER; the dubbing of green and yellow wool mixed, ribbed over with green silk, and a red capon's feather over all.

12. And lastly, a little DUN GRASSHOPPER; the body slender, made of a dun camlet, and a dun hackle at the top.

JULY.

First, all the small flies that were taken in June are also taken in this month.

1. We have then the ORANGE-FLY; the dubbing of orange wool, and the wings of a black feather.

2. Also a little WHITE DUN; the body made of white mohair, and the wings blue, of a heron's feather.

3. We have likewise this month a WASP-FLY; made either of a dark brown dubbing, or else the fur of a black cat's tail, ribbed about with yellow silk, and the wing of the gray feather of a mallard.

4. Another fly taken this month is a BLACK-HACKLE; the body made of the whirl of a peacock's feather, and a black hackle-feather on the top.

5. We have also another, made of a peacock's whirl without wings.

6. Another fly also is taken this month, called the SHELL-FLY; the dubbing of yellow-green Jersey-wool, and a little white hog's hair mixed, which I call the Palm-fly: and do believe it is taken for a palm, that drops off the willows into the water; for this fly I have seen Trouts take little pieces of moss, as they have swam down the river; by which I conclude that the best way to hit the right color is to compare your dubbing with the moss, and mix the colors as near as you can.

7. There is also taken this month, a BLACK-BLUE DUN; the dubbing of the fur of a black rabbit mixed with a little yellow, the wings of the feather of a blue pigeon's wing.

AUGUST.

The same flies with July.

1. Then another ANT-FLY; the dubbing of the black-brown hair of a cow, some red warped in for the tag of his tail, and a dark wing. A killing fly.

2. Next a fly called a FERN-FLY; the dubbing of the fur of a hare's neck, that is, of the color of fern or bracken, with a darkish-gray wing of a mallard's feather. A killer too.

3. Besides these we have a WHITE HACKLE; the body of white mohair, and warped about with a white hackle-feather; and this is assuredly taken for thistle-down.

4. We have also this month a HARRY-LONG-LEGS; the body made of bear's dun and blue wool mixed, and a brown hackle-feather over all.

Lastly, In this month all the same browns and duns are taken that were taken in May.

SEPTEMBER.

This month the same flies are taken that are taken in April.

1. To which I shall only add a CAMEL-BROWN FLY; the dubbing pulled out of the lime of a wall, whipped about with red silk, and a darkish-gray mallard's feather for the wing.

2. And one other, for which we have no name, but it is made of the black hair of a badger's skin, mixed with the yellow softest down of a sanded hog.

October.

The same flies are taken this month that were taken in March.

November.

The same flies that were taken in February are taken this month also.

December.

Few men angle with the fly this month, no more than they do in January; but yet, if the weather be warm,—as I have known it sometimes in my life to be, even in this cold country, where it is least expected,—then a brown that looks red in the hand, and yellowish betwixt your eye and the sun, will both raise and kill in a clear water, and free from snow-broth; but, at the best, 't is hardly worth a man's labor.

And now, Sir, I have done with Fly-fishing, or angling at the top; excepting once more to tell you, that of all these,— and I have named you a great many very killing flies,—none are fit to be compared with the Drake and Stone-Fly, both for many and very great fish. And yet there are some days that are by no means proper for the sport; and in a calm you shall not have near so much sport, even with daping, as in a whistling gale of wind, for two reasons, both because you are not then so easily discovered by the fish, and also because there are then but few flies that can lie upon the water; for where they have so much choice, you may easily imagine they will not be so eager and forward to rise at a bait, that both the shadow of your body, and that of your rod, nay, of your very line, in a hot, calm day, will, in spite of your best caution, render suspected to them; but even then, in swift streams, or by sitting down patiently behind a willow-bush, you shall do more execution than at almost any other time of the year with any other fly; though one may sometimes hit of a day, when he shall come home very well satisfied with sport with several other flies. But with these two, the Green-Drake and the Stone-Fly, I do verily believe I could, some days in my life, had I not been weary of slaughter, have loaden a lusty boy; and have sometimes, I do honestly assure you, given over upon the mere account of satiety of sport; which will be no hard matter to believe, when I likewise assure you that, with this very fly, I have, in this very river that runs by us, in three or four hours, taken thirty, five and thirty, and forty of the best Trouts in the river. What shame and pity is it, then, that such a river should be destroyed by the basest sort of people, by those unlawful ways of fire and netting in the night, and of damming, groping, spearing, hanging, and hooking by day! which are now grown so common, that, though we have very good laws to punish such offenders, every rascal does it, for aught I see, *impunè*.

To conclude, I cannot now, in honesty, but frankly tell you, that many of these flies I have named, at least so made as we make them here, will peradventure do you no great service in your southern rivers; and will not conceal from you but that I have sent flies to several friends in London, that, for aught I could ever hear, never did any great feats

with them; and, therefore, if you intend to profit by my instructions, you must come to angle with me here in the
Peak; and so, if you please, let us walk up to supper; and to-
morrow, if the day be windy, as our days here commonly
are, 't is ten to one but we shall take a good dish of fish for
dinner.

THE THIRD DAY.

CHAPTER IX.

PISCATOR.

A GOOD day to you, Sir; I see you will always be stirring before me.

VIAT. Why, to tell you the truth, I am so allured with the sport I had yesterday, that I long to be at the river again; and when I heard the wind sing in my chamber-window, could forbear no longer, but leap out of bed, and had just made an end of dressing myself as you came in.

PISC. Well, I am both glad you are so ready for the day, and that the day is so fit for you. And look you, I have made you three or four flies this morning; this silver-twist hackle, this bear's dun, this light brown, and this dark brown, any of which I dare say will do; but you may try them all, and see which does best: only I must ask your pardon that I cannot wait upon you this morning, a little business being fallen out, that for two or three hours will deprive me of your company; but I'll come and call you home to dinner, and my man shall attend you.

VIAT. O, Sir, mind your affairs by all means. Do but lend me a little of your skill to these fine flies, and, unless it have forsaken me since yesterday, I shall find luck of my own, I hope, to do something.

PISC. The best instruction I can give you, is that, seeing

the wind curls the water, and blows the right way, you would now angle up the still-deep to-day; for betwixt the rocks where the streams are you would find it now too brisk; and, besides, I would have you take fish in both waters.

VIAT. I 'll obey your direction, and so a good morning to you. Come, young man, let you and I walk together. But hark you, Sir, I have not done with you yet; I expect another lesson for angling at the bottom, in the afternoon.

PISC. Well, Sir, I 'll be ready for you.

THE THIRD DAY.

CHAPTER X.

PISCATOR.

O SIR, are you returned? You have but just prevented me. I was coming to call you.

Viat. I am glad, then, I have saved you the labor.

Pisc. And how have you sped?

Viat You shall see that, Sir, presently: look you, Sir, here are three brace of Trouts, one of them the biggest but one that ever I killed with a fly in my life; and yet I lost a bigger than that, with my fly to boot; and here are three Graylings, and one of them longer by some inches than that I took yesterday, and yet I thought that a good one too.

PISC. Why you have made a pretty good morning's work on 't; and now, Sir, what think you of our river Dove?

VIAT. I think it to be the best Trout-river in England; and am so far in love with it, that if it were mine, and that I could keep it to myself, I would not exchange that water for all the land it runs over, to be totally debarred from it.

PISC. That compliment to the river speaks you a true lover of the art of Angling; and now, Sir, to make part of amends for sending you so uncivilly out alone this morning, I will myself dress you this dish of fish for your dinner; walk but into the parlor, you will find one book or other in the window to entertain you the while; and you shall have it presently.

VIAT. Well, Sir, I obey you.

PISC. Look you, Sir! have I not made haste?

VIAT. Believe me, Sir, that you have; and it looks so well, I long to be at it.

PISC. Fall to, then. Now, Sir, what say you, am I a tolerable cook or no?

VIAT. So good a one, that I did never eat so good fish in my life. This fish is infinitely better than any I ever tasted of the kind in my life. 'T is quite another thing than our Trouts about London.

PISC. You would say so, if that Trout you eat of were in right season; but pray eat of the Grayling, which, upon my word, at this time, is by much the better fish.

VIAT. In earnest, and so it is. And I have one request to

make to you, which is, that as you have taught me to catch Trout and Grayling, you will now teach me how to dress them as these are dressed; which, questionless, is of all other the best way.

Pisc. That I will, Sir, with all my heart; and am glad you like them so well, as to make that request. And they are dressed thus:—

Take your Trout, wash, and dry him with a clean napkin; then open him, and, having taken out his guts, and all the blood, wipe him very clean within, but wash him not; and give him three scotches with a knife to the bone, on one side only. After which take a clean kettle, and put in as much hard stale beer (but it must not be dead), vinegar, and a little white wine, and water, as will cover the fish you intend to boil; then throw into the liquor a good quantity of salt, the rind of a lemon, a handful of sliced horse-radish root, with a handsome little fagot of rosemary, thyme, and winter-savory. Then set your kettle upon a quick fire of wood, and let your liquor boil up to the height before you put in your fish; and then, if there be many, put them in one by one, that they may not so cool the liquor, as to make it fall. And whilst your fish is boiling, beat up the butter for your sauce with a ladleful or two of the liquor it is boiling in. And, being boiled enough, immediately pour the liquor from the fish; and, being laid in a dish, pour your butter upon it; and, strewing it plentifully over with shaved horse-radish, and a little pounded ginger, garnish your sides of your dish, and the fish itself with a sliced lemon or two, and serve it up.

A Grayling is also to be dressed exactly after the same manner, saving that he is to be scaled, which a Trout never is; and that must be done, either with one's nails, or very lightly and carefully with a knife for bruising the fish. And note, that these kinds of fish, a Trout especially, if he is not eaten within four or five hours after he be taken, is worth nothing.

But come, Sir, I see you have dined; and, therefore, if you please, we will walk down again to the little House, and there I will read you a lecture of Angling at the Bottom.

THE THIRD DAY.

CHAPTER XI.

VIATOR.

SO, Sir, now we are here, and set, let me have my instructions for Angling for Trout and Grayling, at the Bottom; which, though not so easy, so cleanly, nor, as 't is said, so genteel, a way of fishing, as with a fly, is yet (if I mistake not) a good holding way, and takes fish when nothing else will.

PISC. You are in the right, it does so; and a worm is so sure a bait at all times, that, excepting in a flood, I would I had laid a thousand pounds that I killed fish more or less with it, winter or summer, every day throughout the year; those days always excepted that, upon a more serious account, always ought so to be. But not longer to delay you, I will begin: and tell you, that Angling at the Bottom is also commonly of two sorts;—and yet there is a third way of angling with a ground-bait, and to very great effect too, as shall be said hereafter;—namely, by Hand, or with a Cork or Float.

That we call Angling by Hand is of three sorts.

The first: with a line about half the length of the rod, a good weighty plumb, and three hairs next the hook, which we call a running-line, and with one large brandling, or a dew-worm of a moderate size, or two small ones of the first,

or any other sort, proper for a Trout, of which my Father
Walton has already given you the names, and saved me a
labor; or, indeed, almost any worm whatever; for if a Trout
be in the humor to bite, it must be such a worm as I never
yet saw that he will refuse; and if you fish with two, you are
then to bait your hook thus. You are first to run the point of
your hook in at the very head of your first worm, and so
down through his body till it be past the knot, and then let
it out, and strip the worm above the arming (that you may
not bruise it with your fingers) till you have put on the
other, by running the point of the hook in below the knot,
and upwards through his body towards his head; till it be
but just covered with the head, which being done, you are
then to slip the first worm down over the arming again, till
the knots of both worms meet together.

The second way of angling by hand, and with a running-
line, is with a line something longer than the former, and
with tackle made after this same manner. At the utmost extremity of your line, where the hook is always placed in all
other ways of angling, you are to have a large pistol or cara-
bine bullet, into which the end of your line is to be fastened
with a peg or pin, even and close with the bullet; and, about
half a foot above that, a branch of line, of two or three
handfuls long, or more for a swift stream, with a hook at the
end thereof baited with some of the forenamed worms; and
another, half foot above that; another, armed and baited
after the same manner, but with another sort of worm,
without any lead at all above: by which means you will always certainly find the true bottom in all depths; which,

with the plumbs upon your line above you can never do, but that your bait must always drag whilst you are sounding (which, in this way of Angling, must be continually), by which means you are like to have more trouble, and peradventure worse success. And both these ways of angling at the bottom are most proper for a dark and muddy water; by reason that in such a condition of the stream, a man may stand as near as he will, and neither his own shadow nor the roundness of his tackle will hinder his sport.

The third way of angling by hand with a ground-bait, and by much the best of all other, is, with a line full as long, or a yard and a half longer than your rod; with no more than one hair next the hook, and for two or three lengths above it; and no more than one small pellet of shot for your plumb: your hook little; your worms of the smaller brandlings, very well scoured; and only one upon your hook at a time, which is thus to be baited: the point of your hook is to be put in at the very tag of his tail, and run up his body quite over all the arming, and still stripped on an inch at least upon the hair; the head and remaining part hanging downward. And with this line and hook, thus baited, you are evermore to angle in the streams; always in a clear, rather than a troubled water, and always up the river, still casting out your worm before you with a light one-handed rod, like an artificial fly; where it will be taken, sometimes at the top, or within a very little of the superficies of the water, and almost always before that light plumb can sink it to the bottom; both by reason of the stream, and also that you must always keep your worm in motion by drawing still

back towards you, as if you were angling with a fly. And believe me, whoever will try it, shall find this the best way of
all other to angle with a worm, in a bright water especially;
but then his rod must be very light and pliant, and very true
and finely made; which, with a skilful hand, will do wonders, and in a clear stream is undoubtedly the best way of
angling for a Trout or Grayling, with a worm, by many degrees, that any man can make choice of, and of most ease
and delight to the angler. To which let me add, that if the
angler be of a constitution that will suffer him to wade, and
will slip into the tail of a shallow stream, to the calf of the
leg or the knee, and so keep off the bank, he shall almost
take what fish he pleases.

The second way of angling at the bottom is with a cork
or float. And that is also of two sorts: with a Worm, or with
a Grub or Cadis.

With a Worm, you are to have your line within a foot, or
a foot and a half, as long as your rod, in a dark water with
two, or, if you will, with three; but in a clear water never
with above one hair next the hook, and two or three for four
or five lengths above it; and a worm of what size you please:
your plumbs fitted to your cork, your cork to the condition
of the river (that is, to the swiftness or slowness of it), and
both, when the water is very clear, as fine as you can; and
then you are never to bait with above one of the lesser sort
of brandlings; or, if they are very little ones indeed, you may
then bait with two after the manner before directed.

When you angle for a Trout, you are to do it as deep, that
is, as near the bottom as you can, provided your bait do not

drag; or if it do, a Trout will sometimes take it in that posture. If for a Grayling, you are then to fish further from the
bottom, he being a fish that usually swims nearer to the
middle of the water, and lies always loose; or, however, is
more apt to rise than a Trout, and more inclined to rise than
to descend even to a ground-bait.

With a Grub or Cadis, you are to angle with the same
length of line, or if it be all out as long as your rod, 't is not
the worse; with never above one hair for two or three
lengths next the hook, and with the smallest cork or float,
and the least weight of plumb you can that will but sink,
and that the swiftness of your stream will allow: which also
you may help, and avoid the violence of the current, by angling in the returns of a stream, or the eddies betwixt two
streams; which also are the most likely places wherein to kill
a fish in a stream, either at the top or bottom.

Of Grubs for a Grayling, the Ash-grub, which is plump,
milk-white, bent round from head to tail, and exceeding
tender, with a red head; or the Dock-worm, or grub, of a
pale yellow, longer, lanker, and tougher than the other, with
rows of feet all down his belly, and a red head also; are the
best, I say, for a Grayling: because, although a Trout will
take both these, the Ash-grub especially, yet he does not do
it so freely as the other, and I have usually taken ten
Graylings for one Trout with that bait; though if a Trout
come, I have observed that he is commonly a very good
one.

These baits we usually keep in bran, in which an Ash-
grub commonly grows tougher, and will better endure bait-

ing; though he is yet so tender, that it will be necessary to warp in a piece of a stiff hair with your arming, leaving it standing out about a straw-breadth at the head of your hook, so as to keep the grub either from slipping totally off when baited, or at least down to the point of the hook, by which means your arming will be left wholly naked and bare, which is neither so sightly, nor so likely to be taken: though, to help that, which will however very oft fall out, I always arm the hook I design for this bait with the whitest horsehair I can choose; which itself will resemble, and shine like that bait, and consequently will do more good, or less harm, than an arming of any other color. These grubs are to be baited thus: the hook is to be put in under the head or chaps of the bait, and guided down the middle of the belly, without suffering it to peep out by the way (for then, the Ash-grub especially, will issue out water and milk, till nothing but the skin shall remain, and the bend of the hook will appear black through it) till the point of your hook come so low, that the head of your bait may rest, and stick upon the hair that stands out to hold it; by which means it can neither slip of itself, neither will the force of the stream, nor quick pulling out, upon any mistake, strip it off.

Now the Cadis, or Cod-bait, which is a sure killing bait, and, for the most part, by much surer than either of the other, may be put upon the hook, two or three together; and is sometimes, to very great effect, joined to a worm, and sometimes to an artificial fly to cover the point of the hook; but is always to be angled with at the bottom, when by itself especially, with the finest tackle; and is for all times of the year the most holding-bait of all other whatever, both for Trout and Grayling.

There are several other baits, besides these few I have named you, which also do very great execution at the bottom; and some that are peculiar to certain countries and rivers, of which every Angler may in his own place make his own observation; and some others that I do not think fit to put you in mind of, because I would not corrupt you, and would have you,—as in all things else I observe you to be a very honest gentleman, a fair Angler. And so much for the second sort of angling for a Trout at the bottom.

VIAT. But, Sir, I beseech you give me leave to ask you one question. Is there no art to be used to worms, to make them allure the fish, and in a manner compel them to bite at the bait?

PISC. Not that I know of: or did I know any such secret, I would not use it myself, and therefore would not teach it you. Though I will not deny to you that, in my younger days, I have made trial of Oil of Osprey, Oil of Ivy, Camphor, Assafœtida, Juice of Nettles, and several other devices that I was taught by several Anglers I met with, but could never find any advantage by them; and can scarce believe there is anything to be done that way: though I must tell you, I have seen some men, who I thought went to work no more artificially than I, and have yet with the same kind of worms I had, in my own sight, taken five, and sometimes ten, for one. But we'll let that business alone, if you please. And, because we have time enough, and that I would deliver you from the trouble of any more lectures, I will, if you please, proceed to the last way of angling for a Trout or Grayling, which is in the middle; after which I shall have no more to trouble you with.

VIAT. 'T is no trouble, Sir, but the greatest satisfaction that can be, and I attend you.

THE THIRD DAY.

CHAPTER XII.

PISCATOR.

ANGLING in the Middle, then, for Trout or Grayling, is of two sorts: with a Penk or Minnow for a Trout; or with a Worm, Grub, or Cadis for a Grayling.

For the first; it is with a Minnow, half a foot, or a foot, within the superficies of the water. And as to the rest that concerns this sort of Angling, I shall wholly refer you to Mr. Walton's direction, who is undoubtedly the best Angler with a Minnow in England: only in plain truth I do not approve of those baits he keeps in salt,—unless where the living ones are not possibly to be had (though I know he frequently kills with them, and peradventure more than with any other, nay, I have seen him refuse a living one for one of them),—and much less of his artificial one; for though we do it with a counterfeit-fly, methinks it should hardly be expected that a man should deceive a fish with a counterfeit-fish. Which having said, I shall only add, and that out of my own experience, that I do believe a Bull-head, with his gill-fins cut off, at some times of the year especially, to be a much better bait for a Trout than a Minnow, and a Loach much better than that: to prove which I shall only tell you, that I have much oftener taken Trouts with a Bull-head or a Loach in their throats (for there a Trout has questionless his first digestion) than a Minnow; and that one day especially, having angled a good part of the day with a Minnow, and that in as hopeful a day, and as fit a water, as could be wished for that purpose, without raising any one fish; I at last fell to it with the worm, and with that took fourteen in a very short space; amongst all which there was not, to my remembrance, so much as one that had not a Loach or two, and some of them three, four, five, and six Loaches, in his throat and stomach; from whence I concluded, that, had I angled with that bait, I had made a notable day's work of 't.

But, after all, there is a better way of angling with a Minnow than perhaps is fit either to teach or to practise: to which I shall only add, that a Grayling will certainly rise at, and sometimes take a Minnow, though it will be hard to be believed by any one, who shall consider the littleness of that fish's mouth, very unfit to take so great a bait; but 't is affirmed by many, that he will sometimes do it, and I myself know it to be true; for though I never took a Grayling so, yet a man of mine once did, and within so few paces of me, that I am as certain of it as I can be of anything I did not see; and, which made it appear the more strange, the Grayling was not above eleven inches long.

I must here also beg leave of your Master, and mine, not to controvert, but to tell him, that I cannot consent to his way of throwing in his rod to an overgrown Trout, and afterwards recovering his fish with his tackle. For though I am satisfied he has sometimes done it, because he says so, yet I have found it quite otherwise; and though I have taken

with the Angle, I may safely say, some thousands of Trouts
in my life, my top never snapped (though my line still continued fast to the remaining part of my rod, by some lengths
of line curled round about my top, and there fastened with
waxed silk, against such an accident) nor my hand never
slacked, or slipped by any other chance, but I almost always
infallibly lost my fish, whether great or little, though my
hook came home again. And I have often wondered how a
Trout should so suddenly disengage himself from so great a
hook as that we bait with a Minnow, and so deep-bearded
as those hooks commonly are; when I have seen by the forenamed accidents, or the slipping of a knot in the upper part
of the line, by sudden and hard striking, that though the
line has immediately been recovered, almost before it could
be all drawn into the water, the fish cleared, and was gone
in a moment. And yet, to justify what he says, I have sometimes known a Trout, having carried away a whole line,
found dead three or four days after, with the hook fast sticking in him; but then it is to be supposed he had gorged it,
which a Trout will do, if you be not too quick with him,
when he comes at a Minnow, as sure and much sooner than
a Pike; and I myself have also, once or twice in my life,
taken the same fish with my own fly sticking in his chaps,
that he had taken from me the day before, by the slipping
of a hook in the arming. But I am very confident a Trout
will not be troubled two hours with any hook, that has so
much as one handful of line left behind with it, or that is
not struck through a bone, if it be in any part of his mouth
only: nay, I do certainly know that a Trout, so soon as ever

he feels himself pricked, if he carries away the hook, goes immediately to the bottom, and will there root like a hog upon the gravel, till he either rub out, or break the hook in the middle. And so much for this sort of angling in the middle for a Trout.

The second way of angling in the middle is with a Worm, Grub, Cadis, or any other ground-bait for a Grayling; and that is with a cork, and a foot from the bottom, a Grayling taking it much better there than at the bottom, as has been said before; and this always in a clear water, and with the finest tackle.

To which we may also, and with very good reason, add the third way of angling by hand with a ground-bait, as a third way of fishing in the middle, which is common to both Trout and Grayling; and, as I said before, the best way of angling with a worm of all other I ever tried whatever.

And now, Sir, I have said all I can at present think of concerning Angling for a Trout and Grayling, and I doubt not have tired you sufficiently; but I will give you no more trouble of this kind whilst you stay; which I hope will be a good while longer.

VIAT. That will not be above a day longer; but if I live till May come twelvemonth, you are sure of me again, either with my Master Walton or without him; and in the mean time shall acquaint him how much you have made of me for his sake, and I hope he loves me well enough to thank you for it.

PISC. I shall be glad, Sir, of your good company at the

time you speak of, and shall be loath to part with you now; but when you tell me you must go, I will then wait upon you more miles on your way than I have tempted you out of it, and heartily wish you a good journey.

LINNÆAN ARRANGEMENT

OF THE FISH

FIGURED IN THIS EDITION OF WALTON AND COTTON'S

COMPLETE ANGLER.

Extracted from General Zoölogy, by GEORGE SHAW, M.D., &c., &c.; and
British Zoölogy, by THOMAS PENNANT, Esq., Edit. Lond., 1812, 8vo.

Fishes form one great division of the Systema Naturæ of
Linnæus; and the most generally received modification
thereof, by Dr. Shaw, arranges them under two great
Classes,—to the former of which alone the present work
has reference,—viz. those which have a Skeleton of *Bone*,
and those which have a Skeleton of *Cartilage.* The Orders
are founded upon circumstances connected with the Fins,
which are named from their situation, *Dorsal,* or *Back Fins;
Pectoral,* or *Breast Fins; Ventral,* or *Belly Fins; Anal,* or *Vent
Fin;* and *Caudal,* or *Tail Fin.*

The Ventral Fins are held to be analogous to the Feet of
Quadrupeds; and from their absence, or relative situation to
the others, the Orders are taken. Such as *want* the *Ventral*
Fins are named *Apodal,* or *Footless;* such as have the *Ventral*
placed *before,* or *more forward* than the *Pectoral,* are named
Jugular; such as have them immediately *under* the *Pectoral*
are named *Thoracic;* and such as have them *behind* or *beyond*
the *Pectoral* are named *Abdominal.*

As the ensuing descriptions of the Fish are placed according to their scientific order, and not according to that

of their occurrence in the preceding work, a reference to the chapter and the page in which they are treated of and represented is placed against each of the following Articles.

ORDER I.
APODAL, OR FOOTLESS.
No Ventral Fins.

Genus ANGUILLA, EEL.

Head smooth. Nostrils tubular. Eyes covered by the common skin. Gill-membrane 10 rayed. Body roundish, smooth, mucous. Dorsal, Caudal, and Anal fins united. Spiracles behind the head or Pectoral fins.

A. vulgaris. Common Eel. Chap. XIII. page 181.

Olive-brown Eel, subargenteous beneath, with the lower jaw longer than the upper.

ORDER II.
JUGULAR.
Ventral Fins before the Pectoral.

No example.

ORDER III.
THORACIC.
Ventral Fins under the Pectoral.

Genus COTTUS, BULL-HEAD.

Head broader than the body, spiny. Eyes vertical, and furnished with a nictitating membrane. Gill-membrane 6 rayed. Body (in most species), without scales, attenuated towards the tail. Dorsal fins (in most species), two.

C. Gobio, River Bull-Head. Chap. XVIII. pp. 223, 225.

Smooth yellowish-olive Bull-Head, variegated with black; beneath whitish. The Head furnished with a spine on each side.

Genus PERCA, PERCH.

Teeth sharp, incurvate. Gill-covers triphyllous (three-leaved), scaly, serrated. Dorsal fin spiny on the fore part. Scales (in most species) hard and rough.

P. Fluviatilis, Common Perch. Chap. XII. page 175.

Olivaceous Perch, with transverse semi-decurrent blackish bands. Dorsal fin subviolaceous, the rest red.

P. Cernua, Ruffe-Perch. Chap. XV. page 197.

Sub-olivaceous Perch speckled with black, with 15 spines in the Dorsal fin.

N. B. The large Eyes (Oculi magni), which are noticed in Linnæus's description, are well expressed in the Plate.

Genus GASTEROSTEUS, STICKLEBACK.

Body somewhat lengthened. Dorsal spines distinct. Ventral fins spiny. Abdomen carinated on the sides, and bony beneath.

G. Aculeatus, Common Stickleback. Chap. XVIII. pp. 223, 226.

Olivaceous Stickleback, silvery-red beneath, with 3 Dorsal spines.

ORDER IV.
ABDOMINAL.
Ventral Fins behind, or beyond the Pectoral.

Genus COBITIS, LOCHE.

Mouth (in most species) bearded. Eyes situated in the upper part of the head. Body nearly of equal thickness, from head to tail. Scales small, easily deciduous. Air-bladder hard, or osseous.

C. Barbatula, Common Loche. Chap. XVIII. pp. 223, 225.

Yellow-gray Loche, with dusky variegations, small compressed head and 6 beards.

Genus SALMO, SALMON.

Head compressed, smooth. Tongue cartilaginous. Teeth, both in the jaws, and on the tongue. Gill-membrane from 4 to 10 rayed. Body compressed, furnished at the hind part with an Adipose fin.

S. Salar, Common Salmon. Chap. VII. page 132.

Silvery-gray spotted Salmon, with the jaws (in the male) incurvated.

S. Fario, Common Trout. Chap. V. page 81.

Yellowish-gray Salmon with red spots, and lower jaw rather longer than the upper.

S. Salmulus, Samlet. Chap. IV. page 65.

Bluish-gray Salmon, with distant reddish spots and forked tail.

Note. Pennant seems to have established this as a distinct species, and not the fry of the Salmon, which some have supposed. One conclusive reason amongst others is, that they are furnished with roes, and are therefore to be considered as full-grown fishes. A similar inference may be made with respect to the *White-Bait* of the Thames.

S. Thymallus, Grayling Salmon. Chap. VI. page 126.

Gray Salmon, with longitudinal dusky blue lines, and violet-colored Dorsal fin barred with brown.

Genus ESOX, PIKE.

Head somewhat flattened above. Mouth wide. Teeth sharp, in the jaws, palate, and tongue. Body lengthened. Dorsal and Anal fins (in most species) placed near the tail, and opposite each other.

E. Lucius, Common Pike. Chap. VIII. page 145.

Grayish-olive Pike, with yellowish spots, and depressed subequal jaws.

Genus CYPRINUS, CARP.

Mouth small and toothless. Teeth in the throat. Gill-membrane 3 rayed. Ventral fins, in general, 9 rayed.

Note. It is remarkable, that of the twenty-one principal Fish which minister to the pleasure of the Angler, ten belong to this single Genus.

C. Carpio, Common Carp. Chap. IX. page 158.

Yellowish-olive Carp, with wide Dorsal fin, with the third ray serrated behind.

C. Brama, Bream. Chap. X. page 164.

Broad olivaceous Carp, with flesh-colored Abdomen; smallish Dorsal fin, and 27 rays in the Anal fin.

C. Rutilus, Roach. Chap. XVII. page 212.

Yellowish-silvery Carp, with olivaceous back. Dorsal fin brown, the rest reddish, and forked tail.

C. Tinca, Tench. Chap. XI. page 173.

Mucous blackish-olive Carp, with very small scales, and nearly even tail.

C. Barbus, Barbel. Chap. XIV. page 192.

Bluish-white Carp, with 4 beards, olive-colored back, and the first ray of the Dorsal fin serrated on both sides.

C. Jeses, Chub. Chap. II. page 54.

Silvery-bluish Carp, with olivaceous back, thick head, and rounded snout.

C. Leuciscus, Dace. Chap. XVII. page 213.

Yellowish-silvery Carp, with olivaceous back, Dorsal fin brown, the rest reddish, and forked tail.

C. Alburnus, Bleak. Chap. XV. page 198.

Silvery Carp, with olivaceous back, 20 rays in the Anal fin, and forked tail.

C. Gobio, Gudgeon. Chap. XV. page 196.

Silvery-Olive Carp, with the upper lip bearded, and the Dorsal fin and tail spotted with black.

C. Phoxinus, Minnow. Chap. XVIII. pages 223, 225.

Blackish-green Carp, with blue and yellow variegations; reddish-silvery Abdomen, and forked tail.

SELECTED NOTES,

ILLUSTRATIVE OF THE COMPLETE ANGLER.

1. *A Conference betwixt an Angler, etc.* The First Edition of the Complete Angler has not any descriptive titles prefixed to the chapters; but the leaf immediately preceding the commencement of the work itself contains a short Table of Contents to the thirteen chapters of which that edition is composed, and which is introduced in the following manner: "Because in this Discourse of Fish and Fishing I have not observed a method, which (though the Discourse be not long) may be some inconvenience to the Reader, I have therefore for his easier finding out some particular things which are spoken of, made this following Table. The first chapter is spent in a vindication or commendation of the Art of Angling." After having gone through the whole number of chapters, the Table concludes with, "These directions the Reader may take as an ease in his search after

some particular Fish, and the baits proper for them; and he will shew himselfe courteous in mending or passing by some few errors in the Printer, which are not so many but that they may be pardoned." In the Second Edition, there were twenty-one chapters, entitled as they are in the foregoing pages; and the Third Edition was the first which had an index.

2. *The Thatched House in Hoddesden.* In the First Edition, there are but two characters introduced in Chapter I.: Viator, or the Wayfarer, whose name in the Second impression was changed to Venator, or the Hunter, and Piscator, the Fisherman. Instead, therefore, of the dialogue as it now stands, the opening passages were originally as follow: "*Piscator.* You are wel overtaken Sir; a good morning to you; I have stretch'd my legs up Totnam Hil to overtake you, hoping your businesse may occasion you towards Ware, this fine, pleasant, fresh, Mayday in the morning. *Viator.* Sir, I shall almost answer your hopes; for my purpose is to be at Hodsden (three miles short of that town) I will not say, before I drink, but before I break my fast: for I have appointed a friend or two to meet me there at the Thatcht-house, about nine of the clock this morning; and that made me so early up, and, indeed, to walk so fast. *Pisc.* Sir, I know the Thatcht-house very well: I often make it my resting place, and taste a cup of ale there, for which liquor that place is very remarkable; and to that house I shall by your favour accompany you, and either abate of my pace, or mend it, to enjoy such a companion as you seem to be, knowing that (as the Italians say,") etc. Pages 3, 4. The Thatcht-house is

stated by the Rev. Moses Browne, in a note in his Third Edition of the Complete Angler, *Lond.* 1772, 12mo, p. 1, to be "seventeen miles from London on the Ware road." It is now quite unknown; but it has been supposed that a thatched cottage, once distinguished by the sign of the Buffalo's Head, standing at the farther end of Hoddesdon, on the left of the road in going towards Ware, about seventeen miles and half distant from London, was the actual building.

3. *Theobald's.* In the county of Hertford, about twelve miles from London, in the parish of Cheshunt; built by Cecil, Lord Burleigh, who often entertained Queen Elizabeth there.

4. *See a hawk, that a friend mews.* From the French word *mué.* It signifies the care taken of a hawk during the moulting-season. The places where hawks were trained and kept were called *mews.*

5. *Mr. Sadler's.* Ralph Sadler, of Standon, a few miles from Amwell, in the County of Herts, the son and heir of Sir Thomas Sadler, Knight. "He delighted much in Hawking and Hunting and the pleasures of a country life, was famous for his noble table, his great hospitality to his neighbours, and his abundant charity to the poor." He died in 1660.

6. *According to Lucian.* The First Edition of the Complete Angler has these verses placed immediately after the extract from Montaigne, which was introduced by the same remarks which now precede it, upon Viator's answer to that speech of Piscator, in which he declares himself an enemy

to the Otter, both on the account of his brother-anglers and his own. At page 6, in the original impression, *Viator*, who is the subsequent Venator, though without his discourse in praise of Hunting, says: "Sir, to be plain with you, I am sorry you are an Angler: for I have heard many grave, serious men pitie, and many pleasant men scoffe, at Anglers." Piscator's reply is then nearly the same as it now appears, with the transposition already mentioned; but at the end of the sentence "and I hope I may take," etc., see page 7, he continues: "But, if this satisfie not, I pray bid the scoffer put this Epigram in his pocket, and read it every morning for his breakfast (for I wish him no better); Hee shall find it fixed before the Dialogues of Lucian, who may justly be accounted the father of the family of all scoffers: And, though I owe none of that fraternitie so much as good-will, yet I have taken a little pleasant pains to make such a conversion of it as may make it the fitter for all of that fraternity."

7. *The learned and ingenious Montaigne says.* The original edition, in this place, reads, "And as for any Scoffer, '*qui mockat, mockabitur.*' Let mee tell you (that you may tell him), what the wittie Frenchman sayes in such a case."

8. *Varro.* Marcus Terentius Varro, a most learned Roman, contemporary with Cicero, and author, it is said, of nearly five hundred volumes. He was one of the best writers on agriculture.

9. *Mr. G. Sandys.* George Sandys, the youngest son of Dr. Edwin Sandys, Archbishop of York, born in 1577. The book referred to by Walton is "A Relation of a Journey begun An. Dom.: 1610."

10. *Macrobius.* Aurelius Macrobius, a learned writer of the fourth century, chamberlain to the Emperor Theodosius.

11. *He that shall view the writings of Macrobius or Varro.* This passage occurs first in the Second Edition of The Complete Angler, 1655; and the materials of it are taken, with little alteration in the language, from lib. iv. sect. 6, p. 434, of Dr. Hakewill's Apology.

12. *Then first, for the antiquity of Angling.* At this place, in Walton's First Edition, p. 12, there is a marginal reference to "J. Da. Jer. Mar." as the authorities which furnished this paragraph; which are certainly meant for John Davors, and Jervis or Gervase Markham. The beautiful verses by the former of these persons, on page 43, have been, however, considered to belong rather to a John Dennys; since those stanzas which in the First Edition of Walton, p. 35, are marked Jo. Da., afterwards extended into Davors, form a part of a very rare poem entitled "The Secrets of Angling, by J. D., Esquire," first printed in octavo in 1613. The passage referred to in Markham, whose opinion Walton says, in the First Edition, he "likes better," is in the "Pleasures of Princes, or Good Men's Recreations, containing a Discourse of the General Art of Fishing with an Angle or otherwise," 4to, 1614, p. 3.

13. *The learned Peter du Moulin.* Dr. Peter du Moulin, Prebendary of Canterbury. His treatise entitled "The Accomplishment of the Prophecies," was translated from the French by J. Hath, and printed in octavo at Oxford in 1613. The passage to which Walton refers is in the Preface to the

Reader: "For as God intending to reveale future events to his prophets, withdrew them aside, and carried them either to the desert or els to the seashore, that so having pluckt them from amidst the presse, he might settle their minds in a quiet repose; so thinke I, that to dive into their prophecies a man need be free from all cares, and to partake of their rest, that he may partake of the cleernesse of their spirit."

14. *And an ingenious Spaniard says.* This passage is commonly supposed to allude to John Valdesso, a Spanish soldier in the service of the Emperor Charles V., of whom, in his old age, he obtained leave to retire by urging the aphorism, "It is fit that between the employment of life and the day of death some space should intervene."

15. *One of no less credit than Aristotle.* In the margin of the First Edition of Walton is inserted at this place, "In his Wonders of Nature."

16. *But I will lay aside my discourse of rivers.* The passage from the words "But I will lay aside" down to "she locks up her wonders," p. 31, was not inserted till Walton's Fifth Edition.

17. *Dr. Casaubon.* Méric, son of Isaac Casaubon, born at Geneva in 1599, but educated at Oxford, was for his great learning preferred to a Prebend in the Cathedral of Canterbury, and the Rectory of Ickham near that city. . . . He died in 1671, leaving behind him the character of a religious man, loyal to his Prince, exemplary in his life and conversation, and very charitable to the poor. *Athen. Oxon.,* vol ii. p. 485, edit. 1721. Casaubon's work "Of Credulity and Incredulity in

Things Natural, Civil, and Divine," was first printed in London in 1668. What relates to the Dolphins is at page 243 of the First Edition.

18. *John Tradescant.* There were three of the *Tradescants,*—grandfather, father, and son. The son is the person here meant; the two former were Gardeners to Queen Elizabeth, and the latter to King Charles the First.

19. *Elias Ashmole, Esq.* Ashmole was at first a Solicitor in Chancery, afterwards was promoted to the office of Windsor Herald, and wrote the "History of the Order of the Garter," published in 1672.

20. *Gesner, Rondeletius . . . Ausonius.* Conrad Gesner, an eminent physician and naturalist, was born at Zurich in 1516. His skill in botany and natural history was such as procured him the appellation of the Pliny of Germany. He died in 1565. Two of his works are "Historia Animalium" and "De Serpentum Naturâ, Tiguri," to both of which Walton frequently refers.

Guillaume Rondelet, also an eminent physician, was born at Montpellier, in Languedoc, in 1507. He wrote a treatise, "Libri de Piscibus marinis," where all that Walton has taken from him is to be found. He died in 1566.

Decius Ausonius, a native of Bordeaux, was a Latin Poet, Consul of Rome, and Preceptor to the Emperor Gratian. He died about 390.

21. *Divine Du Bartas.* Guillaume de Salluste, Sieur du Bartas, was a poet of great reputation in Walton's time. He wrote, besides numerous other productions, a poem in

French, called "Divine Weeks and Works," which was translated into English by Joshua Sylvester.

22. *And there is a fish called a Hermit.* The passage from the words "And there is a fish" down to "most of mankind" was not inserted till the Third Edition of The Complete Angler, 1664.

23. *Ælian.* Claudius Ælianus was born at Præneste, in Italy, in the reign of the Emperor Adrian. He wrote "De Animalium Naturâ," and other works.

24. *The Voyages of Ferdinand Mendez Pinto.* The passage alluded to by Walton occurs in "The Voyages and Adventures of Ferdinand Mendez Pinto, done into English by H[enry] C[ogan], Gent. London, 1633," fol. chap. lxxix. p. 319.

25. *He that reads Plutarch.* These passages, from the words "And for the lawfulness" down to "many others of great learning have been," did not appear until Walton's Second Edition. The anecdote of Antony and Cleopatra given by Plutarch is as follows: "It would be very tedious and trifling to recount all his follies; but his fishing must not be forgot. He went out one day to angle with Cleopatra, and being so unfortunate as to catch nothing in the presence of his mistress, he was very much vexed, and gave secret orders to the fishermen to dive under water, and put fishes that had been fresh taken upon his hook. After he had drawn up two or three, Cleopatra perceived the trick; she pretended, however, to be surprised at his good fortune and dexterity; told it to all her friends, and invited them to come and see him

fish the next day. Accordingly a very large company went out in the fishing vessels, and as soon as Antony had let down his line, she commanded one of her servants to be beforehand with Antony's, and diving into the water, to fix upon his hook a salted fish, one of those which were brought from the *Euxine Sea.*"

26. *Our learned Perkins ... Doctor Whitaker ... Doctor Nowel.* William Perkins was a preacher who flourished at the latter end of the sixteenth century.

Dr. Whitaker was an eminent writer in the Romish controversy, and Regius Professor of Divinity in the University of Cambridge. He flourished toward the close of the sixteenth century. The fact referred to in the text is thus attested by Fuller in his "Holy State," book iii. chap. 13: "Fishing with an angle is to some rather a torture than a pleasure, to stand an hour as mute as the fish they mean to take; yet herewithal Dr. Whitaker was much delighted."

Dr. Alexander Nowel was a learned divine and famous preacher in the reign of Edward VI., upon whose death he, with many other Protestants, fled to Germany, where he lived many years.

27. *Sir Henry Wotton.* This eminent scholar and statesman was born at Breton Hall, in Kent, in 1568, and educated at Winchester School, in New Oxford. He became Secretary to Robert Devereux, Earl of Essex, and afterwards attached himself to the Duke of Florence, who sent him as Ambassador to James VI. of Scotland. When the latter came to be King of England, he knighted Wotton and em-

ployed him as his principal Ambassador. About 1624 he was made Provost of Eton College, and died there in December, 1639. The passage quoted in the text is in his "Remains."

28. *Make conscience of the laws of the nation.* This alludes to a statute made in the 5th of Eliz., which enacts that any person eating flesh upon the usual Fish-days shall forfeit £3 for every offence, or undergo three months' imprisonment without bail. The passages from "Is not mine Host a witty man?" down to "To speak truly," p. 52, are wanting in the First Edition.

29. *At Trout Hall . . . where I purpose to lodge to-night.* At page 73 Piscator tells the milkwoman he is "going to *Bleak Hall* to his bed."

30. *There are Trouts taken of three cubits long.* That is, four feet and a half,—a length scarcely credible (says Jesse), although it is known that trout attain a great size in very large lakes. One of the largest English trout on record was taken in a small stream which runs through the park at Drayton Manor, the seat of Sir Robert Peel. It weighed twenty-two pounds and a half.

31. *Mercator.* Gerard Mercator, of Rupelmonde, in Flanders; a man of intense application to mathematical studies. He engraved with his own hand, and colored, the maps to his geographical writings. He died in 1594.

32. *Albertus.* Albertus Magnus, a German Dominican, and a very learned man. He wrote a treatise "on the Secrets of Nature," and twenty other volumes in folio, and died at Cologne, in 1280.

33. *The Royal Society, etc.* This passage did not appear until Walton's last edition.

34. *Bleak Hall.* A fishing-house on the banks of the Lea, about one mile from Edmonton, was called Bleak Hall, and is presumed to be the place alluded to.

35. *The choice songs, etc.* In Walton's First Edition, this passage is contained in the Third Chapter: which is entitled "In Chapter 3 are some observations of Trouts, both of their nature, their kinds, and their breeding."

36. *Our Topsel.* The Rev. Edward Topsell, Chaplain to Dr. Neil, Dean of Westminster, in the Church of St. Botolph, Aldersgate. He was the author of "The History of four-footed Beasts," and "The Historie of Serpents, or the Seconde Booke of Living Creatures."

37. *Aldrovandus.* Ulysses Aldrovandus, an eminent physician and naturalist of Bologna, who wrote one hundred and twenty books on several subjects, and a treatise "De Piscibus," published at Frankfort, in 1640. The passage alluded to in the text, is in his "Serpentum et Draconum Historiae."

38. *Devout Lessius.* Leonard Lessius, a very learned Jesuit, born at Antwerp, 1554. He wrote several theological tracts, and a book entitled "Hygiasticon, seu vera ratio valetudinis bonae & vitae extremam senectutem conservandae." From this tract, it is probable the passage in the text is cited. He died in 1623.

39. *A most excellent fly-fisher.* Leonard Mascall, from whose "Booke of Fishing with Hooke and Line, &c. 4to. Lond., 1600," the ensuing list of flies is copied verbatim.

THE ANGLER'S SONG.*

SET BY H. LAWES, 1653.

Man's life is but vain; For 'tis sub-ject to

pain, And sorrow, and short as a bubble; 'Tis a

hodge-podge of business and money and care; and

care and mon-ey and trou-ble. But

*Walton himself calls this a "Catch,"—Hawkins styles it a Song,—probably from the nature of the words, although the music is perfectly that of the Madrigal so much in the fashion of the time, and now again revived by persons of the best musical taste. The above version is harmonized for four voices, the Alto and

we'll take no care when the weather proves

fair; Nor will we vex now though it rain; We'll

ban - ish all sor - row, and sing till to-

morrow, and an - gle and an - gle a - gain.

Tenor being now first added. For the convenience of publication, the four parts are given on two staves instead of a stave for each voice,—a *double tail* being added where two voices sing the same note.

40. *Mr. Thomas Barker.* Barker appears to have been an angler by profession, and an experienced cook of fish, since he says he "had been admitted into the most Ambassadors' Kitchens that had come to *England* for forty years, and drest fish for them;" for which, he adds, he was duly paid by the Lord Protector. In 1651, two years before the first publication of Walton's work, he published his "Art of Angling," the third edition of which was issued in 1659, under the enlarged title of "Barker's Delight, or the Art of Angling."

41. *Ch. Harvie.* The verses with this signature do not appear until the Second Edition; for the dialogue in the First passes immediately from Herbert's verses to the Beggars' Song, which is there sung by Viator, without the introductory story.

42. *Dr. Boteler.* Dr. William Butler, a celebrated physician, styled by Fuller, in his "Worthies," the Æsculapius of the age. He was born at Ipswich about 1535 and died in 1618.

43. *Hear my Kenna sing a song.* The reference to the margin indicates that Walton wishes to hear Kenna, his mistress, sing the song "Like Hermit Poor." This song was set to music by Nicholas Laneare, an eminent master of Walton's time. The verses which introduce this song were in all probability the production of Walton; for it may be observed that Kenna is evidently a feminine formation of Ken, the maiden name of his second wife.

44. *Like Hermit poor.* The following is the song to which Walton alludes. It occurs in a Collection of Poems entitled the "Phoenix Nest," published in 1593.

"Like to a Hermite poore, in place obscure,
   I meane to spend my daies of endles doubt,
To waile such woes as time cannot recure,
   Where none but Love shall ever finde me out.

My foode shall be of care and sorrow made,
   My drinke nought else but teares falne from mine eies;
And for my light, in such obscured shade,
   The flames shall serve, which from my hart arise.

A gowne of graie my body shall attire,
   My staffe of broken hope whereon Ile staie;
Of late repentance, linct with long desire,
   The couch is fram'de whereon my limbes Ile lay;
     And at my gate Dispaire shall linger still,
     To let in Death, when Love and Fortune will."

45. *Our late English Gusman.* This allusion occurs in the Second Edition, 1655, and is to a work which had appeared three years before: "The English Gusman; or, the History of that unparalleled Thief, James Hind, written by G. F. [George Fidge]. 4to. Lond., 1652."

46. *Ben Jonson in his Beggar's Bush.* The comedy of "The Royal Merchant, or Beggar's Bush," was written by Fletcher, and not by Ben Jonson. It was first printed with the title of "The Beggar's Bush," only.

47. *Frank Davison.* Francis Davison was the eldest son of Secretary Davison. He was born about the year 1575, and published the "Poetical Rhapsody" in 1602, in which miscellany he inserted the "Beggar's Song."

48. *Gaspar Peucerus.* A learned physician and mathemati-

cian, born at Bautzen in 1525. He married the daughter of Melancthon, wrote many books, and died in 1602.

49. *Learned Doctor Hakewill.* This paragraph did not appear until the Second Edition of Walton.

50. *Advise anglers to be patient, and forbear swearing, lest they be heard and catch no fish.* This saying occurs in "Sicelides a Piscatory [by Phineas Fletcher], as it hath been acted in King's College in Cambridge. Lond., 1631." 4to.

"Nay, if you sweare, we shall catch no fish."

51. *The umber and grayling.* The larger grayling (says Browne) is called an umber, as the full-grown jack is called a pike. Jesse states that there are three very distinct sizes of grayling: the pink, so called from its not much exceeding the minnow in size; the skett, or skate, which average about five to the pound; and the half-pound fish, which then takes the name of "grayling."

52. *Salvian.* Hippolito Salviani, an Italian physician of the sixteenth century. The book referred to by Walton is "Aqvatilivm Animalivm Historiae, Rom., 1554."

53. *Dubravius.* Janus Dubravius Scala, Bishop of Olmutz in Moravia, in the sixteenth century, was born at Pilsen, in Bohemia. The Latin title of the book cited by Walton is "De Piscinis, et Piscium qui in eis aluntur naturis."

54. *Cardanus.* Hieronymus Cardanus, an Italian physician, naturalist, and astrologer, who died at Rome, 1576.

55. *Sir Richard Baker, in whose chronicle, etc.* Not in Walton's First Edition.

56. *Jovius.* Paulus Jovius, an Italian historian of doubtful authority, who lived in the sixteenth century, and wrote a small tract "De Romanis Piscibus." He died in 1552.

57. *Venerable Bede.* The most universal scholar of his time, born at Durham about 671. He died in 734. The passage referred to in the text is in his "Ecclesiastical History of the English Nation," lib. iv. cap. 19.

58. *Lobel.* Mathieu de Lobel, or L'Obel, an eminent physician and botanist of the sixteenth century, was a native of Lille, in Flanders. He was a disciple of Rondeletius, and, being invited to London by James I., published there his "Historia Plantarum," and died in the year 1616.

59. *Gerard.* John Gerard, a surgeon in London, and one of the most celebrated of English botanists, born at Namptwich, Cheshire, in 1545. The passage referred to in the text is from his "Herball or Generall Historie of Plantes," Lond. 1633, lib. 3, p. 1587, chap. 171, which is entitled "Of the Goose tree, Barnacle tree, or the Tree bearing Geese."

60. *How to make this Eel a most excellent dish of meat.* Neither the instructions for dressing the Eel, nor the observations on the Flounder, the Char, and the Guiniad, occur in the First Edition.

61. *Gasius.* Antonius Gazius, of Padua. His principal work, to which Walton probably alludes, was his "Corona Florida Medicinæ, sive De Conservatione Sanitatis," first published at Venice in 1491.

62. *Doctor Sheldon.* Dr. Gilbert Sheldon, Warden of All-Souls College, Chaplain to Charles I., and after the

Restoration Archbishop of Canterbury, born July 19, 1598, at Stanton in Staffordshire. He died in 1677.

This passage is not in Walton's First Edition, and the Second reads, "Doctor Sh."

63. *Phineas Fletcher.* The son of Giles Fletcher, LL.D., and Ambassador from Queen Elizabeth to the Duke of Muscovy, said to have been born about 1584. In 1633 was published his "Purple Island, or the Isle of Man; together with Piscatoric Eclogs." He died about 1650.

64. *Either to Mr. Margrave,* etc. There is printed upon the reverse of the last leaf of Cotton's Second Part of the Complete Angler, Edit. 1676, the following memorandum concerning this person: "*Courteous Reader.* You may be pleas'd to take notice, that at the Sign of the Three Trouts in St. *Paul's* Church-Yard, on the North side, you may be fitted with all sorts of the best Fishing-Tackle, by *John Margrave.*"

The four earlier editions of Walton read, "I will go with you either to Charles Brandon's (neer to the Swan in Golding-Lane); or to Mr. Fletcher's, in the Court which did once belong to Dr. Nowel, the Dean of St. Paul's, that I told you was a good man and a good Fisher; it is hard by the West end of St. Paul's Church; they be both," etc. Viator selects Charles Brandon. This is in the last chapter of the First Edition. The marginal note on the value of an Angler's Tackle did not appear until the Second Edition.

65. *Matthiolus.* Petrus Andreas Matthiolus, an eminent physician, born at Siena, in Tuscany, in 1501, famous for his

Commentaries on some of the writings of Discorides. He died at Trent in 1577.

66. *Chap. XIX.* No portion of this chapter occurs in the First, but was added in the Second and subsequent editions.

67. *Dr. Wharton.* One of the most eminent physicians of his day, born at Winston, county of Durham, 1614, died in 1673.

68. *Chap. XX.* The whole of this chapter was added to the Second Edition.

69. *Doctor Lebault.* The work here alluded to is "L'Agriculture et Maison Rustique de M.M. Charles Estienne, et Iean Liebavlt, Docteurs en Médicin," a translation of which, under the title of "Maison Rustique, or the Country Farme," appeared in London in 1600, and a second edition, with large additions, by Gervase Markham in 1616. The latter is no doubt the "large discourse" to which Walton alludes. The XXth Chapter of Walton is contracted from Chapters XI. to XIV. of Liébault's fourth book.

70. *But first for your line.* This and the two following paragraphs first appeared in the Second Edition.

71. *Caussin.* Nicholas Caussin, a native of Troyes, in Champagne, author of a book called "The Holy Court," of which there is an English translation in folio. He died in July, 1651.

72. *I have heard a grave divine say.* Dr. Donne, in his Sermons.

73. *Cotton's Fishing-House.* Cotton, in his "Epistle to John Bradshaw, Esq." printed in his "Posthumous Poems," thus alludes to his Fishing-House:

"My River still through the same channel glides
Clear from the tumult, salt, and dirt of tides,
And my poor Fishing-house, my Seat's best grace,
Stands firm and faithfull in the self same place,
I left it four months since, and ten to one
I go a fishing ere two days are gone."

74. *Tom Coriate.* The son of the Rev. George Coriate, born at Odcombe, in Somersetshire, in 1577. He travelled almost all over Europe on foot, and in that tour walked nine hundred miles with one pair of shoes, which he got mended at Zurich. Afterwards he visited Turkey, Persia, and the Great Mogul's dominions; proceeding in so frugal a manner that, as he tells his mother in a letter, in his ten months' travel between Aleppo and the Mogul's Court, he spent but three pounds sterling, living reasonably well for about twopence sterling a day! He died of the flux, occasioned by drinking sack at Surat in 1617; having, in 1611, published his Travels in a quarto volume, which he called his *Crudities;* in which, on the reverse of b. 1. in "a Character of the Author," is the passage alluded to in the text. *Hawkins.*

75. *Now, Sir, you are come to the door.* This celebrated Fishing-House is formed of stone, and the room within is a cube of fifteen feet, paved with black and white marble, having in the centre a square black marble table. The roof, which is triangular in shape, terminates in a square stone sun-dial, surmounted by a globe and a vane. It was originally wainscoted with walls of carved panels and divisions, in the larger spaces of which were painted some of the most interesting scenes in the vicinity of the building; whilst the

smaller ones were occupied with groups of fishing-tackle. In the right-hand corner stood a large beaufet with folding-doors, on which were painted the portraits of Walton and Cotton attended by a servant-boy; and beneath it was a closet, having a Trout and a Grayling delineated upon the door. Such was the original appearance of the Fishing-House, as collected from a description given by Mr. White, of Crickhowel, to Sir John Hawkins, in 1784; although it was then considerably decayed, especially in the wainscoting and the paintings. To this, the following account of its state in 1811, written from actual observation by W. H. Pepys, Esq., F.R.S., etc., will form an appropriate and an interesting counterpart:

"It was in the month of April, 1811, that I visited the celebrated Fishing-House of Cotton and Walton. I left Ashbourne about nine o'clock in the morning, accompanied by several Brothers of the Angle: we took the Buxton road for about six miles, and, turning through a gate to the left, soon descended into the valley of the Dove, and continued along the banks of the river about three miles farther, when we arrived at Beresford Hall. The Fishing-House is situated on a small peninsula, round which the river flows, and was then nearly enveloped with trees. It has been a small, neat stone building, covered with stone slates, or tiles, but is now going fast to decay: the stone steps by which you entered the door are nearly destroyed. It is of a quadrangular form, having a door and two windows in the front, and one larger window on each of the other three sides. The door was secured on the outside by a strong staple; but the bars and casements of the windows being gone, an easy entrance was obtained. The marble floor, as described by White in 1784, had been removed: only one of the pedestals upon which the table was formerly placed was standing, and that much deteriorated. On the left side was the fireplace, the mantle-piece and sides of which were in a good state. The chimney and recess for the stove were so exactly on the Rumford plan, that one might have supposed he had lived in the time when it was erected. On the right-hand side of the room is an angular excavation or small cellar, over which the cup-board, or beaufet, formerly stood. The wainscot of the room is wanting, the ceiling is broken, and part of the stone-tiling admits both light and water. Upon examining the small cel-lar, we found the other pedestal which supported the mar-ble table; and against the door on the inside, three large fragments of the table itself, which were of the Black Dove Dale Marble, bevelled on the edges, and had been well pol-ished. The inscription over the door, and the cipher of Wal-ton and Cotton in the key-stone, were very legible."

COMMENDATORY VERSES.

TO MY DEAR BROTHER
IZAAK WALTON

UPON HIS

"COMPLETE ANGLER."

ERASMUS in his learned Colloquies
Has mixt some toys, that by varieties
He might entice all readers: for in him
Each child may wade, or tallest giant swim.
And such is this Discourse: there's none so low
Or highly learn'd, to whom hence may not flow
Pleasure and information; both which are
Taught us with so much art, that I might swear,
Safely, the choicest critic cannot tell
Whether your matchless judgment most excell
In angling or its praise: where commendation
First charms, then makes an art a recreation.

　'T was so to me: who saw the cheerful spring
Pictur'd in every meadow, heard birds sing
Sonnets in every grove, saw fishes play
In the cool crystal springs, like lambs in May;
And they may play, till anglers read this book,
But after, 't is a wise fish 'scapes a hook.

JO. FLOUD, M.A.

TO THE

READER OF THE "COMPLETE ANGLER."

First mark the title well: my friend that gave it
Has made it good; this book deserves to have it.
For he that views it with judicious looks,
Shall find it full of art, baits, lines, and hooks.
    (The world the river is; both you and I,
And all mankind, are either fish or fry.)
If we pretend to reason, first or last
His baits will tempt us, and his hooks hold fast.
Pleasure or profit, either prose or rhyme,
If not at first, will doubtless take in time.
    Here sits, in secret, blest theology,
Waited upon by grave philosophy
Both natural and moral; history,
Deck'd and adorn'd with flowers of poetry,
The matter and expression striving which
Shall most excell in worth, yet seem not rich.
There is no danger in his baits; that hook
Will prove the safest that is surest took.
    Nor are we *caught* alone,—but, which is best,
We shall be wholesome, and be toothsome, drest;
Drest to be fed, not to be fed upon:
And danger of a surfeit here is none.
The solid food of serious contemplation
Is sauc'd, here, with such harmless recreation,
That an ingenuous and religious mind
Cannot inquire, for more than it may find
Ready at once prepared, either t' excite
Or satisfy a curious appetite.
    More praise is due: for 't is both positive
And truth—which, once, was interrogative,

And utter'd by the poet, then, in jest—
Et piscatorem piscis amare potest.

Ch. Harvie, M.A.

TO MY DEAR FRIEND MR. IZAAK WALTON;

IN

PRAISE OF ANGLING; WHICH WE BOTH LOVE.

Down by this smooth stream's wand'ring side,
Adorn'd and perfum'd with the pride
Of Flora's wardrobe, where the shrill
Aërial choir express their skill—
First, in alternate melody;
And, then, in chorus all agree—
Whilst the charm'd fish, as extasy'd
With sounds, to his own throat deny'd,
Scorns his dull element, and springs
I' th' air, as if his fins were wings.
    'T is here that pleasures sweet and high
Prostrate to our embraces lie:
Such as to body, soul or fame,
Create no sickness, sin or shame:
Roses, not fenc'd with pricks, grow here;
No sting to th' honey-bag is near:
But, what 's perhaps their prejudice,
They difficulty want and price.
    An obvious rod, a twist of hair,
With hook hid in an insect,—are
Engines of sport would fit the wish
O' th' epicure, and fill his dish.
    In this clear stream, let fall a grub;

And, straight, take up a dace or chub.
I' th' mud, your worm provokes a snig;*
Which being fast, if it prove big,
The Gotham folly will be found
Discreet, ere ta'en she must be drown'd.
The tench, physician of the brook,
In yon dead hole expects your hook;
Which having first your pastime been,
Serves then for meat or medicine.†
Ambush'd behind that root doth stay
A pike; to catch—and be a prey.
The treacherous quill in this slow stream
Betrays the hunger of a bream.
And that nimble ford, no doubt,
Your false fly cheats a speckled trout.
  When you these creatures wisely choose
To practise on, which to your use
Owe their creation,—and when
Fish from your arts do rescue men,—
To plot, delude, and circumvent,
Ensnare and spoil, is innocent.
Here by these crystal streams you may
Preserve a conscience clear as they;
And when by sullen thoughts you find
Your harassed, not busied, mind
In sable melancholy clad,

---

*A small eel.
 †The following four lines were here added to the second edition, but are
omitted in all the others:—

    "And there the cunning carp you may
    Beguile with paste; if you'll but stay,
    And watch in time, you'll have your wish,
    For paste and patience catch this fish."

Distemper'd, serious, turning sad;
Hence fetch your cure, cast in your bait,
All anxious thoughts and cares will straight
Fly with such speed, they'll seem to be
Possest with the hydrophobie.
The water's calmness in your breast,
And smoothness on your brow shall rest.

 Away with sports of charge and noise,
And give me cheap and silent joys.
Such as Actæon's game pursue,
Their fate oft makes the tale seem true.
The sick or sullen hawk, to-day,
Flies not; to-morrow quite away.
Patience and purse to cards and dice
Too oft are made a sacrifice:
The daughter's dower, th' inheritance
O' th' son, depend on one mad chance.
The harms and mischiefs which th' abuse
Of wine doth every day produce,
Make good the doctrine of the Turks,
That in each grape a devil lurks.
And by yon fading sapless tree,
'Bout which the ivy twin'd you see,
His fate 's foretold, who fondly places
His bliss in woman's soft embraces.
All pleasures but the angler's bring
I' th' tail repentance like a sting.

 Then on these banks let me sit down,
Free from the toilsome sword and gown;
And pity those that do affect
To conquer nations and protect.
My reed affords such true content,
Delights so sweet and innocent,

As seldom fall unto the lot
Of scepters, though they're justly got.

Tho. Weaver, M.A.* 1649.

TO THE READERS

OF

MY MOST INGENIOUS FRIEND'S BOOK,

"THE COMPLETE ANGLER."

He that both knew and writ the Lives of men,
 Such as were once, but must not be again;
 Witness his matchless Donne and Wotton, by
 Whose aid he could their speculations try:
He that conversed with angels, such as were
 Ouldsworth† and Featly,‡ each a shining star
 Showing the way to Bethlem; each a saint,
 Compar'd to whom our zealots, now, but paint.
He that our pious and learn'd Morley§ knew,
 And from him suck'd wit and devotion too.
He that from these such excellencies fetch'd,
 That he could tell how high and far they reach'd;
 What learning this, what graces th' other had;
 And in what several dress each soul was clad.
Reader, this he, this fisherman, comes forth,
And in these fisher's weeds would shroud his worth.

---

*The son of Thomas Weaver, of Worcester.
†Dr. Richard Holdsworth. See an account of him in Wood's "Fasti Oxon."
and in Ward's "Lives of the Gresham Professors."
‡Dr. Daniel Featley.
§Dr. George Morley, Bishop of Winchester.

Now his mute harp is on a willow hung,
With which when finely touch'd, and fitly strung,
He could friends' passions for these times allay,
Or chain his fellow anglers from their prey.
But now the music of his pen is still,
And he sits by a brook watching a quill:
Where with a fixt eye, and a ready hand,
He studies first to hook, and then to land
Some trout, or pearch, or pike; and having done,
Sits on a bank, and tells how this was won,—
And that escap'd his hook, which with a wile
Did eat the bait, and fisherman beguile.
Thus whilst some vex they from their lands are thrown,
He joys to think the waters are his own;
   And like the Dutch, he gladly can agree
To live at peace now, and have fishing free.

                  EDW. POWEL, M.A. APRIL 3, 1650.

TO MY DEAR BROTHER MR. IZAAK WALTON

ON HIS

"COMPLETE ANGLER."

THIS book is so like you, and you like it,
For harmless mirth, expression, art and wit,
That I protest, ingenuously 't is true,
I love this mirth, art, wit, the book and you.

                        ROB. FLOUD, C.

CLARISSIMO AMICISSIMOQUE

FRATRI, DOMINO ISAACO WALTON

ARTIS PISCATORIÆ PERITISSIMO.

Unicus est medicus reliquorum piscis, et istis,
    Fas quibus est medicum tangere, certa salus
Hic typus est salvatoris mirandus Jesu,
    Litera* mysterium quælibet hujus habet.
Hunc cupio, hunc cupias, bone frater arundinis, ἰχθὺν;
    Solverit hic pro me debita, teque Deo.†
Piscis is est, et piscator, mihi credito, qualem
    Vel piscatorem piscis amare velit.

HENRY BAYLEY, A.M.

AD VIRUM OPTIMUM ET PISCATOREM PERITISSIMUM,

ISAACUM WALTONUM.

Magister artis docte piscatoriæ,
Waltone, salve! magne dux arundinis,
Seu tu reducta valle solus ambulas,
Præterfluentes interim observans aquas,
Seu fortè puri stans in amnis margine,
Sive in tenaci gramine et ripâ sedens,
Fallis perità squameum pecus manu;
O te beatum! qui procul negotiis,

---

*ΙΧΘΥ` Σ, *Piscis.*
 Ι Ἰησοῦς, *Jesus.*
 Χ Χριστὸς, *Christus.*
 Θ Θεοῦ, *Dei.*
 Υ Ὑιὸς, *Filius.*
 Σ Σωτήρ, *Salvator.*
†Matt. xvii. 27, the last words of the chapter.

Forique et urbis pulvere et strepitu carens,
Extraque turbam, ad lenè manantes aquas
Vagos honestâ fraude pisces decipis.
Dum cætera ergo pœnè gens mortalium
Aut retia invicem sibi et technas struunt,
Donis, ut hamo, aut divites captant senes,
Gregi natantûm tu interim nectis dolos.
Voracem inescas advenam hamo lucium,
Avidamve percam parvulo alberno capis,
Aut verme ruffo, musculâ aut truttam levi,
Cautumve cyprinum, et ferè indocilem capi
Calamoque linoque, ars at hunc superat tua,
Medicamve tincam, gobium aut escâ trahis,
Gratum palato gobium, parvum licet,
Prædamve, non æque salubrem barbulum,
Etsi ampliorem, et mystace insignem gravi.
Hæ sunt tibi artes, dum annus et tempus sinunt,
Et nulla transit absque lineâ dies.
Nec sola praxis, sed theoria et tibi
Nota artis hujus; unde tu simul bonus
Piscator, idem et scriptor; et calami potens
Utriusque necdum et ictus, et tamen sapis.
Ut hamiotam nempe tironem instruas!
Stylo eleganti scribis en Halieutica
Oppianus alter artis et methodum tuæ, et
Præcepta promis rite piscatoria,
Varias et escas piscium, indolem et genus.
Nec tradere artem sat putas piscariam,
(Virtutis est hæc et tamen quædam schola
Patientiamque et temperantiam docet,)
Documenta quin majora das, et regulas
Sublimioris artis, et perennia
Monimenta morem, vitæ et exempla optima,—
Dum tu profundum scribis Hookerum; et pium

Donnum ac disertum; sanctum et Herbertum, sacrum
Vatem; hos videmus nam penicillo tuo
Graphicè, et perità, Isace, depictos manu.
Post fata factos hosce per te Virbios.*
O quæ voluptas est legere in scriptis tuis!
Sic tu libris nos, lineis pisces capis,
Musisque litterisque dum incumbis, licet
Intentus hamo, interque piscandum studes.†

AD ISAACUM WALTONUM,

VIRUM ET PISCATOREM OPTIMUM.

ISAACE, Macte hâc arte piscatoriâ;
Hâc arte Petrus principi censum dedit;
Hâc arte princeps nec Petro multo prior,
Tranquillus ille, teste Tranquillo,‡ pater
Patriæ, solebat recreare se lubens
Augustus, hamo instructus ac arundine.
Tu nunc, amice, proximum clari es decus
Post Cæsarem hami, gentis ac Halieuticæ:
Euge O professor artis haud ingloriæ,
Doctor cathedræ, perlegens piscariam!
Næ tu magister, et ego discipulus tuus,
Nam candidatum et me ferunt arundinis,

---

*VIRBIUS *quasi* BIS VIR, is an epithet applied to Hippolytus, because he was
by Diana restored to life after his death. *Vide* Ovidii Met. lib. xv. v. 536, et seq.;
Hoffmanni "Lexicon Universale," art. Virbius.—H.
†These verses are written by Dr. James Duport.
‡*i. e.* Suetonius Tranquillus.

Socium hâc in arte nobilem nacti sumus.
Quid amplius, Waltone, nam dici potest?
Ipse hamiota Dominus en orbis fuit!

Jaco. Dup. D.D.*

---

*James Duport, S.T.P., Master of Magdalen College, Cambridge, in 1668, and Dean of Peterborough, July, 1664. Dean Duport was son of John Duport, whom we are told by Fuller ("Church Hist." lib. x.) assisted in the translation of King James's Bible.—ED.

INDEX

A NOTE ON THE TYPE

The principal text of this Modern Library edition was set in a digitized version of Caslon, a typeface first designed in 1722 by William Caslon. Its widespread use by most English printers in the early eighteenth century soon supplanted the Dutch typefaces that had formerly prevailed. The roman is considered a "workhorse" typeface due to its pleasant, open appearance, while the italic is exceedingly decorative.